NARRATIVES OF
BARBARY CAPTIVITY

Burning of the Frigate *Philadelphia* in the Harbor of Tripoli,
February 16, 1804, *oil painting by Edward Moran*

The Lakeside Classics

NARRATIVES OF BARBARY CAPTIVITY

Recollections of
James Leander Cathcart,
Jonathan Cowdery, and
William Ray

EDITED BY ROBERT J. ALLISON

The Lakeside Press

R.R. DONNELLEY & SONS COMPANY

DECEMBER 2007

PUBLISHER'S PREFACE

Although the narratives in this year's Lakeside Classic were written two hundred years ago, the subject—the relationship of America to the Arab states of the Middle East and North Africa—is just as relevant today. In 1783, with the signing of the Paris Peace Treaty, the United States won its independence from Great Britain, but lost the protection of the Royal Navy. The Barbary States of North Africa (Algiers, Tripoli, Tunis, and Morocco), who for centuries had preyed upon shipping in the Mediterranean Sea, noted the weakness of this new country and began seizing its vessels, imprisoning its sailors, and demanding ransom. Stopping these depredations, freeing its citizens, and protecting its vital commercial interest in the region became the first foreign relations challenge for the United States.

It took more than thirty years for America and the Barbary States to reach a lasting peace. In the process the United States created a navy, fought its first foreign war, conquered its first foreign city, and added new heroes like Stephen Decatur to its pantheon. The most well-known souvenir of this conflict is the opening lines of the Marine Hymn: *From the halls of Montezuma / To the shores of Tripoli*, which commemorates the attempt by William

Eaton, two midshipmen, and seven marines to free Barbary captives by marching across Egypt to capture Derne in Tripoli.

Barbary captivity narratives, like the three in this volume, arguably deserve recognition as a genre of American literature alongside the better known Indian captivity and slave narratives, some of which have been published as Lakeside Classics. Like those volumes, certain descriptions in this year's edition are neither pretty nor what today would be considered acceptable. We present them as the perceptions of their time in the hope that they will enable us to better understand our past. A member of the Donnelley family has said that part of the value of the form of The Lakeside Classics—first-person narratives—is that it allows us to see history "with all its warts."

The editor of this year's Classic is Robert J. Allison, chairman of the History Department at Suffolk University, Boston, where he teaches American history, constitutional history, cultural contact in world history, and the history of Boston. Professor Allison is the author of *The Crescent Obscured: The United States and the Muslim World 1776–1815, A Short History of Boston,* and *Stephen Decatur: American Naval Hero, 1779–1820,* a biography of a leader in the wars against the Barbary States. He has edited a number of other books focused primarily on the American Revolutionary War period.

The Cowdery narrative is published in full; the

Cathcart and Ray narratives have been abridged to fit this edition. As always, we are grateful to the many academic libraries and historical collections—listed in the credits—that provided images to enrich this volume.

The publication of this latest Lakeside Classic follows an exciting year of expansion and change at RR Donnelley.

For several years, RR Donnelley has increased our capabilities and revenues by complementing organic growth with targeted acquisitions. Between February 2004 and June 2007, RR Donnelley completed a dozen acquisitions, expanding our resources on three continents. As of this writing, this year alone thousands of talented new employees had come to RR Donnelley through the acquisitions of Banta Corporation, Perry Judd's, and Von Hoffman. Banta, an innovative Wisconsin-based provider of printing and supply management services, enhanced RR Donnelley's capabilities to produce and deliver books, magazines, catalogs, literature management, direct mail, premedia, and other services. Also in the United States, Perry Judd's added its respected magazine and catalog printing resources to RR Donnelley's, and Von Hoffmann expanded our book and business-to-business catalog offering with its exceptional capabilities.

During the past several years, RR Donnelley has

built an unparalleled ability to provide end-to-end solutions that address virtually all of our customers' needs for printing and complementary business services. Without missing a beat, our facilities have installed new presses, finishing equipment, computer systems, logistics capabilities, and more. All of this enables us to offer a unique resource for integrated solutions—or put more simply, we have become the industry's best one-stop-shop.

This year we unified our brand under the RR Donnelley name, as we honorably retired venerable names such as Moore, Moore Wallace, Banta, Perry Judd's, Von Hoffmann, and Office Tiger. Now the RR Donnelley logo and name represent our complete offering, worldwide.

This change, though it will result in many new signs and logos being applied to buildings throughout the world, is anything but merely cosmetic. It reflects our proven ability to develop creative solutions for customers across the entire breadth of the value chain. For example, RR Donnelley can nurture the creative process, with capabilities ranging from digital photography to digital asset management. Perhaps you own a digital camera and have encountered the challenge of organizing all of the pictures that you take. For large organizations, the task is even more daunting; but RR Donnelley helps—with powerful, Internet-based systems. We help to manage more than 2.3 million digital images and keep up-to-date information associated with each. For some customers, we provide creative services, such as copywriting, layout, and design. As our customers become increasingly global, we help them to communicate in multiple languages. In just one year, our in-house team managed the translation of nearly 38 million words into an astonishing 71 languages.

Once materials are ready to be printed, customers the world over turn to RR Donnelley's unmatched global platform. We produce a remarkable range of printed materials, in quantities that range from one to more than a billion. For example, when a popular musical group won a Grammy Award, we used sophisticated digital printing equipment to print a single colorful full-size poster that was put up on a billboard along a Los Angeles freeway. On the other end of the spectrum, for a global cosmetics and fashion brand, we produced more than 983 million brochures worldwide. In Asia, Latin America, North America, Europe, and the Middle East, the RR Donnelley brand stands for excellence in printing.

We were delighted that our employees' printing craftsmanship was recognized by a variety of customers, as well as by peer and industry organizations. Wal-Mart selected RR Donnelley as its Gravure Printer of the Year. *GRAVURE* magazine echoed that appraisal of our work as it presented two of our facilities with Golden Cylinder Awards. At the prestigious Gold Ink Awards, our facilities won mentions for manuals; textbooks; dimensional printing; catalogs; consumer, tabloid, and specialty magazines; event programs; point-of-purchase displays; direct mail packages; digital printing; and more.

Customers turn to RR Donnelley for services that extend far beyond the end of a press. For example, when you open your Sunday newspaper, you'll find a range of colorful advertising inserts inside. We not only print inserts, but our logistics professionals also coordinate their delivery to hundreds of newspapers so that they can be placed inside: all on the tightest of deadlines. RR Donnelley helps customers to speed magazines to your door, to arrange that vital business documents are accurately printed and mailed, and that our customers can accomplish all of this at the best postal rate.

We even help to close the loop with a variety of business services. For example, we might help a customer to craft a direct-mail offer that invites prospects to open a new account. When prospects respond, RR Donnelley can help process the return mail, set up the account, and mail the new customer a welcome kit of forms and brochures. Around the world, and around the clock, RR Donnelley's service professionals complement our customers' in-house resources.

Our deep commitment to sustainability was reflected as RR Donnelley's facilities achieved Forest Stewardship Council certification. In doing so, these operations joined all of our North American printing plants in offering customers the ability to choose papers that are certified to originate from responsibly managed forest resources.

Among our employees' many accomplishments during 2007, none were more important than the safety milestones achieved by so many of our facilities. Across the world, operations set new records by working millions of hours without a day-away injury. We apply OSHA's exacting metrics to all of our facilities across the world. Although we are very pleased that our global safety performance is significantly better than the printing industry's as a whole, our goal remains to have our facilities be 100-percent injury-free. There is no more important measure of operational excellence than safety.

In early 2007, Thomas J. Quinlan III became RR Donnelley's President and Chief Executive Officer, following the retirement of Mark A. Angelson, who had served as CEO and as a member of the Board of Directors since 2004. This year, Robert F. Cummings also completed his years of service on our Board of Directors. We are grateful to Messrs. Angelson and Cummings for their contributions to RR Donnelley.

T. E. Donnelley, one of founder Richard Robert

Donnelley's sons, began the Lakeside Classic series in 1903. His vision was in part to convey "that machine-made books are not a crime against art." The blend of engineering, technology, and craftsmanship that went into the making of the volume that you hold in your hands illustrates wonderfully that we continue to bring his vision to life, in these books and in the many other products that we produce.

We wish you all the blessings of the holiday season and a happy, safe, and peaceful new year.

THE PUBLISHER
December 2007

CONTENTS

Contents

Book III
Horrors of Slavery; or
The American Tars in Tripoli
by William Ray

ILLUSTRATIONS

xv

Illustrations

LIST OF MAIN CHARACTERS

AMERICANS

William Bainbridge (1774–1833). Naval officer. Commanded the *Philadelphia* when it ran aground off Tripoli. Held captive in Tripoli with his officers and crew. In War of 1812, led USS *Constitution* to victory over HMS *Java*. Returned to Mediterranean in 1815 to conduct negotiations with Algiers, Tripoli, and Tunis.

Joel Barlow (1754–1812). Businessman, diplomat, and poet. Sent to Algiers in 1796, where he eventually negotiated the release of the captives.

James Barron (1769–1851). Naval officer. Served in Tripolitan War with his brother. Court-martialed for failure to prevent British attack on the *Chesapeake* in 1807; suspended from navy. Killed Stephen Decatur Jr. in a duel, 1820. Reinstated in the navy, but never again given active command of a ship.

Samuel Barron (1765–1810). Naval officer. Served in U.S. Navy during Revolutionary and Tripolitan wars. Later, commanded gunboat fleet in Hampton, Virginia.

James Leander Cathcart (1767–1843). Sailor and diplomat. Captured by the Algerians with the *Maria* in July 1785; held until 1796.

Zachariah Coffin (?–1787). Merchant marine officer. Passenger on the *Dauphin* when it was captured by Algiers; died in captivity.

Jonathan Cowdery (1767–1852). Naval officer and author. Surgeon's mate on the *Philadelphia*, captured and imprisoned in Tripoli.

James Decatur (c. 1782–1804). Naval officer. Younger brother of Stephen Decatur. Killed in action in Tripoli.

Stephen Decatur Jr. (1779–1820). Naval officer. Led daring raid into Tripoli harbor on February 16, 1804, and destroyed the *Philadelphia* to keep Tripolitans from using it. Led American fleet into Mediterranean in 1815, making peace with Algiers, Tunis, and Tripoli.

Joseph Donaldson Jr. (c. 1745–?). Businessman sent to Algiers in 1795 to negotiate release of captives.

William Eaton (1764–1811). Soldier and diplomat. Led U.S. marines and mercenaries across the desert from Egypt to capture Derne in hopes of replacing Yusuf Qaramanli Pasha with his elder brother, Achmed (Hamet). Elected to one term in Massachusetts Legislature.

David Humphreys (1772–1818). Diplomat and poet. Aide to General George Washington during the American Revolution. Resident minister to the court in Lisbon, Portugal; responsible for negotiations with Algiers that freed the captives.

John Lamb (1735–1800). Connecticut mule-trader; connections with Alexander Hamilton led to his appointment as agent to negotiate with Algiers in 1785–86.

Tobias Lear (1762–1816). Diplomat. Successfully negotiated treaties with Algiers and Morocco. Tripoli proved more difficult, taking him two years to conclude the treaty freeing the *Philadelphia* captives.

Richard O'Brien (1758–1824). Merchant marine officer and diplomat. Captain of the *Dauphin*, captured by Algerians. Returned to Algiers in 1798 as American consul. Later served in Pennsylvania Legislature.

Edward Preble (1761–1807). Naval officer. In 1803, commanded Third Squadron from his flagship *Constitution*, on the Barbary Coast, where he promoted a treaty with Morocco and established a blockade off Tripoli.

William Ray (1771–1827). Sailor and writer. Captured with the *Philadelphia* and held prisoner in Tripoli.

James S. Ridgely. Naval surgeon. Joined the navy July 2, 1803. Senior medical officer on the *Philadelphia*. Held with officers and crew in Tripoli until 1805. Stayed on in Tripoli after captives were released. Resigned from the navy August 26, 1808.

John Rodgers (1772–1838). Naval officer. Commanded the *John Adams* in the battles with Tripoli. Became commodore of the Mediterranean squadron in 1805.

Richard Somers (1778–1804). Naval officer. Commanded the *Nautilus* during operations against Tripoli. Volunteered to sail the *Intrepid* into Tripoli harbor and blow it up to destroy enemy fleet. The ketch exploded prematurely—perhaps accidentally, perhaps intentionally to avoid capture—killing Somers and his entire crew.

Isaac Stephens. Merchant sailor. Captain of *Maria* out of Boston. Held in Algiers with Cathcart.

List of Main Characters

BARBARY STATES

Micaiah Cohen Bacri (d. 1805). Banker; member of a prominent Jewish family in Algiers. Helped negotiate and fund the release of the American captives. Killed in 1805 coup d'etat that overthrew Mustafa Dey.

Muhammad D'Ghies. Tripolitan foreign minister. Opposed Tripoli's war against the U.S.; helped negotiate treaty of 1805; influential in Tripolitan politics into 1830s.

Shoush Hammad. Tripolitan official; rais of the marine, or harbormaster.

Hassan Bey. Tripolitan soldier; commanded Yusuf Qaramanli's forces at Derne.

Hassan Dey. Ruler of Algiers, 1791–98. Minister of the marine in 1780s; Cathcart's employer as dey.

Suleiman Mellimelli Sidi. Tunisian diplomat. First Muslim envoy to the United States in 1805.

Achmed (Hamet) Qaramanli (d. 1811). Deposed elder brother of Yusuf. Plotted unsuccessfully with Eaton to depose his brother. Yusuf forgave him, later installing him as governor of Derne.

Yusuf Qaramanli (1766–1838). Ruler of Tripoli, 1795–1832. Held crew of the *Philadelphia* captive.

Murad Reis (?–1832). Tripolitan naval officer. Born Scotsman Peter Lisle. Captured by the Algerians, converted to Islam, and married the pasha's daughter. Became admiral of Tripoli's navy.

Muhammad ibn Uthman Dey (c. 1710–91). Ruler of Algiers, 1766–91.

List of Main Characters

Jean-Baptiste Michel de Kercy (1751–1801). French general consul to Algiers.

Marquis de Lafayette (1757–1834). French aristocrat, soldier, and statesman. Fought in American Revolution. Offered to assist Jefferson in negotiations with Barbary States, but forestalled by his government.

Charles Logie. British consul to Algiers.

Bryan McDonough. British consul to Tripoli.

Nicholas C. Nissen. Danish consul to Tripoli.

Mattias Skjöldebrand. Swedish consul to Algiers.

Pierre Eric (Peter Erick) Skjöldebrand. Brother of Swedish consul to Algiers.

Commodore Stephen Decatur Jr. by Orlando S. Lagman

HISTORICAL INTRODUCTION

SEVEN HUNDRED American sailors were taken captive by the Barbary States of North Africa (Morocco, Algiers, Tunis, and Tripoli) between 1785 and 1815. Among them were the men who tell their stories in this book—James Leander Cathcart, Jonathan Cowdery, and William Ray. Their captivity prompted the newly independent United States to build a navy in the 1790s and to fight its first foreign war—against Tripoli—in the first decade of the nineteenth century.

The Mediterranean had long been an important market for American wheat, flour, and dried fish. In the years immediately preceding the War of Independence, more than a thousand American sailors, manning eighty to one hundred ships, sailed to the Mediterranean annually, selling about $3.5 million worth of goods and buying about $1 million worth to bring home. One-quarter of the dried or pickled fish and one-sixth of the grain Americans exported went to the Mediterranean, mainly to Spain, France, and Italy.

The Barbary States not only were trade competitors—also producing wheat and exporting grain, olive oil, and African slaves—but also had the strategic advantage of being situated at the Mediterranean outlets of the Saharan caravan trade, connecting Europe, Africa, and the Ottoman Empire. Their populations were diverse, with Berbers and Arabs, exiled Moors and Jews from Spain, African slaves, and European traders and renegades. Though the rulers were nominally Muslims, the focus of each state was control of the various populations, trade, and competition with its neighbors.

All these principalities had been part of the historic struggle between Christian Spain and the Islamic Ottomans. Based in Istanbul (then called Constantinople), the Ottoman Empire stretched from the states of North Africa eastward into present-day Iraq and Saudi Arabia. The Ottoman sultans claimed the allegiance of all the diverse peoples of the empire, exacting tribute from the rulers, although by the end of the eighteenth century, the sultans were not directly governing the states of North Africa. Some of these principalities, however, continued to threaten Spain and the coasts of Italy, and Spain continued to attempt to seize territory in North Africa. From west to east, the Barbary States of Morocco, Algiers, Tunis, and Tripoli each set its own course, and each had its own relationship with the newly independent United States.

Each also had its own distinctive government. Morocco had been an independent kingdom since 788. Its emperor recognized American independence in 1777—the second nation in the world to do so— and his descendants still govern the kingdom.

Algiers, a city of 50,000 (New York's population then was 33,000), had been governed by a janissary garrison since the 1500s. These janissaries, or soldiers, mainly came from the sultan's Balkan or Greek provinces; westerners called the ruler a dey, from the Turkish *dayi* (unit commander; literally, *maternal uncle*), but the local population called him pasha (often *bashaw* in English), or head.

Tunis also had been governed by Turkish janissaries. In 1705, their captain, Husayn bin Ali, had created a political dynasty in Tunis, which his descendants governed as beys, or princes, until the French occupied Tunis in 1881.

The city of Tripoli (population 40,000) also had a pasha, originally the leader of the janissary garrison. In 1711, Achmed Qaramanli, Tripolitan-born son of a janissary, had overthrown the janissaries and sworn allegiance to the sultan, establishing himself as pasha of the coastal area between Tunis and Egypt stretching for several hundred miles into the desert. His family would govern most of present-day Libya until the Ottomans resumed control in 1835.

During the Crusades, and throughout Spain and Portugal's continuing wars against the Barbary States, captured Christians had been put to work in the galleys (ships) of the Muslims, while captured Muslims had been forced to work on the sugar plantations of the Christian Mediterranean. In the

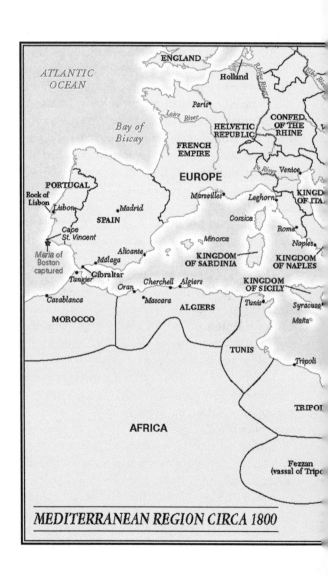

MEDITERRANEAN REGION CIRCA 1800

centuries that followed, Barbary corsairs—privateers sent out against enemy merchant ships—continued to attack the coasts of Italy, Spain, and the islands of Sicily, Majorca, Sardinia, and Corsica, bringing back Christian captives. Portugal guarded the Strait of Gibraltar to prevent corsairs from entering the Atlantic, and Spain used its military base at Oran to mount offenses against Algiers. The novelist Miguel de Cervantes transformed the story of his own captivity into "The Tale of the Captive" in his great novel *Don Quixote*, and Wolfgang Amadeus Mozart composed an opera, *Abduction from the Seraglio,* the story of a European woman held captive in the Ottoman Empire.

Britain and its American colonies were pulled into this conflict. In 1625, raiders from Salé, on Morocco's Atlantic coast, seized a British/American ship, and in the 1640s a ship built in Massachusetts defeated an Algerian ship in a sea battle. When Britain went to war against Algiers in the 1670s, many New Yorkers wound up as captives in Algiers; churchgoers in their hometown ransomed them. Joshua Gee, a Massachusetts sailor taken captive in Morocco in the 1670s, was ransomed and returned to Boston; his son became Cotton Mather's assistant in the North Church.

When Britain made peace with Algiers in 1686, British ships—many of them from the American colonies—sailed into the Mediterranean. Other European states also made peace with the Barbary States, finding it worth their while to pay Algiers, Tunis, Tripoli, and Morocco to leave their shipping alone. Barbary cruisers instead would attack the merchant shipping of their rivals: Spain, Naples, Russia, and Genoa. By the end of the eighteenth century, Venice, Sweden, Holland, and Denmark each paid Algiers about a quarter of a million dollars a year. France also paid a tribute; England made presents when appropriate.

"If there were no Algiers, we would have to build one" was a phrase variously attributed to Louis XIV of France, to the merchants of Holland, and to the British ministry. In fact, it was worthwhile for each of these states to pay Algiers to hold its rivals in check.

*   *   *

Before the Revolution, American colonial shipping operated under the protection of the British flag and the Royal Navy. With the signing of the Treaty of Versailles, the ships of the newly minted United States lost this protection; moreover, the British actually encouraged the Barbary corsairs to prey upon them. American shipping was made even more vulnerable by the weakness of the central

American government operating under the loose Articles of Confederation before the implementation of the constitutional government in 1789.

In October 1784, a Moroccan ship seized the American merchant ship *Betsey*. Although Emperor Moulay Muhammad had recognized American independence in December 1777, extending most-favored-nation trading status to the new republic, the Americans had not sent a negotiator to work out a treaty. As a way to get American attention, the emperor had the American merchant vessel brought into port. Moulay Muhammad notified the Americans that he would not allow the crew to be enslaved and would not sell the ship, but was holding them until the United States negotiated a treaty.

John Adams, American commissioner to France, called on France's foreign minister, the Comte de Vergennes, for advice. A cagey diplomat who had been French minister to the Ottoman Empire, Vergennes told Adams that Morocco's emperor was "the most [self-] interested man in the world" and only wanted an American treaty in order to receive American presents. Adams asked if it was true that France had recently renewed its own treaty with Algiers; Vergennes only smiled. He was amused that Adams knew this, yet would not confirm it. Adams realized that France had no interest in aiding the United States in the Mediterranean.

Spain, however, now saw the United States as a potential ally against the British in North America, and Morocco as a potential ally in its own war against Algiers. So Spain interceded with Moulay Muhammad, who released the *Betsey* in March 1785. The Americans promised to send a negotiator. Thomas Barclay negotiated a treaty with Morocco in 1786, under which the United States would pay no tribute to the emperor. This peace treaty between the United States and Morocco has endured for more than two centuries, making it the longest-standing contract in American diplomatic history. The American legation building in Tangier is the only national landmark on foreign soil.

Algiers was a different story. Spain, after an unsuccessful attack on Algiers in 1783, made a truce in 1785, paying Algiers $3 million (equivalent to $45 million today). Almost immediately after this, Britain's consul to Algiers, Charles Logie, alerted the Algerians to the possibility of seizing American ships. By the first of August the merchant ships *Maria*, a six-man schooner out of Boston, and *Dauphin*, with a crew of fifteen out of Philadelphia, were in Algerian custody.

Isaac Stephens of Braintree, Massachusetts, captain of the *Maria*, and Richard O'Brien of Maine, captain of the *Dauphin*, wrote to the American diplomats in Europe—Thomas Jefferson and John Adams—stating that Algiers had captured them for the purpose of extorting ransom from their friends or their country and that the British had instigated the capture to keep Americans out of the Mediterranean.

News of these captures and rumors of others drove up insurance rates and forced American merchants to turn to British carriers to ship goods to Europe. British newspapers even reported that Benjamin Franklin, returning to Philadelphia from France, had been captured and was bearing his "slavery to admiration" in Algiers.

*   *   *

It fell to Jefferson, the American minister to France and so the official closest to Algiers, to shape the American response. Jefferson was wary of showing too much interest for fear that he would encourage Algiers to capture more Americans. Better to let these two dozen men languish than to have Algiers fill her prisons with more ransomable Americans.

Jefferson did arrange through the Mathurin religious order to give a small allowance of about seven cents (equivalent to $1 today) a day to each prisoner. When the French Revolution abolished the Mathurins and other religious orders, William Carmichael, the American minister to Spain, arranged their allowance. Carmichael relied on the generosity of either the Bacri family of Jewish bankers or Swedish consul Mattias Skjöldebrand.

When David Humphreys, American minister to Lisbon, became involved with the prisoners in 1794, he raised their stipend to $3 a month for sailors, $6 for mates, and $8 for captains (roughly $46, $92, and $116 today).

Wary of showing too much concern for the plight of the captives, Jefferson advocated using force against the Barbary States. He saw the Barbary States not only as a threat to American trade, but also as a lesson to the Americans. For Jefferson and other enlightened thinkers, the region from modern Iran through Turkey and from Egypt to Morocco presented a puzzle. Although they had great natural resources, these birthplaces of great civilizations now were desolate. Egypt and Mauritania, home to the world's first universities, now were backwaters of indolence and poverty. The Barbary States, sitting astride the trade routes between Europe and Africa, supplied grain to southern Europe. Why did they have to resort to capturing ships? Why were these societies seemingly stagnant?

Jefferson was not alone in wondering about this. After traveling through Egypt and Syria in the 1780s, French philosopher Abbé Constantin François de Chasseboeuf Volney blamed the decline of Egypt and Syria on Turkish despotism. Tyranny ruined the "labours of past ages" and destroyed "the hopes of future times." Additionally, Volney believed that religious intolerance in Muslim countries had stifled free inquiry and that the spirit of fatalism made men unwilling to exert themselves. While Islamic fatalism made Muslim rulers good-hearted, humane, just, and less avaricious than Christian rulers, this same spirit of fatalistic acceptance made society as a whole indolent. Jefferson was so impressed with Volney's message that, while he was president of the United States, he helped translate Volney's book *The Ruins* into English.

For Jefferson, Volney's lesson was not so much aimed at reforming Egypt and Syria as it was a warning to America. If Americans simply accepted the status quo, allowing someone else to govern them, they would become indolent and complacent, suffering the fate of either the people in the Ottoman Empire, governed by the tyrannical power of the sultan, or of the Tripolitans, Tunisians, and Algerians, separately caught between the superpowers of England and France. Either option was possible if Americans were not careful first in constructing a stable government, then in conducting it according to its own rules and principles.

*   *   *

Jefferson saw a need for the United States to act. If the United States wanted to trade in the Mediterranean—with the British closing the West Indies to

American ships, commerce in the Mediterranean was crucial—it would have to protect its merchants from Algiers. The best way to do this was to build a navy. The alternative was for American merchants to send their goods on British or French ships, which would not benefit Americans. "We ought to begin a naval power," Jefferson wrote to Virginia congressman James Monroe, "if we mean to carry on our own commerce." Algiers, the principal threat to American trade in the Mediterranean, would be the first target of this navy. "Can we begin it on a more honourable occasion or with a weaker foe?"

Congress wanted to pursue diplomacy first. Even before Algiers captured the two American ships, Congress had sent Connecticut mule-trader John Lamb to negotiate with Algiers. Lamb did not reach Algiers until March 1786, nearly a year after the two captures. Although he spent a month in Algiers, he failed to free the captives or negotiate a treaty.

As Lamb's mission failed, Jefferson and John Adams considered what policy the United States should follow. Adams wrote that the "Policy of Christendom has made Cowards of all their Sailors before the Standard of Mahomet." He thought the real issue was not religion, but economics. Annual tribute, he thought, would be about £200,000 ($37 million today), yet American merchants could make an annual Mediterranean profit of £1 million (or $192 million today). Nonetheless, the Americans did not have the money to protect their trade.

"This is not good Economy," Adams wrote. Adams thought that the United States should raise money immediately to pay Algiers. "Perhaps you will say," Adams wrote to Jefferson, "fight them, though it Should cost Us a great Sum to carry on the war, and although at the end of it we should have more Money to pay as presents. If this is your Sentiment, and you can persuade the Southern States into it, I dare answer for it that all from Pennsylvania inclusively northward, would not object." Adams knew that most Virginians, unlike Jefferson, opposed building a navy; moreover, as the largest state, Virginia carried a great deal of influence in the American republic.

Jefferson disagreed with Adams on paying tribute and with most Virginians on building a navy. He thought it would be "best to effect a peace thro' the medium of war . . . ." Fighting Algiers would satisfy justice and honor, and would "procure us respect in Europe, and respect is a safe-guard to interest." Jefferson also thought that war would be less expensive than buying a peace.

Jefferson believed that the United States would not have to bear the cost alone. He saw the importance of a multinational alliance to secure a common objective—in this case, free commerce in the

Mediterranean. Also, the way the Americans would secure this trade—by working with other non-aligned nations—would be a lesson to the great powers of Europe as to the value of cooperation. "Were only two or three to begin a confederacy of this kind, I think every power in Europe would soon fall into it except France, England, and perhaps Spain and Holland," he wrote to Monroe. Only England, though, would "give any real aid to the Algerines [Algerians]."

He worked to enlist the support of small European states—Naples, Venice, and Sweden. All of these countries suffered because England and France used Algiers, Tunis, and Tripoli to drive up the cost of trade in the Mediterranean. Jefferson also thought Spain and Portugal might support this effort.

Jefferson enlisted the Marquis de Lafayette in the plan to act as an intermediary not only with European diplomats, but also with American officials. Lafayette wrote to George Washington, by then retired from public life yet still very influential, and to Minister of War Henry Knox, proposing that John Paul Jones command a multinational naval force to blockade Algiers. It was Jefferson's idea, but Lafayette proposed it to minimize the apparent differences between Jefferson and Adams, and Jefferson and Congress.

Unfortunately for the bold idea, France forbade it. Foreign minister Vergennes summoned Lafayette to Versailles, telling him to abandon the plan. Both the British and French government profited from Algerian raids on their commercial rivals. France would not allow this plot against Algiers to be framed on French soil.

Though Lafayette had to back out, Jefferson did not. He tried to enlist the Portuguese and the Russians in the alliance. When John Paul Jones went to Russia to serve in the war against Turkey, he proposed this plan to Catherine the Great. Nothing came of it, though, as Russia, like the other powers of Europe, had its own interests and agenda.

Though the nations of Europe would not embrace Jefferson's idea, Virginia's delegates to Congress in July 1787 nonetheless proposed that Jefferson "form a Confederacy with the powers of Europe who are now at War with the piratical states." Then John Jay, the American minister of foreign affairs, also rejected the idea. "It will be said there is no money in the treasury," Jefferson wrote to Monroe. "There never will be money in the treasury till the confederacy shews it's [*sic*] teeth." It would not be able to show its teeth until the United States adopted the Constitution in 1788, which created a stronger national government. When the new government went into operation, shipowner Mathew Irwin (owner of the captive *Dauphin*) lost no time. He called on President Washington, urging him to support a private relief effort. Irwin wanted to raise money to redeem the captives. He warned the president about the stigma that would fall on a government unable to protect its own citizens. Washington agreed on the need to protect citizens, but he did not think his public position should be used to support private philanthropy.

Washington also was wary of having private individuals such as Irwin, with a vested interest in a certain policy, using their influence with elected officials. The American people had elected Washington, not Irwin, to direct American policy. Washington also feared that raising money for the captives would encourage Algiers to capture more ships. In addition, some families whose loved ones had been lost at sea reported to Washington that an unscrupulous character named James Reynolds had approached them, reporting that he had seen their relatives in Algiers and promising to redeem them for a certain price. For all these reasons, Washington believed that the president should oversee the return of captive Americans; their return should be part of a broad American policy, not motivated by sentimental self-interest.

Washington appointed Jefferson to be the first secretary of state; in March 1790, they discussed "the unfortunate Christians in Captivity among the Barbarians." Jefferson prepared a report to Congress, assembling all the available information on the captives in Algiers, on the value of Mediterranean trade, and on the cost of the various ways proposed to secure it. Jefferson's report to Congress dealt both with the Algerian negotiations and with the more pressing issue of Mediterranean trade, which had been severely restricted since the Revolution.

Jefferson presented Congress with three options. First, the United States could agree to pay Algiers a fixed sum for the release of the captives. This was not a good option, as it would tempt Algiers to capture more American ships.

The second option was to "obtain Peace by purchasing it." The United States would be following the "Example of rich and powerful Nations" who counted "their Interest more than their Honor." Estimates of cost ranged from the $325,000 suggested by Richard O'Brien (about $5 million today) to $15 million. Still, even if the United States paid, every time a new consul was sent or a dey died (Muhammad ibn Uthman Dey, nearly eighty, would die the following year), "Occasion must be made of renewing Presents."

Finally, the "third Expedient is to repel Force by Force." Jefferson gave a detailed account of Algerian forces, including what times of year the Algerians cruised, and proposed a "Concert of Operation" among the nations at war with Algiers—Russia, Austria, Portugal, Naples, Sardinia, Genoa, and

Malta. It was up to Congress, Jefferson said, to choose "between War, Tribute, and Ransom . . . ."

Though Jefferson stated his position as forcefully as he could, Congress decided on paying tribute and ransom. It authorized Washington to spend $400,000 on ransom (approximately $6 million today) and annual payments of $100,000 each ($1.5 million today) to Algiers, Tunis, and Tripoli. Congress also authorized the president to send an agent to negotiate. Perhaps to show that the United States had not altogether given up on the option of force, Jefferson appointed John Paul Jones as the American negotiator. Unfortunately, Jones died before he received his commission.

Jefferson next turned to Thomas Barclay, who had successfully negotiated the American treaty with Morocco. Barclay, however, also died before receiving his instructions. So it was not until spring 1793 that Jefferson commissioned David Humphreys, the American minister to Portugal, to negotiate with Algiers. Humphreys received his instructions in September, leaving immediately for Algiers.

Five days before Humphreys left Lisbon, Britain's consul in Algiers, Charles Logie, arranged a fraudulent truce between Algiers and Portugal. Logie issued passes to Algerian ships that would allow them to slip through Portugal's blockade at Gibraltar. At this moment the British and the French were on the verge of war, and the Algerians could neutralize the Americans, who were trading with the French. By the time the Portuguese government denounced the truce and resumed its blockade, Algiers had taken eleven more American ships and more than one hundred sailors.

Hassan Dey, who had come to power after Muhammad Dey's death in 1791, refused to issue a passport for Humphreys to enter Algiers. From Alicante, Humphreys corresponded with O'Brien and with the Swedish consul, Mattias Skjöldebrand. Humphreys forwarded this correspondence to Jefferson, sending along O'Brien's dispatches. "From these communications," Humphreys wrote, "it will be but too evident, that no choice is left for the United States but to prepare a naval force, with all possible expedition," as the Algerian corsairs "will infest the channel of England, and even the coasts of America, in another season, unless the most vigorous and decisive measures are taken."

By this time, when the wisdom of Jefferson's original policy had become painfully obvious, he had retired from his post as secretary of state. Congress now voted to build a small navy. Construction began on six frigates, built in Portsmouth, New Hampshire; Boston; New York; Philadelphia; Baltimore; and Gosport, Virginia. Washington named the ships the *Constitution, Constellation, United States, President, Congress,* and *Chesapeake.* Still, it would take more than two years to complete them.

Congress also appropriated another $800,000 to spend on a peace treaty with Algiers.

Meanwhile, public sentiment was stirring on behalf of the captives. Philadelphia shipping magnate Stephen Girard formed a committee to raise money for their relief. Girard, who also supported the French in their war against the British, saw the British collusion with Algiers as further evidence of their perfidy. Less politically charged Americans, such as an anonymous writer calling himself Benevolence, wrote to Secretary of State Edmund Randolph urging Washington to sponsor a national contribution for the relief of the captives. Washington would not endorse private contributions; with pro-French activists like Girard behind the campaign, Washington clearly saw the need to stay away.

Humphreys complicated the issue by publishing a plea for contributions to a national lottery to relieve the captives, seemingly giving it official sanction. In February 1795, churches in New England collected money to relieve the captives.

Boston playwright Susanna Haswell Rowson, author of the best-selling novel, *Charlotte Temple,* wrote a play, *Slaves in Algiers: or a Struggle for Freedom,* highlighting the issue of captivity. Rowson's play, borrowed from Cervantes's "Tale of the Captive," has the Americans persuade the dey of Algiers not only to free his captives and renounce attacks on merchant ships, but also to reform his government. He rejects "all power but such as my united friends shall think me incapable of abusing." Royall Tyler, lawyer and writer (his play *The Contrast* is considered the first play written by an American), wrote a novel, *The Algerine Captive,* which drew the connection between captivity and enslavement of Americans in Algiers and the enslavement of Africans in America. The connection was hard to miss. Americans denounced Algiers for enslaving a hundred sailors; yet nearly 700,000 Africans and African Americans were enslaved in the United States. The Americans could not condemn Algiers for brutal despotism without considering slavery at home. The campaign to free the American captives in Algiers brought to public consciousness the brutal fact of slavery in America.

In September, negotiator Joseph Donaldson, suffering from gout, arrived in Algiers. Cathcart had risen in the Algerian bureaucracy and now was secretary to Hassan Dey. He assisted Donaldson in the negotiations, which resulted in a treaty on September 5, 1795. Under terms of the treaty, the United States would pay Algiers $585,000 (approximately one-twelfth of the federal budget at the time, equivalent to $9 million today). Donaldson also promised to build the dey a new frigate, the *Crescent.* Donaldson sent O'Brien to Lisbon to get the gold

(Cathcart fumed that he himself should have gone on this mission) and then waited.

Raising the funds in Europe was more difficult than the Americans imagined. The French Revolution and England's war against France had absorbed most of the gold supply. O'Brien went from Lisbon to London, then to Hamburg, and back to Lisbon, unsuccessfully trying to borrow the gold. Back in Algiers, the prisoners anxiously waited while the dey grew annoyed and angry at the delay in payment. When in February 1796 three of the captive Americans got into a drunken scuffle, and one fell from the apartment gallery to his death, Hassan Dey called it God's judgment against the Americans who did not fulfill their treaty obligations.

Just as Ramadan was beginning, in early March 1796, Joel Barlow, a poet and diplomat, arrived in Algiers. Even though he did not bring the money to fulfill the treaty, he had $30,000 in gifts for the dey. Although Barlow was able to accomplish little during Ramadan, he placated Hassan and interceded between Donaldson and Cathcart, who had come to despise each other. Having smoothed the way to release the captives, Cathcart approached Barlow about the position of American consul general to Algiers. He hoped to stay in Algiers and continue to engage in trade. Barlow, however, wrote to the secretary of state, "I am told that Mr. Cathcart has hopes of obtaining the consulate for this place. He has neither the talents nor the dignity of character necessary for the purpose . . . ." Barlow thought Richard O'Brien would be better suited as American consul, though Cathcart would be a useful diplomatic courier. Without telling Cathcart this was his opinion, he sent Cathcart to America in May 1796 with dispatches for President Washington. Cathcart sailed on his own ship, the *Independent,* anticipating this as the beginning of a lucrative career in international trade and diplomacy.

Finally, in July 1796, Barlow came up with $200,000 in gold for Hassan. It was a complicated arrangement: the new French consul arrived in June with elaborate presents for Hassan Dey, who then lent the French consul $200,000. The consul deposited this money with the Bacris; they loaned this money to Barlow, who used it to pay Hassan. When he received this significant payment, which he did not realize came from his own treasury, Hassan agreed to release the American prisoners.

Barlow chartered the ship *Fortune* from the Bacri fleet; on July 13, 1796, it sailed from Algiers, carrying away more than sixty of the surviving captives. The *Fortune* was well on its way to Marseilles when Hassan learned that Barlow had, in fact, paid him with his own money. Sixty of the prisoners ultimately returned to the United States in February 1797; others stayed in the Mediterranean, working aboard the *Fortune*, shipping the Bacris's wheat from Algerian ports into France.

O'Brien finally returned to Algiers, having taken advantage of an unplanned stop in Tripoli to negotiate a treaty there. He had then stopped in Tunis to negotiate a treaty with that regency. By the end of 1797, when the sixty surviving captives had been returned home, the United States was at peace with the Barbary States.

Barlow, though, had warned the secretary of state that peace treaties were not regarded as binding among the Barbary powers. In Algiers, Tunis, and Tripoli, money promised under a treaty was paid into the public treasury, while the gifts given on signing a treaty went directly to the ruler. So it was in the interest of the dey of Algiers, pasha of Tripoli, or bey of Tunis to go to war against a commercial nation, as that would start the cycle of treaty negotiation and gift-giving. Barlow, like Jefferson, advised building a navy to protect American commerce, as he knew that the recently signed treaties would not last forever. France and England could make permanent peace in Algiers because their navies patrolled the Mediterranean, protecting their merchant ships.

The United States was building a small fleet; it was also building ships for Algiers. Under terms of the treaty, the United States was building a frigate, the *Crescent,* and two smaller vessels, the *Skjölde-*

brand and the *Hassan Bashaw,* for the dey. O'Brien returned to Algiers in February 1798 on board the *Crescent,* coming this time as American consul general to Algiers responsible for all American relations with the Barbary States.

Cathcart was appointed consul to Tripoli. William Eaton, appointed as consul to Tunis, was the only one of the three with no experience in diplomacy or in the Barbary States; he had served in the army along the Cherokee and Creek frontiers of Georgia. Court-martialed after he accused his superior officers of corruption, Eaton was fortunate to have a long-standing friendship with Secretary of State Timothy Pickering, who agreed to send him to Tunis.

Eaton and Cathcart sailed from Philadelphia on the *Sophia,* on what proved to be an eventful crossing. Cathcart had been in Philadelphia only briefly between his return from Algiers and sailing for Tripoli. While there, he had met and married fifteen-year-old Jane Bancker Woodside; by the time the *Sophia* sailed, Jane was already pregnant with their first child.

According to Eaton, Cathcart's "sour, forbidding, self-conceited personality" and his "repulsive manners" disgusted everyone, particularly the captain, who was offended by Cathcart's offer to run the ship. The Cathcarts' maid, Elizabeth Robeson, also became disgusted with her employer (he may have tried to seduce her at sea). When the *Sophia* reached Algiers, Elizabeth Robeson refused to leave the ship, insisting that she be allowed to return immediately to Philadelphia.

O'Brien persuaded Miss Robeson to come ashore, promising her the safety of his consulate. The Cathcarts were appalled that first evening on shore when O'Brien insisted that Betsy Robeson sit down with the party to dinner. She was, after all, their maid, not a social equal. The Cathcarts refused to sit at the table with her, so O'Brien had their meals sent to their rooms. Fuming to Eaton that O'Brien had insulted him, Cathcart was told by the amused Eaton that it was "useless to resent an injury which cannot be chastised—either knock the aggressor down, slap him, or pass the injury unnoticed."

Two months later, when Cathcart was in Tripoli, O'Brien married Elizabeth Robeson. Cathcart had been offended when his servant was treated as his equal; he was outraged when she became his superior.

*   *   *

This personality conflict among the consuls did not help a difficult situation. The United States was slow in sending its tribute to the Barbary States; by 1800, it was so far in debt to Algiers that when the

Commodore William Bainbridge, oil on wood by John Wesley Jarvis

frigate *George Washington* arrived with the American tribute, Mustafa Dey forced Capt. William Bainbridge to convey Algiers's own tribute to Istanbul.

Bainbridge was a young captain—in fact, he had been commissioned a captain just a few days shy of his twenty-sixth birthday, making him the youngest captain in the navy. It was either his age, being younger than many of his crew, or his temper that made him a brutal disciplinarian. In addition to his youth, he had another more dubious distinction. He was the only American naval officer to surrender his ship to an enemy: during the war against France in 1798, Bainbridge had surrendered the sloop *Retaliation* to a French ship.

Now, in 1800, Bainbridge was forced to sail the *George Washington* under the Algerian flag. Though he was the first American naval captain to visit Istanbul, his cruise was not an auspicious one. The cargo included African slaves, exotic animals, and Algerian goods, as well as the Algerian delegation that reportedly grew angry with Bainbridge for altering his course as they were praying toward Mecca. Ultimately they reached Istanbul, where port officials in the Golden Horn seemed puzzled at the origins of the ship. Told that the *George Washington* came from the United States, the minister of marine gave a blank look. He had never heard of such a place. Upon further explanation, his eyes widened—"You mean *the New World!*"

The Algerian tribute was late, and the Algerians had allied themselves with the French while the Ottomans were fighting against Napoleon in Egypt. This meant for a tense reception for the Algerian delegation. The Americans, however, were received warmly. Not only were they also at war with France, but observers noted an auspicious sign of future harmony between the Ottomans and the Americans: the Ottoman flag had a star and a moon; the American flag had many stars. Sharing this celestial connection boded well for future relations.

Cruising through the Bosporus into the Black Sea, Bainbridge hosted a banquet aboard the *George Washington* for the diplomats and officials of Istanbul. To their delight, he served four different decanters of water—one drawn in America, one from Africa, one from Europe, and another from Asia. On this American warship brought to Istanbul under duress, Bainbridge was able to bring together the waters of the earth, perhaps for the first time.

Before leaving Istanbul, Bainbridge was given a letter of safe conduct by the Ottoman admiral. This gave the Americans more prestige in Algiers on their return.

Secretary of State Madison thought that sending the *George Washington* to Istanbul "by force, under the Algerine flag" was too serious an indignity to ignore. But for the moment, the newly inaugurated

Jefferson administration was preoccupied with Tripoli.

*   *   *

Yusuf Qaramanli Pasha of Tripoli was at war with Sweden and threatening American ships as well. He resented the fact that Algiers and Tunis had received much more in the way of tribute than he had in their 1796 treaties (he had received about $50,000; Tunis, he heard, had received $60,000). Yusuf also resented the fact that the American treaty suggested that Tripoli was in some way subservient to Algiers. Yusuf informed Cathcart that unless the United States negotiated a new treaty and gave him $250,000, he would declare war on the United States. On May 14, 1801, he sent a crew of men to cut down the flagpole in front of the American consulate, equivalent to a declaration of war. Cathcart and his family, now consisting of his wife and two children, packed up their belongings and sailed for Italy.

Yusuf had no way of knowing that the United States had already embarked on a new policy in the Mediterranean. Thomas Jefferson, who had become president on March 4, 1801, was prepared to undertake the policy he had begun advocating sixteen years earlier. When Jefferson learned of Yusuf's threats, he dispatched Commodore Richard Dale

Tripolitans cut down the American flagpole

with four ships—the frigates *President, Essex,* and *Philadelphia,* and the schooner *Enterprise*—to the Mediterranean. Dale could give Yusuf $10,000 to keep the peace; otherwise, the squadron would assist Sweden in a blockade of Tripoli or, if Tripoli had declared war, the squadron would protect American shipping.

Commodore Richard Dale appeared off Tripoli on July 24. He imposed a blockade yet did not go ashore to negotiate with Yusuf. Lt. Andrew Sterrett on the *Enterprise* engaged in a three-hour battle with the Tripolitan ship *Tripoli.* The *Enterprise* disabled the *Tripoli,* killing or wounding fifty of its eighty-man crew. As he was not certain that the United States and Tripoli were at war, Sterrett could not capture the ship. He had his men toss its cannon overboard.

Reporting to Congress in his first annual message, Jefferson said that Tripoli, "the least considerable of the Barbary States," had issued "demands unfounded either in right or in compact" and threatened to declare war. "The style of the demand admitted but one answer." He had sent a small squadron to the Mediterranean "with assurances to that power of our sincere desire to remain in peace, but with orders to protect our commerce against the threatened attack." This measure was "seasonable and salutary," for Yusuf had declared war and sent out his cruisers. American commerce was blockaded in the Mediterranean, but the "arrival of our squadron dispelled the danger."

Then Jefferson turned to Lt. Sterrett. "One of the Tripolitan cruisers having fallen in with and engaged the small schooner *Enterprise*," the Tripolitan was "captured, after a heavy slaughter of her men, without the loss of a single one on our part." Jefferson hoped that the "bravery exhibited by our citizens" on the ocean would demonstrate to the world that it was "not the want of that virtue which makes us seek their peace, but a conscientious desire to direct the energies of our nation to the multiplication of the human race, and not to its destruction."

Jefferson pointed out that, although the Constitution did not authorize Sterrett to do more than defend his ship, he thought Congress might consider "authorizing measures of offense also, they will place our force on an equal footing with that of its adversaries." The power to declare war or increase the country's offensive capabilities was "confided by the Constitution to the Legislature exclusively," so he sent Congress the information they would need to make an informed judgment. On February 6, 1802, Congress declared war on Tripoli.

The Tripolitan operation fit in with Jefferson's long-standing views of how to deal with the Barbary States. By closing off the Mediterranean to American trade, Algiers and now Tripoli had imposed a barrier even more effective than the British Navigation Acts. Jefferson believed these states acted, if not under the direction of England and France, at least with their complicity. It was vital that the Americans demonstrate to England and France that the United States would not tolerate these kinds of barriers. So Jefferson sent the American squadron to the Mediterranean. Also, Jefferson wanted the squadron to cooperate with Sweden or other nonaligned nations, as he had proposed sixteen years earlier.

Jefferson did not mention the hypocrisy of previous American administrations. Although President Adams had sent negotiators to make peace with France in 1797, officials in the French foreign ministry—called "Mssrs. X, Y, and Z" in the American dispatches—demanded bribes before they would begin to negotiate. Despite blustering "Millions for Defence, Not one Cent for Tribute," the Adams administration meekly promised tribute to Algiers. Noting that his predecessors had failed to send the tribute they had promised, Jefferson vowed to take "immediate measures" to fulfill American agreements and so "vindicate to ourselves the right of considering the effect of departure from stipulation on their side."

*   *   *

Jefferson sent Commodore Richard Valentine Morris with five ships to relieve Dale's squadron. Morris, on the flagship *Chesapeake*, took his duty to escort merchant vessels very seriously, his obligation to blockade Tripoli less so. In fact, the *Chesapeake* never reached Tripoli. Morris had brought along his wife and young son, spending most of his tour cruising the Mediterranean. British-controlled Malta became the home port of the American fleet; there Morris rented an apartment where his wife gave birth to another child. Yusuf Qaramanli mocked the Americans for making love, not war. Morris returned home in 1803 to be court-martialed, and President Jefferson sent a new commander, Edward Preble, on the *Constitution,* to fight the war.

Preble was determined to use his small fleet to fight the enemy. With just two frigates, *Constitution* and *Philadelphia,* and several smaller vessels, he would have one constantly on patrol off Tripoli. The other would escort merchant ships or refit in Syracuse. Preble based his squadron in Syracuse, where the Americans were the only fleet in port.

Before Preble could implement his strategy, disaster struck. Capt. Bainbridge, commanding the *Philadelphia,* was off Tripoli at the end of October, when a fleet of smaller vessels surrounded the frigate. Unfamiliar with the coast of Tripoli, Bainbridge sailed the *Philadelphia* onto a reef. The smaller Tripolitan ships closed in on the stranded frigate. Bainbridge surrendered. In the navy's short history, only two ships had surrendered to enemies; William Bainbridge commanded both. Not a man had been wounded on either side. Tripoli now had the second-largest ship in the American fleet, and more than three hundred American prisoners, including Jonathan Cowdery, an assistant surgeon, and William Ray, a marine, whose narratives are included in this volume. When they were all ashore, the rising tide lifted the undamaged *Philadelphia* from the reef, and the Tripolitans sailed it into their harbor.

"If it had not been for the capture of the *Philadelphia*," Preble wrote, "I have no doubt but we should have had peace with Tripoly [*sic*] in the Spring." He did not hide his fury. "Would to God," he wrote, "that the Officers and crew of the *Philadelphia* had one and all, determined to prefer death to slavery."

Bainbridge knew how bad this was. He wrote his wife, Susan, telling her about his capture and predicting that this would be the end of his naval career. He had been the first and only captain in the U.S. Navy to surrender his vessel (see page li); now he became the second, and still the only one to do so. In neither engagement had his men resisted. He wrote to Preble and the secretary of the navy, informing them of the capture. Preble tried to be conciliatory in his responses to Bainbridge, assuring him that he had no alternatives. Bainbridge wrote back to Preble, inserting secret messages between the lines in lime juice, giving Preble what intelligence he could of Tripoli's fortifications and troop strength. He also proposed a way to free some of his men. Some could claim to be British subjects, and so could be released into British custody. When Adm. Horatio Lord Nelson, commanding the British fleet off the south coast of France, heard the idea, he made it known that he would hang these men as deserters from the Royal Navy.

Preble negotiated with Tripolitan agents in Malta, trying to free the prisoners, although he knew that would be futile. Yusuf would not give up the advantage of having three hundred American bargaining chips. The *Philadelphia* itself was another matter—the Americans believed Yusuf would fit it out to use against them. In truth, he was arranging to sell the *Philadelphia* to Tunis.

In January 1804, Preble captured the Tripolitan ship *Mastico*. Among its seventy passengers were the Tripolitan officers who had captured the *Philadelphia*. Now Preble had something to bargain with, though Yusuf rebuffed offers for an exchange. Lt. Stephen Decatur proposed a bold plan. Disguising the *Mastico* as a trading vessel renamed *Intrepid*, he would sail it into Tripoli, overpower the Tripolitans aboard the *Philadelphia,* and destroy it. Decatur sailed the *Intrepid* into Tripoli harbor on the night of February 16, 1804. He led his men onto the *Philadelphia,* forced the Tripolitan crew overboard, and then set the frigate on fire. A Tripolitan guard would later recall how the "great smoke cloud spreads its wings like some evil bird over the harbor and soars to the upper regions of the darkness . . . . Soon the red devil tongues make the harbor light as day and redder than the sands of the Sahk-ra [Sahara] when the sun is low in the west . . . . They make its red walls and ramparts red like blood and like some monster dragon as it spits back its fire guns."

The batteries of Tripoli and the guns on the ships in the harbor opened up on Decatur and his men; he navigated away from the blazing ship and out of the harbor without losing a man. Commodore Preble was so impressed with Decatur's heroic action—his ability to steal into the enemy's harbor and destroy the largest ship in it without losing a man—that he immediately requested that President Jefferson promote Decatur to captain. At age 25 years and a few days, Decatur became the youngest man commissioned a captain in the U.S. Navy. Bainbridge's tenure as the navy's youngest captain had lasted seven years; Decatur's has endured for more than two hundred.

The Americans were wise, the Tripolitan guard

said. "When they lose their ship, they lose it to everybody."

*   *   *

Destroying the *Philadelphia* was a great feat, but it did not end the war. Preble maintained his blockade of Tripoli and in the early summer sent Richard O'Brien into Tripoli to negotiate with Yusuf. O'Brien offered the pasha $60,000; Yusuf, remembering that O'Brien had gotten the better of him in the 1796 treaty, angrily rejected the offer.

Preble borrowed gunboats from the king of Naples, planning another assault on Tripoli for early August. Yusuf mocked the Americans, saying they had no notion of fighting; nonetheless, Preble's fleet did considerable damage to Tripoli's navy. It also nearly killed Bainbridge, when a shell hit his room in the palace. Yet at the end of the day, Tripoli still had more guns and men than the Americans. Preble planned another assault at a different point, west of the city. His intelligence was wrong, though—the Tripolitans had fortified the position Preble attacked, and his forces were rebuffed.

The day after this bombardment, a group of American prisoners petitioned Yusuf for better treatment. A former American captive, Lewis Heximer—known as Hamet Amerikan since his conversion to Islam (five of the American captives converted and won better treatment)—presented the petition in which the prisoners complained of being beaten, pelted with stones, spat upon, insulted by soldiers, made to carry impossible burdens, and so "chased and bruised" it was impossible to work. The pasha forbade his guards from striking the prisoners.

Lt. Richard Somers, anxious to earn the same honors as Decatur, loaded the *Intrepid* with 150 barrels of gunpowder, planning to bring the ketch under the shore batteries of Tripoli, light the fuse, and row away. The vessel *Nautilus* would cover their escape and pick them up outside the harbor.

Assisted by midshipmen Henry Wadsworth and Robert Israel, and ten sailors, Somers brought the vessel into Tripoli harbor on the night of September 4. At ten o'clock, the men on the *Nautilus* saw a blinding flash and felt the shock of the explosion. The *Nautilus* waited all night, under fire from the Tripolitan shore batteries, for survivors. There were none.

Preble speculated that, when Somers realized the enemy had discovered his boat, he destroyed it rather than be taken prisoner. Through their disastrous deaths Somers, Israel, and Wadsworth became heroes. Wadsworth's sister, then living in Portland, Maine, married a man named Longfellow; when their first son was born in 1807, they named him Henry Wadsworth Longfellow in honor of his heroic uncle.

Unable to defeat the Tripolitans, Preble maintained the blockade. He also knew American reinforcements were coming; while this brought the promise of victory, it also brought Capt. Samuel Barron. As Barron was senior to Preble, he, not Preble, would command the combined force. Preble would return home, disappointed in not bringing the war to a conclusion. He did not have great confidence in Barron's ability to succeed.

The fleet also would bring William Eaton, former consul to Tunis. Eaton had gone to the United States with a bold plan: the United States should join forces with Achmed Qaramanli, the pasha's older brother, whom Yusuf had deposed in 1795. Achmed would be brought from Egypt to Derne, today in northern Libya. The people of Tripoli would rally to his cause and depose Yusuf, reinstalling Achmed as pasha. Achmed would then make a favorable treaty with the United States.

Eaton, with seven marines and two midshipmen, went to Egypt. Turkish authorities promptly arrested him as a British spy. Released, Eaton and his marines and midshipmen tracked down Achmed 150 miles south of Cairo. On February 21, 1805, Eaton and Achmed signed an agreement under which Eaton, a captain in the U.S. Army, declared himself a general and promised to install Achmed as pasha. Achmed promised to reimburse the United States for expenses incurred on his behalf.

Achmed (Hamet) Qaramanli, William Eaton,
and the U. S. Marines

On March 6, the expedition—Eaton and Achmed, the seven marines and two midshipmen, three hundred Arab horsemen, seventy-five Christian mercenaries, and more than a thousand camels—set out from Alexandria for the five-hundred-mile march across the desert to Derne. Amazingly, Eaton was able to overcome constant problems of provisions, threatened desertions, and dissension within these ranks. In mid-April they reached the Bay of Bomba, where two American ships waited with supplies.

Eaton's army reached Derne on April 27. With two American ships providing artillery support, Eaton's army captured Derne after a 2-½ hour battle. Although only marine John Wilton died in the fight, marine Lt. Presley O'Bannon raised the American flag over the city gate—the first time it had ever flown over a captured foreign city.

Yusuf sent forces to retake the city. On May 8, the Tripolitan army defeated Achmed's cavalry just outside Derne's walls, though the marines and the Arabs loyal to Achmed repulsed Yusuf's infantry from inside the city. Yusuf sent more reinforcements, who were not able to break the resistance, which had American ships off the coast supporting O'Bannon and Achmed's forces in Derne.

Although Yusuf could not take Derne, it was also clear Achmed could not march on to Tripoli. On June 11 the frigate *Constellation* reached Derne.

Eaton and Achmed thought it brought reinforcements. They were stunned that it brought news of a treaty the United States had made with Yusuf. The pasha agreed, for a sum of $60,000 (approximately $700,000 today), to release the prisoners and not to take any more Americans captive. The United States would drop its support of Achmed. Achmed, Eaton, and the marines boarded the *Constellation*; Achmed's remaining forces were left to fend for themselves in Derne.

Negotiator Tobias Lear had arranged the treaty, which was signed aboard the *Constitution* on June 4. While Lear and Tripolitan foreign minister Muhammad D'Ghies negotiated, the ship's carpenter fashioned a new flagpole; at eleven in the morning on June 5, the American flag was raised once more in front of the American consulate, and Tripoli's batteries fired a twenty-one-gun salute.

Some of the naval officers were dissatisfied with the treaty, as was William Eaton. Eaton mocked "Aunt Lear and her Lieutenants," comments that provoked Commodore Barron's brother James to challenge Eaton to a duel.

Decatur thought he could have landed two thousand men in Tripoli, bringing off Yusuf in the light of day. But peace was peace, and the prisoners on shore prepared to leave Tripoli. A group of sailors pooled their resources, coming up with $300 to release a friendly Neapolitan prisoner. Bainbridge was pleased to hear of their generosity (contributing the rest of the money they needed to free their friend). He would not allow his sailors to leave Tripoli, however, until they had cleaned up and sobered up—news of the peace had brought with it "the intoxication of Liberty & Liquor," according to Lear, and Bainbridge wanted them "quite clean and in Order" before they boarded the American vessels.

Five of the men—those who had converted to Islam—were marched out of Tripoli, never to be seen again. The others returned to a heroic welcome in the United States.

Though it was not an unambiguous victory—Yusuf renounced tribute, but the Americans paid him a hefty ransom for their prisoners—the United States celebrated the conclusion of the war. Heroes like Decatur and Eaton sparked national celebrations. While Britain, France, and Spain were content to pay off the Barbary powers, Americans had challenged them and emerged victorious.

Paintings and prints of Decatur's destruction of the *Philadelphia,* his hand-to-hand combat with a Tripolitan officer during the battle of Tripoli, and Somers's death on the *Intrepid* gave the public vivid and heroic images of the war. Congress presented swords to Decatur and Preble, and at testimonial dinners throughout the republic the naval heroes were celebrated in song.

Maryland lawyer Francis Scott Key wrote a song

Stephen Decatur Jr. fighting on a Tripolitan gunboat

in December 1805 for a testimonial dinner in Decatur's honor. To the tune of "Anacreon in Heaven," a popular English drinking song, Key praised this band of brothers who had braved desert and ocean to secure the nation's honor.

> *In conflict resistless each toil they endur'd*
> *Till their foes shrunk dismay'd from the war's*
>   *desolation:*
> *And pale beam'd the Crescent, its splendor*
>   *obscur'd*
> *By the light of the star-spangled flag of our*
>   *nation,*
>   *Where each flaming star gleam'd a meteor of*
>   *war,*
>   *And the turban'd heads bowed to the terrible*
>   *glare.*
> *Then mixt with the olive the laurel shall wave*
> *And form a bright wreath for the brow of the*
>   *brave.*

Nine years later, in September 1814 in Baltimore, Key would watch British forces bombard Fort McHenry. He would revise this song, using the same tune, the imagery of naval bombardment, the "star-spangled" banner, the rhyming of *wave* and *brave*, to create the national anthem.

Algiers, allied again with Britain, declared war on the United States in 1807. Afterward, though, the

United States withdrew its fleet from the Mediterranean and, under threat from Britain and France, closed its own ports in the embargo of 1808. When the United States and England went to war in 1812, Haj Ali Dey of Algiers also declared war on the United States, convinced by the British that the Royal Navy would sweep the minuscule American fleet off the seas. It seemed a reasonable expectation. The British fleet had nearly a thousand ships; the Americans, fewer than twenty. But unexpected American victories at sea (and on the Great Lakes), as well as decisive victories against the British-supported Creek and Shawnee Indians, and against British forces at New Orleans, allowed the United States to survive the war. In early 1815, President Madison ordered the largest American fleet ever built up to that time to sail to the Mediterranean and secure peace with Algiers and the other Barbary States.

William Bainbridge was given command of this squadron and expected to secure his new reputation as a naval hero earned when the *Constitution*, under his command, defeated the *Macedonian*. In Boston he oversaw the construction of the seventy-four-gun *Independence*, the largest warship the Americans had built, which would lead the forces in the Mediterranean. Once again, he was upstaged by Decatur. Before Bainbridge was ready to sail, Decatur led a fleet of ten ships to the Mediterranean. He captured the brig *Estedio* and Algerian frigate *Meshouda*, killing the admiral Hamidou Ra'is, before sailing into Algiers on June 28. Within forty-eight hours, Omar Dey had released ten American prisoners and agreed to a treaty that promised not to take American ships, sparing Americans from paying tribute to Algiers. The dey said he would not have agreed to such terms with any other power "except the man who went in a dark night and burnt the *Philadelphia*—that there was no knowing what such a person might do."

From Algiers, Decatur sailed to Tunis, which had allowed a British warship to seize two British vessels that Americans had lawfully captured during the war. Decatur demanded that the bey pay $46,000 for the two vessels. On receiving the demand, the bey said, "I know this admiral [Decatur]. He is the same one who in the war with Sidi Yusuf, of Trablis [Tripoli], burnt the frigate." The bey paid.

On August 5, Decatur sailed into Tripoli. Yusuf Qaramanli had twenty thousand soldiers manning the batteries of the city, but when he learned that Algiers and Tunis had agreed to Decatur's terms, he released ten hostages—two Danes and eight Sicilians—paid $25,000 for ships he had allowed the British to retake during the war, and fired a twenty-one-gun salute to Decatur's fleet.

*   *   *

Cathcart, Cowdery, and Ray were just three of the Americans involved in this encounter with the Barbary States. Merchant captains like Richard O'Brien, interested in trade, made the first contacts between the United States and the Muslim world. Naval commanders like Preble and Decatur fought against Tripoli and Algiers, not to subdue them but to establish peace. Barlow's and O'Brien's treaty with Tripoli in 1796 declared simply that because the United States was not founded on the Christian religion, there should be no conflict between the new republic and the Barbary States of North Africa. Americans were seeking the right to trade with, not the power to govern, others. These men—Jefferson, Preble, Decatur, Cathcart, Cowdery, and Ray—were not conquerors or missionaries, seeking to subdue or to convert. They merely wanted to make their own way in the world and to allow others to do the same.

Robert J. Allison
Associate Professor of History
and Chair, History Department
Suffolk University
Boston, Massachusetts
June 2007

NARRATIVES OF
BARBARY CAPTIVITY

The Captives
Eleven Years a Prisoner in Algiers

BY
James Leander Cathcart

James Leander Cathcart

INTRODUCTION

By the time he was eighteen, James Leander Cathcart had twice been a prisoner of war. Born in County Westmeath, Ireland, in 1767, he was brought to America by his seafaring uncle, and by the age of twelve was a midshipman aboard the American frigate Confederacy. *Taken prisoner by the British, he was held on one of their prison ships in New York harbor under conditions every bit as unpleasant as those he would later experience in Algiers. He escaped in 1782 but signed on to the merchant service. As a seaman on the schooner* Maria, *out of Boston, Cathcart was taken prisoner by the Algerians in July 1785.*

In Algiers, Cathcart came to the notice of the minister of the marine, Hassan, who became dey of Algiers in 1791. Although still a prisoner, he served as Hassan Dey's chief Christian secretary, responsible for correspondence with Christian nations. When American negotiator Joseph Donaldson arrived in 1795, Cathcart acted as an intermediary. In May 1796, he was released to carry the draft treaty to the U.S. government, sailing for Philadelphia on a ship he owned—acquired through wealth earned in his captivity.

In Philadelphia, Cathcart lobbied for appointment as the new American consul general to Algiers, hoping to exploit the commercial ties he had already made there. Instead, in July 1797, he was appointed consul to

Tripoli, considered to be the least important of the Barbary States.

Cathcart and his young bride, Jane Bancker Woodside, sailed for Tripoli on the Sophia *in December 1798. His diplomatic stint in Tripoli was not a success. When Tripoli declared war on the United States in May 1801, the Cathcarts—now with two children—left for Italy. Though Cathcart was finally appointed consul general to Algiers in 1802, the dey refused to receive him and, in fact, refused to allow him off the ship. He was sent instead to Tunis to replace William Eaton, but the bey of Tunis twice refused to receive Cathcart, calling him an* embroglione, *or a troublesome, litigious trifler.*

Yet, when the bey sent Suleiman Mellimelli Sidi to negotiate with the Americans in 1806, Cathcart was hired to escort him. Mellimelli created a sensation on his American tour, accompanied by a secretary, a barber, a cook, a steward, and three slaves. He was housed at the expense of the U.S. government, though the cost was defrayed by the stud fees charged for use of the four Arabian horses brought as gifts for President Jefferson. The United States even provided Mellimelli with the services of "Georgia, a Greek." Though Mellimelli successfully resolved the issues between the United States and Tunis, he and Cathcart parted on unfriendly terms, with the Tunisian accusing Cathcart of being drunk, dishonest, and disrespectful.

Cathcart and his growing family (in all, he and

Jane had twelve children) were sent on a series of missions to minor outposts such as Madeira and Cadiz. In 1818, after the United States purchased Florida, he was sent there to inspect live oak timber for the naval fleet; in 1823 he was given a desk job in Washington as a clerk in the Treasury Department, spending his spare moments filing futile claims against the government for his services in Algiers and during the Tripolitan War.

The family estate, Cathcart's Seat, to be funded with the elusive claims money, near LaPorte, Indiana, where his son had established a political career, was never built. The mansion house was modeled on the country estates Cathcart had seen near Boston, and below the sketch of his dream home, he wrote in bold letters, "NO CLAIMS, NO HOUSE!" Two years after Cathcart's death, his son Charles, born in Madeira in 1809, was elected to the U.S. Congress.

Cathcart's greatest success had come in Algiers. He had risen to be one of the most powerful men in the regency, though his power derived from his connection to the dey. Forever afterward, he pursued success that was always elusive. In James Leander Cathcart's final letter, written shortly before his death in 1843, he lamented bitterly that he had spent his life "faithfully serving an ungrateful country."

Ironically, Cathcart is remembered today for his Barbary captivity narrative that was not even published in his lifetime. Fifty years after his death, his *daughter Jane B. Newkirk edited and privately printed both this memoir of his captivity and a journal of her father's negotiations with Tripoli. Although first edited by his daughter and then extensively excerpted by the current editors, Cathcart's verbose style, notorious to his diplomatic contemporaries, comes through loud and clear.*

Political State of Algiers

THE *Maria* of Boston, on which I had embarked, was captured three miles southeast of Cape St. Vincent (southeast point of Portugal) on the 25th of July, 1785, and arrived at Algiers on the 4th of August following. The *Dauphin* of Philadelphia was captured seventy leagues to the westward of the Rock of Lisbon[1] on the 30th of said month and arrived at Algiers on the 12th of August, being captured by the admiral's ship, and the *Maria,* by a xebec[2] of fourteen guns.

On being boarded, the Mahometans[3] [Muslims] asked us for our flag and papers. Of the first they had no knowledge, the papers they could not read, and Mediterranean pass we had none; consequently, they conceived us to be a good prize, but my feelings were very different from the rest of my fellow sufferers. I understood the Spanish language, which they all spoke, and was the only person on board who had any knowledge of the Barbary States. I knew that a few months before, Spain was at war with the eastern states and prevented their cruisers from coming into the western ocean; and, not having spoken [hailed] any vessel at sea to inform us of that event, I conjectured that this boat must belong to some pirate from that part of Morocco which was then at [civil] war with the

emperor⁴ and that they concluded that the Kingdom of Heaven⁵ was at hand. They were twenty-one
in number and we were only six, which precluded
the possibility of overpowering them had we been
so imprudent as to have made an attempt.

In this state of mind I remained more than two
hours before we joined the xebec, there being very
little wind; and the first salutation we received was a
shout from the whole crew of the cruiser indicative
of our being a good prize. We were then driven into
the boat without being permitted to go into the
cabin, and taken on board the cruiser and conducted to the quarterdeck, every person having a
pull at us as we went along in order to benefit by
our capture. Our hats, handkerchiefs, and shoes
were the first articles that were taken from us and
which we most wanted, as we could not endure the
scorching heat of the sun on our heads, nor were
our feet calculated to bear the heat of the deck.

We were welcomed on board by the *rais*, or captain, a venerable old Arab, who had been a captive
for several years both in Spain and Genoa, and who
was really a good man. "Christians," said he, "be
consoled; this world is full of vicissitudes. You shall
be well used. I have been a slave myself and will
treat you much better than I was treated. Take some
bread and honey and a dish of coffee; and God will
redeem you from captivity, as he has done for me
twice. And when you make your peace with your

father, the king of England, the dey of Algiers will liberate you immediately."[6]

He informed me that they were a cruiser of Algiers; that they had come through the straits in consequence of their having concluded a peace with Spain; and of the arrival of a British consul (Charles Logie) who informed them that they might take all such vessels that had not passports of a particular cut. They had taken several Portuguese fishermen; two pretty large vessels, the crews of the whole amounting to thirty-six men; and one woman, a Spaniard by birth, a facetious creature who seemed perfectly reconciled to her situation and endeavored to reconcile everyone to theirs.

I had entered into a conversation with her and began to thank God that our situation was no worse, when a sail was descried from the masthead and we were all ordered down to the sail room, except the woman. It is impossible to describe the horror of our situation while we remained there. Let imagination conceive what must have been the sufferings of forty-two men, shut up in a dark room in the hold of a Barbary cruiser full of men and filthy in extreme, destitute of every nourishment, and nearly suffocated with heat; yet here we were obliged to remain every night until our arrival in Algiers and wherever we were—either chased or in chase. The vessel proved to be a friend and was liberated immediately, the prize master and crew taking the captain's quadrant perspective glass, charts, and some wearing apparel to indemnify themselves for the trouble of examining their papers.

We were permitted to come upon deck and were regaled with some very bad black olives, mixed with a small quantity of rank oil and some vinegar, to which was added some very coarse bread and water, which was corrupted and which we were literally obliged to strain through our teeth and, while we drank, to stop our noses. This was all our allowance except twice they served us burgul,[7] which we could not eat; notwithstanding, the calls of nature were very great. We must inevitably have perished had it not been for some Turks more charitable than the rest, who gave us some onions, oranges, raisins, and figs from their own private stores. I likewise received relief several times for standing at the helm for the sailors, and actually learned to smoke by the kindness of the ship's steward, who gave me a pipe and tobacco, and whom I lived to repay at Algiers more than two years after.

Whether the Algerine [Algerian] cruisers were apprehensive that Portugal would fit out a squadron to cruise against them or were content with the booty they already had made, I know not; but, fortunately for us, they made but a short cruise and returned to the Mediterranean the first westerly wind after our capture. Had they remained thirty days longer in the western ocean, they would undoubtedly have captured as many American vessels as they could have manned and, probably, several rich Portuguese.

We arrived in Algiers on the eve of the feast that follows Ramadan and, being private property, were conducted to the owner of the cruiser's house, having been first entirely stripped of the remnant of our clothes which remained. I was furnished in lieu thereof with the remains of an old dirty shirt and brown cloth trousers, which formerly belonged to a Portuguese fisherman and were swarming with myriads of vermin, which, with the crown of an old hat, composed the whole of my wardrobe. The rest of my brother sufferers were in no better condition.

We were first carried to the *kieuchk,* or admiralty office, and were permitted to regale ourselves with as much good water as we pleased, which flowed from a neat marble fountain and was as clear as crystal. My desire was so great to partake of this refreshment that I really believed that I should have expired had I been refused this gratification. Those who have been on long voyages know how to appreciate this greatest of luxuries and how grateful it must have been to people in our situation. It has made so permanent an impression on my mind that I shall remember the Fountain of the Kiosk of the marine [harbor] of Algiers to the latest hour of my existence.

We were marched from the *kieuchk* through the

principal streets and marketplace of Algiers and to several of the grandees'[8] houses, followed by the mob who had gathered to view Americans—we being the first they had ever beheld—and, at last, arrived at our owner's house, having received no refreshment but water since the evening before. Here we remained but a few minutes, when we were visited by Christian slaves of all denominations, they not being at work in consequence of the festival. Those who could afford it brought us the fruits of the season, wine, bread, and everything that was cooked or could be eaten without cooking.

At our owner's house, we were all put into an empty room on the ground floor, where we all sat or lay on the bare bricks. In the center of the area was placed a large cauldron—in which clothes had lately been boiled—filled with water and a quantity of coarse flesh, which we supposed to be ordinary beef but afterwards were informed was camel's flesh, which prevented us from tasting it. This enraged our master considerably, and he declared he never would put himself to so much expense again to accommodate Christian slaves. To this again was added a quantity of burgul and some grease, which was extremely rank, and then served up in wooden platters, which, with a quantity of black bread, composed the whole of our nourishment until that time the next day, as the Mahometans of his rank seldom eat themselves or feed their slaves above once a day—and that is after sunset.

Thus forlorn, without food or raiment, anticipating the horrors of a miserable captivity, we stretched ourselves on the bare bricks, where we remained all night, tormented with vermin and mosquitoes, and at daylight were driven down to the marine to unbend the sails and do other necessary work on the cruisers that had captured us. Here we received some biscuit and olives, such as was given us at sea, and plenty of good water.

In the evening we were marched back to our master's house and passed the night in the same manner we had done the one before, with the exception that we got, in lieu of camel's flesh, some boiled mumsa,[9] vegetables, and fruits, with which, with some wine and provisions given by Christian slaves, we made out tolerably well. But still our fate was not decided, and we did not know whether we would be placed at the oar in the galleys or sold to the Arabs in the interior of the regency.[10] Although our fears proved groundless, they prevented us from enjoying the least repose for, when we slumbered, our imagination painted the horrors of our situation in such lively colors that we started from the arms of Morpheus very little refreshed.

The next day we were taken, in a kind of procession, to several of the grandees' houses whom we had not visited on our arrival and who were curious to see Americans—having supposed us to be the aborigines[11] of the country, of which some of them had an imperfect idea from viewing figures which ornament charts of that continent—and were much surprised to see us so fair or, as they expressed themselves, so much like Englishmen. Ultimately we were taken to the British consul's house, who ordered us some refreshments and passed his word to our master that he would be answerable for our conduct while in his house but advised him to leave a person to prevent us from strolling about the streets. But, even here, we were made sensible of indignities which we did not expect and therefore felt in a superlative degree.

We remained here two days and on the third, in the morning, were marched to the *bedistan*, or slave market, where we remained from daylight till half past three o'clock without any refreshments, and were treated thus for three days successively, the first and second nights being lodged in our master's house and having no better accommodations than we had the first day of our arrival.

On the afternoon of the third, we were taken into the dey's palace and paraded before His Excellency when, of our crew, he took five, only leaving Capt. Stephens;[12] and of the Portuguese, eight, for the service of the palace; and the others sent to the slave prison, as the regency purchased them all,

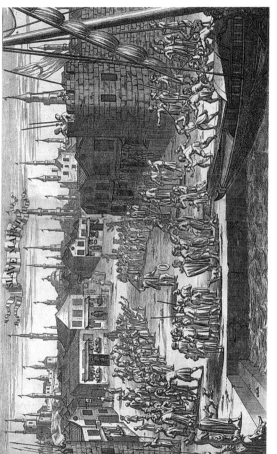

A Barbary slave market

except four or five old men who had been sold at vendue [auction]. The woman, who immediately on her arrival had been sent to the Spanish hospital, there to remain until ransomed, was purchased by the regency.

We were now taken to the hot bath by the other Christian slaves and cleansed from the filth of the cruiser. Our old rags were changed for a large shirt with open sleeves and a large pair of cotton trousers, a pair of shoes, and red cap, all made in Turkish fashion, in which no doubt we made a curious appearance. We were allowed to remain together that night and fared sumptuously in comparison to what we had some time before, and, being clean, slept for several hours as sound as any people could do in our situation. In the morning, we awakened much refreshed and were stationed at our respective duties: two were retained as upper servants; one was sent to the kitchen; and myself and another were doomed to labor in the palace garden, where we had not a great deal to do, there being fourteen of us, and—the taking care of two lions, two tigers, and two antelopes excepted—the work might have very well been done by four.

Here I had sufficient time to bewail my unfortunate situation but was ignorant of its full extent. Had I known the different vicissitudes I was to experience and the length of my captivity, I should have sunk beneath the weight of such accumulated woe. But hope, that sweet soother of all earthly cares, represented that our situation was really not so bad as we had expected and that we had not been used worse than many of our fellow citizens had been during the Revolutionary War in the different British prisons. Being confident that our country would immediately redeem us, I resolved to bear my captivity with as good a grace as possible and not give the Mahometans the satisfaction of seeing me dejected. But alas! I had seen the best part only. I had as yet experienced but few of the bitters of slavery in comparison to what I afterwards suffered.

NOTES

1. The Capa de Roca in Portugal is Europe's westernmost point.

2. Xebec: a small three-masted sailing vessel.

3. Once a common reference for Muslim, the word Mahometan (or Muhammadan) is now regarded by some as offensive because it implies worship of the Prophet Muhammad rather than of God.

4. Muhammad bin Abdallah Sidi, emperor of Morocco.

5. Kingdom of Heaven: the end of the world; deliverance of this ship into their power.

6. Algiers did not recognize American independence from Britain.

7. Burgul: boiled and cracked wheat.

8. Grandees: wealthy or notable people.

9. Mumsa: couscous, the national dish of Algeria, made of boiled wheat and other ingredients. To Cathcart, it resembled mum, an old English brew of wheat, oatmeal, and mashed beans.

10. Regency: a term for Algiers as a political unit. From the city of Algiers (population 50,000), the government's power extended approximately 480 miles along the coast of North Africa and

approximately 100 miles into the interior, where the Atlas Mountains formed a barrier with the Sahara.

11. Aborigines: American Indians, the continent's native peoples.

12. Isaac Stephens, from Braintree, Massachusetts, had been the captain of the *Maria*.

Limited Privileges of the Slaves

O N T H E 12th of August arrived the cruiser that captured the *Dauphin,* with her crew on board. Being fifteen in number, they had been used nearly in the same manner that we had but, being public property, were brought from the cruiser direct to the palace, where they remained all night. It was a consolation to find us here, as we informed them of many particulars very pleasing to people in their situation, especially that there were no galleys in Algiers; that they would not be made to wear chains any longer than the ships of war of England and France were in the bay, unless they committed crimes to deserve them; and that the officers would be sent to work in the sail loft and the seamen in the marine. This was so much better treatment than they expected that they began to reconcile themselves to their situation. And, as the clothes which they had on were not taken from them in consequence of their having an old English Mediterranean passport, when washed and cleaned they made a much better figure than we did.

When paraded before the dey the next morning, His Excellency chose several of them for the palace and the rest were sent to the slave prison. Capts. O'Brien and Stephens, and Coffin—the latter was a passenger on board the *Dauphin*—were immedi-

A dey of Algiers

ately taken to the British consul's house to serve as domestics, where they remained suffering every indignity that inhumanity could devise to render their situation humiliating in the extreme, until the arrival of the Count de Expilly[1] who, by the orders of Mr. [William] Carmichael, chargé d'affaires at Madrid, took them under his protection and hired a small house, where they lived very comfortably for some time upon the supplies furnished them by Mr. Carmichael and their friends in the palace. The mates were likewise taken out of the marine and placed with the captains, but the marines were left at hard labor and were only allowed three *masoons*[2] a day to clothe and maintain them, which is equal to seven-and-a-half cents.

I shall now return to the palace. The slaves in the upper apartments received two suits of elegant clothes trimmed with gold; those in the palace garden had the same quality of clothing with less gold; and the cooks were supplied with clothing somewhat inferior, trimmed with silk. Those that are sent to the marine to hard labor receive one suit of clothes which is seldom worth more than one dollar and a half; and each slave receives two coarse blankets, which is supposed to last them the whole of their captivity. The slaves in the palace never receive anything else from the dey, but those who work at hard labor are allowed a suit of clothes every year of the same value as is given them on their arrival, but no blankets.

The first two months I was stationed in the palace garden nothing very particular happened. We watched the wild beasts in rotation and performed the other duties assigned us without murmuring, and were generally or individually abused by the chamberlains once or twice a day when they came to wash in order to purify themselves before they said their prayers; and very often some were bastinadoed[3] from mere caprice.

As I understood the French and Spanish languages sufficiently to read their authors, I employed myself in reading such books as I could borrow from the other slaves, and writing, or teaching some of my companions practical navigation. This procured me the title of the false priest, the *moshabbe*, and many other names of a similar nature from the chamberlains; and as the lower class, to ingratiate themselves with their superiors, generally imitate them, these appellations proved a great source of disquiet and involved me in continual disputes both with the chamberlains and Christians. As I always refuted their arguments, it ultimately procured me many enemies, among whom was Ciddi Aly,[4] the chief chamberlain, who uniformly persecuted me through the rest of my captivity until he was ultimately expelled from the regency by Hassan Bashaw.[5]

The garden of the dey of Algiers

A little more than two months after my admission into the dey's garden, the slaves were permitted to go out into the town in consequence of the great festival of which the first and last day is celebrated in the palace with feasting, music, wrestling, and fireworks of very poor construction, before the palace gate. In the morning of the first day, the banner of Mahomet is hoisted on the palace and the national flag on the fortifications; and the cannon of the fortifications are fired, those next to the sea with ball.

When the wrestling is ended, the officers of the regency and inhabitants kiss the dey's hand while [he is] seated on his throne, having the *Hasnagi Agas* at *Hodga Beitelmel* and *vikilharche*[6] of the marine standing on his left hand, and the *chauxes*[7] and other inferior officers behind them. After the Mussulmen [Muslims] have all performed this act of humiliation and respect, not even excepting the hangman and scavengers, the consuls have that honor conferred on them, next to them the head clerk, and then the chief of the Jew brokers of the palace and their dependents. The dey then invites the five grandees to dine with him in his apartments; they are joined by the chief cook. After dinner they retire to their respective houses, and the dey generally goes to visit his lady if he is married; if not, he retires to sleep.

The second day is a day of recreation for the

slaves, and the third is celebrated in the same manner as the first except the firing of the cannon and visits from the consuls. On the second day of the festival, the slaves are permitted to visit their friends and to absent themselves from six or seven in the morning until one in the afternoon, but are generally excused if they return by three, some few in particular employment excepted.

By special grace, we were permitted to visit our countrymen at the British consul's garden, which was about three miles from the city. There, to our surprise, we found Capt. O'Brien with a hoe, digging a hole to plant a tree in the consul's garden; Stephens, with the capote [hooded coat] given him by the regency tied around his middle with a straw rope, driving a mule loaded with manure for the root of the tree; and Coffin, who was consumptive, feeding the hogs and poultry. We could not refrain from tears at viewing their humiliating situation, which affected us the more as they suffered this indignity from a person (the British consul) who ranked among Christians and gentlemen, was of the same religion and spoke the same language, and from whom a more humane treatment might naturally have been expected.

We stayed but a short time, shared the money that had been given to us in the palace among them, and returned to town; visited the poor fellows in the prison; borrowed some money from our comrades to give them; and returned to the palace with a heavy heart, in order to be immured for ten months, where I remained without once being permitted to go out, and was then sent to the marine in consequence of some young Hollanders being captured on board a Russian prize.

I had not been long in this garden before the persecutions of the chamberlain became intolerable. I was prevented from reading or writing except by stealth, and likewise forbidden to speak to any of my countrymen who were stationed in other parts of the palace. This was occasioned by my frequently retorting on them their insolence and barbarity, and in consequence of my observing in conversation that those who were base enough to renegade [abandon] the faith of the forefathers generally became the most bitter enemies of those who continue faithful, in order to induce the secretaries, whose tenets they embrace, to believe that they were really converted and had renounced their former opinions or convictions, [and] that they were really erroneous and thus made up for their ignorance by hypocrisy and a pretended zeal for what they did not understand. This was reported to Ciddi Aly and Ciddi Mahomed (who were both renegades from the Greek church), probably with additions, and afterwards they continued my most inveterate enemies.

These deprivations (being prevented from reading and writing) I felt most sensibly; and having nothing now to divert my mental faculties, I really became a victim to melancholy reflections. My spirits were so much depressed that I fainted several times in a day and, ultimately, was obliged to keep my bed. This was construed by the chamberlain as a pretense in order to be sent to the hospital to divert myself. The Spanish surgeon petitioned for me without effect; however, he rendered me assistance and, with the help of a good constitution, I soon recovered. During my illness, the Portuguese and Spaniards were continually persuading me to change my religion, to confess immediately to restore myself to the bosom of the Holy Mother Church.[8]

I had been about four months in captivity when, one evening, I heard a noise in another part of the garden. Induced by curiosity to know the cause, I went to where the sound proceeded from and found to my no small astonishment the two chamberlains diverting themselves, beating with two sticks on the soles of the feet of a Portuguese, who roared most tremendously. I asked his crime but received no answer before I was seized by four stout Moors[9] who threw me down; and the same game was played on the soles of my feet to the tune of twenty-eight hard blows, which produced the most excruciating pain and left me with four toenails less than I had before this game commenced. All fourteen were served in the same manner; none were pardoned for age or infirmity, but old men of sixty and children of ten years of age received the bastinado without ever knowing what it was for.

After some days had elapsed, we found that we were indebted to the head gardener, a native of Malta, for this refreshment. It seems he had complained that he could not keep us in subjection, that we made use of the fruit which was intended for the dey, and several frivolous charges; but, as he could not particularize the offenders, the chamberlains concluded that by chastising the whole, they would undoubtedly find those who had offended. As for the innocent suffering unjustly, that was a trifle of such little moment that it either entirely passed their notice or was deemed unworthy of attention.

Twice more was I bastinadoed while I remained in the palace: once for writing, and the last time for speaking to some of the Americans who belonged to the upper apartments. In the last were involved seven or eight. My comrade was included—a simple, ignorant lad who was so much terrified that it had a sensible effect on his mind; and I am sure it was the first step which caused him to lose his reason.

I could never have endured the anxiety and degradations under which I labored for any length of time had I not placed the greatest confidence in the generosity of my country. I thought it impossible that a nation just emerged from slavery herself would abandon the men who had fought for her independence to an ignominious captivity in Barbary, when they could be immediately redeemed for less than $50,000. I was not ignorant of the embarrassments that our government labored under before the adoption of the present Constitution. Yet the sound policy of redeeming their citizens immediately appeared so evident that I was confirmed in my hopes; and, although I knew the treasury at that period was poor, I was so sanguine as to believe that the sum would be loaned immediately to the government by individuals or that our fellow citizens would have raised it by subscription. But I reckoned "without my host," as I lived more than ten years after this in captivity, experiencing every indignity that barbarians could invent to render the life of a Christian miserable in the extreme. I hesitate not to assert that no class of men suffered in any degree so much by the consequences attending the American Revolution as those who were captured by the Algerines in 1785.

The period now approached that was to put an end to my sufferings in the palace and to give birth to a new species of indignity. Two large vessels—the one a Russian and the other a Leghornese[10]—were captured by the cruisers of Algiers, on board of which were several handsome youths who were taken into the palace. Eight of the oldest and ugliest were sent into the slave prison called the Bagnio Beylique in order to be sent to hard labor the next day, among whom was myself and my American comrade before mentioned. But as we had not committed any crime, we had none of our clothes taken from us but were permitted to depart with all our wardrobe. This closes the first year of my captivity, and the next opens with fresh scenes of horror.

NOTES

1. The Count de Expilly was Spain's ambassador to Algiers. Nothing more is known of this shadowy figure.

2. *Masoon*: from the Arabic *mawzuna*, or Turkish *mevzuna*.

3. Bastinado: beat with a stick, usually on the soles of the feet.

4. Ciddi Aly: Ali Sidi, an Algerian official.

5. Bashaw is a Western corruption of pasha, title of high rank in the Ottoman Empire. Hassan succeeded Mustafa as dey in 1791.

6. The *Hasnagi* (*khaznaji*) was the treasurer; the *Beitelmel* (*Bayt al-malji*), the keeper of forfeited property; and the *vikilharche* (*wakil al-kharj*), in charge of maritime affairs, essentially the foreign minister of Algiers. *Aga*, or sir, is a term of respect.

7. *Chauxes*: shawushes, ushers or guards.

8. Cathcart, who is Protestant, is referring to the Roman Catholic Church.

9. Moor: a Muslim of mixed Berber and Arab descent, living chiefly in northwest Africa; descendant of Muslims who occupied Andalusia in Spain from the eighth century until the late fifteenth century.

10. Leghornese: Leghorn, Italy, now known as Livorno.

Commodore Lamb's Arrival at Algiers

I SHALL GIVE a circumstantial detail of Mr. Lamb's negotiation with the regency of Algiers, which proved extremely detrimental to the captives, as it fed them with false hopes of obtaining their liberty soon and prevented their friends from exerting themselves to procure their ransom. By deceiving the dey with unwarranted expectations, he committed the honor and dignity of his country and led the dey and grandees to believe that the government of the United States was trifling with them. In the event a negotiation for peace prevented that explicit confidence being placed in the promises of the negotiators on the part of the United States, a sacred adherence to, and compliance with, ought forever to characterize the public operations of contracting powers, especially those divided by so great a distance as the United States and the regency of Barbary.

On the 25th of March, 1786, John Lamb, Esq., ambassador plenipotentiary from the United States of America, and Mr. Randall,[1] secretary, arrived at Algiers in a Spanish brig commanded by Capt. Basilini.

The Count Expilly, His Catholic Majesty's[2] ambassador, and Monsieur du Kersey, His Christian Majesty's[3] consul general, advised Mr. Lamb to make application to the dey at once as the least expensive way of negotiating, though not the most successful. Mr. Lamb took their advice and requested them to wait upon the dey and request His Excellency to permit him to deliver his credentials from the government of the United States and to receive him as their ambassador plenipotentiary for negotiating a treaty of peace between the said states and the regency of Algiers. The dey answered that there were many insurmountable obstacles to be removed before he could receive an ambassador from the United States of America to treat [negotiate] on terms of peace; but if Mr. Lamb would content himself to treat only for the redemption of his countrymen in captivity, he would receive him in a few days.

On the 1st of April, 1786, Mr. Lamb was introduced to the dey by Monsieur du Kersey and Mr. John Woulfe.[4] Mr. Lamb requested His Excellency to inform him what he exacted for the ransom of twenty-one Americans which he held in captivity. The dey answered that he did not consider them in the same point of view that he did the subjects of other nations at war with him, that he would expect a much higher price for them and would give an answer at his next audience.

On the 3rd, Mr. Lamb waited upon the dey, who asked him what he was willing to give for the ransom of his countrymen. When he replied

A view of the flat roofs of Algiers

"$10,000," the dey answered, "You may have them for $50,000 if you think proper, but nothing less. I am not anxious to dispose of them; they are wanted to work at the marine; they are the best sailors we have and beylique has plenty of bread and olives to give them." Mr. Lamb observed that the price was exorbitant and double the price that any other nation paid for their people in the same situation. "You are at liberty to leave them," said the dey. Mr. Lamb promised to give His Excellency an answer at his next audience and retired.

On the 5th, Mr. Lamb went again to the palace and offered the dey $30,000 for the ransom of the captives. The dey was displeased with this, supposing him to be capable of huckstering [peddling] like a Jew, and answered, "I should conceive that I was defrauding the *hasna* (treasury) were I to abate one dollar in my demand; but as my own perquisite is at my own disposal, I will remit that sum which is 10 percent, and if you are not satisfied, I desire you will not trouble me any more on the subject. I told you already that we have plenty of bread and olives to give them." Mr. Lamb promised to consider the dey's demand and to give him an answer in a few days.

On the 7th, Mr. Lamb waited upon the dey, and, finding him inflexible, he agreed to pay the sum already mentioned for the redemption of the captives but specified that, as the United States were at a great distance, he could not promise to return with the cash in less than four months from his departure from Algiers. The dey answered, the sooner he paid the money, the sooner he should have the captives.

Mr. Lamb retired to the French consul's house, where the dey sent his own dragoman [interpreter] a short time afterwards to desire him to come to the palace. He immediately complied, and the dey interrogated him to know whether he was perfectly contented with the agreement he had made. He answered that he would have been better content had the terms been more favorable but that he ratified the agreement and hoped His Excellency, in consequence thereof, would be disposed to listen to his proposals of peace on the part of the United States when he returned with the cash. "Make peace with your father, the king of England," answered the dey, "and then come to me, and I will make peace with you."[5]

Mr. Lamb took leave of the dey and returned to the French consul's house. The American prisoners were in a manner reanimated and resolved to bear the remaining four months of their captivity with becoming patience and fortitude.

Mr. Lamb left Algiers without making any further application to any person and left the prisoners in the lively hope of seeing him with the money for their ransom in four months, the limited time.

They little imagined they were to remain over ten years longer in captivity after the honor of their country was pawned for their redemption; but, nevertheless, that was the case. I was not informed at this time by whom Mr. Lamb was empowered to negotiate or whether he was empowered at all, but that he made the agreement and that the government of the United States never ratified it; the consequences of which—no confidence was placed in anything that was said in our behalf and we remained nearly eleven years in the vilest slavery—are facts as incontrovertible as they are lamentable.

NOTES

1. Paul R. Randall of New York had been sent as Lamb's secretary to keep an eye on the diplomat.

2. His Catholic Majesty: King Charles III of Spain.

3. His Christian Majesty: King Louis XVI of France.

4. John Woulfe was a British merchant residing in Algiers.

5. The dey is suggesting that the United States renounce its independence and return to British rule.

The Slave Prisons

O<small>N THE EVENING</small> of the 29th of July, 1786, the Christian chief clerk of the dey and regency informed the captives in the palace garden that he had orders to conduct eight of them to the Bagnio Beylique, as the dey had thought proper to replace them with the captives newly arrived. Accordingly, two Portuguese, two Americans, and four Spaniards—among whom were myself and unfortunate companion—were selected and ordered to prepare ourselves immediately. My wardrobe consisted of a small basket, which, with two blankets, a few books and papers, a four-dollar gold coin, and two *sequins*[1] in gold, constituted the whole of my worldly possessions.

We left the palace without regret, as we were ignorant of the situation we were destined for, but we were soon undeceived. For myself, I candidly own that I found a great difference between the Bagnio Beylique and hard labor at the public works, and the palace garden with all its evils; but the nature of mankind is such that they are never sensible of the blessings they enjoy until they are deprived of them, when they learn to appreciate their value by comparison. We rejoiced that we had escaped the humiliation of taking care of wild beasts and keeping the garden in order, and the tyranny of the two *hasnadars*[2] [supervisors], but did not consider that, seeking to avoid Scylla, we had fallen upon Charybdis and were now exposed to the more ferocious Ibram Rais, guardian bashaw, and his numerous minions, a more motley crew than whom never breathed the ambient air.

I observed that the regency only allows the slaves in the palace their living on their first arrival. They are ever afterwards obliged to furnish themselves with every article of apparel from the perquisites they receive, which are collected from the *coffeegies* [coffee servers] in the following manner: When the beys, caliphs, *alcaides*, sheiks,[3] and, in general, every stranger who is permitted the honor of drinking coffee with the dey—including Christian ambassadors and sometimes consuls—are presented with coffee, when they return the cup they put a quantity of gold according to their rank into it and give it to the *coffeegie*, who deposits it in a box in the dey's apartment. His Excellency generally makes a small addition to it himself and divides it twice a year among the captives, according to his own pleasure. It sometimes amounts to $3,000 annually and is seldom less than $2,000, which is sufficient to supply all their wants as well as to enable them to assist their brother sufferers at hard labor in the nauseous prisons called the bagnios.

On our arrival at the Bagnio Beylique, we were introduced to Ibram Rais, who acted as the guardian bashaw; in consequence of his age and sickness, he was soon afterwards confirmed in the post, the superior guardians having died of the plague. I shall only take notice of him in that station where he remained during the rest of my captivity and several years afterwards. He was, at this period, guardian of the large pontoon for cleaning out the harbor and was generally supposed to be the most cruel, unrelenting guardian that had ever been in Algiers. He had lately returned from Malta, where he had remained in captivity for fourteen years; and, having been cruelly treated himself on board the Maltese galleys, he was determined to retaliate on the slaves whom he had under his command.

The reception we received from this petty tyrant will both characterize the man and delineate the horrors of our situation. He was sitting under the gallows at the outer gate. In the porch were a double row of guardian *sbirri*,[4] all armed with sticks, thick rope, and other offensive weapons, the guardians who were soldiers being also armed with *attagans* (swords) and pistols; and the walls of the porch were decorated with clubs, halters, chains, shackles, and handcuffs, the whole forming the most dejecting coup d'oeil [sight] that imagination can possibly conceive.

"Well, gentlemen," commenced Ibram Rais, "so you were not content with your situation in the palace and have preferred my acquaintance to the *hasnadar's*. You are all young and healthy and too well clothed for slaves. You shall have something to divert you tomorrow at Bebal Wey'd; I will show you there how I was treated at Malta. Here, *sbirro*, put stout rings on these gentlemen's legs and let them be awakened and brought to me before daylight at the marine gate."

The head clerk now interfered and informed him that we had committed no fault and that the *hasnadar* had ordered him to have them sent to the marine. "They shall go to the marine," answered the surly guardian, "but from thence I will send them where I please. They don't know what slavery is yet; it is time they should learn. I have not forgot the treatment I received from Christians when I was a slave."

I observed that I was an American and that it would be extremely hard for me to suffer for the injuries he had received from the Maltese, who were situated at the distance of six thousand miles from my country and were likewise of a different religion, which taught them from time immemorial to view the Mahometans with enmity; but that in America there probably had never been a Mussulman and that we never had been at war with any nation of that religion.

"True," answered he (curling his whiskers), "but you are Christians; and if you have not injured

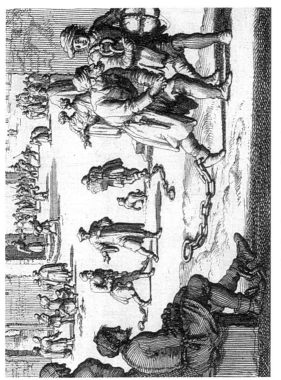

Christian slaves wearing heavy chains

Mussulmen, it was not for the want of will, but for want of power. If you should chance to take any of our cruisers, how would you treat our people?"

"That will entirely depend on how you treat those of my nation whom you have captured," I answered, "and you may be assured, sir, that my nation will retaliate upon those who treat their unfortunate citizens with undeserved cruelty."

"Slave!" answered he, "I am not accustomed to listen to the arguments of infidels. You are too loquacious for a young man. Retire immediately, and for the future be silent and obey."

"I shall obey, sir, but never be silent while there remains a higher tribunal to appeal to."

My fellows by this time had all kissed this tyrant's hand, and we were ushered into the prison yard and there left to shift for ourselves, having first had a large iron shackle bolted and riveted above our ankles, which weighed about twenty ounces. The *sbirro* informed us that we might have it changed for a small iron ring by paying a *sequin* each to the guardian bashaw and twelve *masoons* to him for his trouble and for the ring. I felt too indignant to give him any answer, and my American companion did not understand him.

No sooner had this ceremony ended than we were obliged to give in our names to the clerk of the prison and were ordered to hold ourselves in readiness to march to the marine gate at daylight the next morning. At the same moment, the *sbirro* called out in a most tremendous tone thrice distinctly, *"Capi capar,"* which in the Turkish language means "We are closing the gate," when immediately emerged from the taverns a motley crew of Turks, Moors, Arabs, and even some Jews—all intoxicated; some half-naked, having sold or pawned their clothes to the Christian tavern keepers for liquor; others singing or shouting; some with drawn swords, swearing they would kill the first person that offended them; and some few reeling peacefully to their habitations or, if soldiers, to the public barracks. The gates of the prison were then shut for the night, a heavy chain was drawn across the inside of the outer gate, and the inner one was bolted and locked. The prison was now under the control of the Christian corporals, who were all deserters from the Spanish garrison of Oran,[5] where they had been banished from their country, either for murder or theft, and, before their appointment here, had in general signalized themselves as the most hardened villains in the regency.

The Bagnio Beylique is an oblong hollow square, 140 feet in length and sixty in breadth, is three stories high, and may be about fifty feet high to the top of the terrace. The whole of the apartments are built upon arches and have no windows, except a small iron grating in each of the upper apartments, and receive the light and air from the doors.

Christian slaves in a Barbary dungeon

The lower story has no grating and is converted into taverns, which are kept by the Christian slaves who pay their rent and very high duties for permission to sell liquors and provisions in them. They are perfectly dark and in the day are illuminated with lamps; and, when full of drunken Turks, Moors, Arabs, Christians, and now and then a Jew or two—especially on Fridays, the day the Christians are sometimes permitted to rest in the prison from their labor—forms the most disgusting coup d'oeil that can be imagined, especially when you add to the noise an instrument called a *triboocca*, a tabor or *quinterra*, and a guitar, and sometimes a fiddle and Turkish guitar; and not infrequently an Italian mandolin and Spanish guitar; each singing, or rather shouting, in different languages, without the least connection; the place filled with the smoke of tobacco, which renders objects nearly impervious to the view; some wrangling with the tavern keepers for more liquor and refusing to pay for it, that, upon the whole, it must resemble the infernal regions [hell] more than any other place in the known world, especially when they frequently quarrel among themselves and proceed to blows. Even murder often takes place in these receptacles of vice and immorality, which generally occasions the tavern keeper to lose all his property, as the tavern is in the most instances seized by the regency and the tavern keeper sent to hard labor unless he bribes the guardian to make a favorable report of the case.

In all the prisons in the evening may be seen different tradesmen at work, among which shoemakers, tailors, carpenters, coopers, sawyers, and some hucksters are those who meet with the most constant employment and make the most money.

The second and third story of this dungeon is surrounded by a small corridor, or gallery, from whence are entrances into long, narrow rooms where the slaves sleep. [The rooms] are hung in square frames one over another, four tier deep. [The slaves] repose as well as miserable wretches can be supposed to do who are swarming with myriads of vermin of all sorts, many nearly naked, and few with anything more than an old tattered blanket to cover them with in the depth of winter; for those who have the means of subsistence either live in the tavern or little boxes, called rooms, built of boards hanging round the galleries for which they pay the regency from twelve to fifty-four *masoons* per month.

In the center of the prison, or very near, is the well from which water is drawn from the cistern, which is nearly as large as the whole prison and was formerly supplied from the terrace of the prison with rainwater but is now partially supplied, when necessity requires it, from the waterworks of the city. The whole of the building is covered with a terrace which has only two communications with the prison. It would be a great recreation to the slaves, especially in the summer, were they permitted to sleep there; but that is strictly prohibited.

There are two other prisons. The Bagnio Gallera, or the prison of the galley slaves, was so called because those who formerly used to row in the Algerine galleys were here confined, and after it was rebuilt, the name was continued. It was built on the same plan as the former but is only two stories high and not so long; the taverns are the same and so are the long rooms. But on the terrace are two tiers of small rooms, one above the other, inhabited by those who are able to pay for them, which is one great reason why the better sort of slaves prefer this prison to any of the others. The greatest inconvenience in this prison is in consequence of the lions and tigers being kept there, which creates an insufferable stench which, joined to the common shore of the hospital which communicates with that of the prison, corrodes the atmosphere that in the summer season is nearly suffocating.

The Bagnio Ciddi Hamouda is the smallest bagnio of the three and has every misery common with the other two but is not regularly built, being composed of three or four old houses with communications made from one to the other. It takes its name from its former owner.

I now return to my initiation into the dungeons

of Algiers. While ruminating on the horrors of my situation, I received an invitation from the dey's chief clerk to stay in his apartments until I had time to provide for myself, which I thankfully accepted but could not enjoy his civilities, my imagination wound up to such a degree that I was nearly insane. I retired to rest on his sofa but slept but little, and awaited the approach of day in anxious expectation of knowing my fate. About 3 o'clock in the morning, the awful summons was given from the tremendously cadaverous lungs of the *sbirro*, "Arise! all those who sleep; the day approaches!" and a short time afterwards, "Depart, sleepers! each one to his daily labor."

We all marched out at this warning and proceeded through a narrow street towards the gates of the marine just at the time that the gates of the city were opened; and the influx of camels, mules, asses, and laborers was so great that we could hardly pass. The animals were loaded with provisions for the market, palace, and grandees' houses; and the slaves, instigated by hunger, were endeavoring to steal as much as they could, which produced such a scene as I have no words to describe. The Moors uttered curses and threats, of which "Christian dog, infidel dog without faith, I will have you bastinadoed to death" were the most distinguishable among this motley crew.

We proceeded until relieved by the turn of the

street towards the mole,[6] and then marched at my ease to the gate, where we were all paraded in rows, the guardians being in front, seated on a brick seat made for the purpose. Here we waited about a quarter of an hour, when the *vikilharche*, beylique bashaw, captain of the post, and other officers made their appearance and marched through the gate, followed by the guardians and slaves who, on the *vikilharche*'s first appearance, must stand uncovered until he passes them some distance. The dey's chief clerk took us to the guardian bashaw, who presented us to the *vikilharche*. After he asked a number of questions and received a favorable account of us from the clerk, we were ordered to our respective destinations.

My comrade and myself were sent to the carpenter's shop. I was immediately apprenticed to a genteel-looking Spaniard, a native of Barcelona. He had been a cadet in the Spanish service, but for some irregularity was sent to serve in the garrison at Oran, from whence he deserted in hopes of regaining his liberty. He was taken into custody by the Arabs of the western province and sold to the bey of Mascara,[7] who brought him with a number of others as part of his triennial present to the regency of Algiers.

This man, despairing of ever being redeemed by Spain, abandoned by his relatives, had applied himself to learn the trade he was put to on his first arrival at Algiers so effectually that, at present, he was really the best house carpenter in the regency, and consequently was employed on the outdoor business, such as working in the grandees' houses, and was very much in favor. The eight months I was with him I constantly accompanied him; and, as I understood French, Spanish, and Portuguese tolerably well, I had an opportunity to get much information and to study the manners and customs of the people to whom Divine Providence had made me subject.

During the period that I worked in the city or for the marine, I was well-provided with one good meal a day, which the regency paid for exclusive of the allowance which we had in common with the rest of the slaves. Had our duties been confined to the duties of the carpenter's shop alone, there would have been no reason to complain of hard usage. But that was not the case, for whenever any hard loads were to be carried—the ships of friendly powers that brought presents to be discharged; the ballast, guns, and ammunition to be taken out of the cruisers or put on board again, which was done every cruise, be it ever so short—then the apprentices in all the shops in the marine were taken out and employed on that duty as well as in clearing out the magazines, fortifications, and other occasional jobs. Not infrequently they were sent on board the pontoons to clear the harbor of mud and stones and likewise to bring heavy stones from the Ponto Pis-

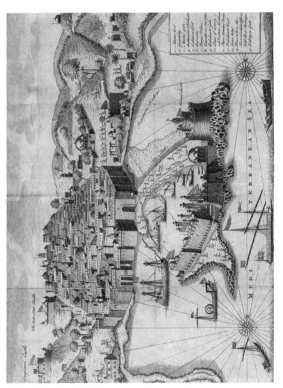

A view of Algiers

cado to throw at the back of the mole to prevent the sea from breaking over in stormy weather or, at this period, to a large magazine war building adjoining the *vikilharche* garden at Bebal Wey'd, about one mile from the city, large enough to contain all the gunboats belonging to the regency. This magazine was built upon arches, and the earth that was dug out to lay the foundation was afterwards used to form the terrace. During this work, frequent drafts of men were sent from the marine; and on Friday, the Mahometan Sabbath, all the slaves that worked at the marine, with the exception of a few favored workmen, were sent to this employment, which was much worse than the labor of the whole week.

NOTES

1. *Sequin:* an Algerian gold coin, weighing approximately three grams. (The 1790 U.S dollar contained 1.6 grams of gold.) Today, it would have a purchasing power of about $40.

2. The *khazinedar* was responsible for keeping the books within the household of an official.

3. These are titles of Muslim officials: a bey is a governor; the caliph, a religious or civil ruler; an *alcaide (al-qadi),* a judge; and a sheik, the chief of a family or tribe.

4. *Sbirri* (singular, *sbirro*): derogatory Italian slang for private guards.

5. Spain had maintained its base at Oran, approximately 200 miles west of Algiers, since the 1500s. Algiers had retaken it in 1708; the Spanish returned in 1732.

6. Mole: a massive stone pier or breakwater in Algiers harbor.

7. Mascara was a city approximately forty-five miles southeast of Oran.

Continuation of My Situation

I HAVE ALREADY stated that when I was sent from the palace garden, my whole wardrobe was contained in a small basket; and, in cash, my funds did not amount to quite eight dollars, two of which I was obliged to pay to the corporals to make interest to procure me leave to go to the Bagnio Gallera, where the rest of the American prisoners were and as many as it could hold of the most respectable prisoners. I, therefore, and my companions in adversity took leave of Bagnio Beylique for the present.

A large ring of iron, which was put on my leg there, I got changed for a small one, and my next occupation was to look out for quarters. Some of the Americans were fortunate enough to have a small room to themselves, but this was so crowded that it was impossible to hold any more inhabitants, and most of them slept on tables in the taverns. We arrived so late that all the berths in the tavern where we put up were taken. I was obliged to spread my blanket on the interstice of the bilge of a large wine cask and the wall, with my basket containing all my worldly possessions under my head to serve for a pillow and prevent the contents from being stolen. The weather being very sultry, the stench of the prison, the quantity of rats which were continually running over us, joined to myriads of fleas which attacked on all sides, did not render the night's lodging very agreeable, and I was glad when I was summoned to work in the morning.

From this to the month of March 1787, I continued in nearly the same situation, working in the carpenter shop in the daytime, occasionally sent to carry heavy loads to disarm the cruisers; load vessels with wheat; carry ballast on board the cruisers; and, on Friday, either be sent to Bebal Wey'd to work at the magazine or to the Ponto Piscado to load the pontoon with heavy stone to throw at the back of the mole, to prevent the sea from breaking over it— in short, every other sort of labor which the most common slave in the regency was obliged to do; but this was not all. The guardians, or slave drivers, supposing we had money, would send us to the worst work, abuse us in the worst manner, using the most opprobrious language and often giving us cuts with their twisted rattans, *en passant* [in passing], in order to oblige us to purchase our peace with them, which generally could be done for thirty or forty cents; but for those who had it not to give, it might as well have been a million.

It might be supposed that my treasury was soon exhausted and that the clothes which I got in the palace were disposed of to supply my most urgent wants. It is true, we were allowed seven-and-a-half cents a day for some time from our own country;

but that allowance was soon withdrawn from us, and for years no more notice was taken of us than if no such unfortunate men were in existence. It may therefore well be imagined that our situation could not well be worse, especially as the plague, which had been introduced from the Levant, began to make its appearance in the slave prisons. This, however, produced no mitigation of our labor—as long as we lived we must work.

I continued in this miserable situation until the 17th of March, 1787, when the king of Naples redeemed all his subjects who were taken at sea, except those who were taken in the galleys which fled from Naples. A Neapolitan frigate arrived with the cash on board, and they were permitted to embark under a flag of truce. They were about three hundred in number; and many of them being employed in the most eligible situations, many vacancies remained to be filled by those unfortunate men who remained, among whom my fellow prisoner and myself were taken from the carpenter's shop and ordered to attend on the intendant [superintendent], or *vikilharche,* of the marine.

There were generally from six to nine Christians in this department whose duty it is to attend to the *vikilharche* at meals, to take care of the stores, carry the keys for the beylique bashaw, serve the oil and bread out to the slaves, and, in general, whatever the intendant and the beylique bashaw order them to do; but they are not subject to the guardians nor to the orders of anyone else. They are well-fed and receive some emolument from the intendant's visitors, especially the beys, caliphs, *alcaides,* ambassadors, and Christian consuls, who are expected to put some money into the cup every time they take coffee with him; and this money is divided among these Christians every Thursday night—and they always have Friday to themselves. This was no small alleviation from our sufferings, especially as we were nearly naked; and now we received two pieces of cotton sufficient to make two jackets and two pair of trousers, and money to pay for making them. Although you are subject to hard labor, sometimes, in clearing out the stores, it is nevertheless considered one of the best situations, and a great deal of interest is made to get there.

Although peace with Spain took place in June 1785, still the Spaniards remained in captivity. The plague had commenced, and in January, there died sixteen Christian slaves; in February, forty-one; and in March, the number was increasing when the Neapolitans were redeemed. The Spanish priests now thought seriously of their captives, as they became very refractory and blamed the priests for their being detained so long in captivity after peace had taken place, and even threatened their lives. They, therefore, with the assistance of the Spanish ambassador, became security to the dey for the ran-

Priests ransom Christian prisoners from Barbary captivity

som of all the Spaniards who were taken at sea, to the number of about four hundred.

On the 19th of March, they were embarked on board a large Russian prize vessel, which was purchased for that purpose, and soon sailed for Minorca to perform quarantine. The slaves who had deserted from Oran, who were about one thousand of all nations, had always been expected to have been included in the general redemption. Some of these unfortunate men had been in captivity for fifty years, and certainly had suffered sufficiently to have expiated any crimes which they might have committed in their youth; and finding this not so, all their hopes vanished, and they gave themselves up to despair.

When the Spaniards who had been redeemed embarked, the scene was truly affecting: they separated from their countrymen who were left behind, with embraces and tears for their speedy liberation; they divided their clothes and money with them—some even gave away their all—and probably never was generosity more conspicuous or carried to a greater length. With the ship sailed, she was followed by the eyes of those poor captives. When she disappeared in the horizon, a universal groan was heard from those unfortunate men and they sank into despondency, declaring that now their last hope of ever being redeemed had vanished and they cared not how soon they were struck with the plague and terminated their existence.

The plague still increased, notwithstanding more than seven hundred captives were redeemed, which lessened the number considerably. Forty-three died this month and 105 in April; nevertheless, the usual work was carried on and, the labor being increased, no doubt exposed the poor slaves to the miasma of infection more than otherwise they would have been.

By the redemption of the Spaniards, the places of the *coffeegie* and clerk of the marine department became vacant. Giovanni de la Cruz, a native of Leghorn who had been chief mate of a large Leghornese ship which I had left at Boston and who was captured last year, and with whom I was acquainted, was appointed to the latter situation; and I was appointed to the former. His duty was to keep the books, and mine to make coffee and hand it to the intendant and his visitor. I likewise had the superintendency of the other slaves, was accountable for their good behavior, and was obliged to report them if they behaved improperly.

The clerk of the marine is allowed a small room in the Bagnio Gallera, gratis. I took up my quarters with him, and, with the exception of people dying with the plague all around us, our situation was very tolerable. We were obliged to be in the prison at the same hours as the other slaves were and to go to the marine as soon as the gate was opened, in order to have the intendant's seat made and coffee ready for him on his arrival. On Fridays, as we were confidential slaves, we could generally get leave to go out of town as far as the consuls' country seats.

In May, 114 Christian slaves died, and in June, 155 died, among whom was my friend Giovanni de la Cruz. He lingered a few days and on the 11th of June departed this life, regretted by all who knew him. He was a most amiable young man. During his illness, I rendered him all the service in my power but to no effect. When he was struck with the plague, I was ordered to take charge of the books of the marine department until he died or recovered, and on the 12th, I was appointed clerk of the marine. Here I remained until all the people of the magazine, the *vikilharche* of the marine excepted, had died and been replaced three different times.

My former shipmate had been sent out of the magazine, soon after he was taken into it, for incapacity, as he was a very simple, ignorant lad and could not learn the duty exacted from him. The beylique bashaw died; another was appointed. He died also; and a Turk, a fisherman (in the Turkish language, *baluckgee*), was appointed in his stead.

This man had never been in any office before and was in rank only a common soldier. He was extremely ignorant, poor, and proud, and very morose in his manners, finding fault without reason and not over-honest. Several things were missing from the stores, but no person dare accuse him of purloining them; besides, they wanted proof.

My situation was then rendered very unpleasant. I remained, however, at my post until April 1788, when one Thursday, having made out a *tischera,* or account, of the money to be delivered to the treasury that day by the beylique bashaw, it amounted to a considerable sum more than he had in his possession. He first tried to persuade me that I had made some mistake and requested me to alter it without making any noise. This I positively refused to do, and read to him all the items of the money he had received and what he had paid away. He then endeavored to throw the blame on the Christian slaves, saying that they must have taken the money out of his drawer, although he had always kept the key himself. This produced altercation when he complained to the *vikilharche*, saying that I had accused him of embezzlement and that either he or I must leave the marine. The *vikilharche* endeavored to pacify him, but without effect; and the policy of these people being never to take part with a Christian against one of themselves—especially if he is a Turk or a soldier—occasioned him to order me to leave the marine and remain in my tavern, declaring that he never would appoint another clerk in my place. This promise he kept, and the duties of my place were done by the Turkish clerk until the beylique bashaw was removed, which happened shortly after. Frequently I met him with his cane and basket coming, after this time, from fishing.

I remained in the tavern some time when, in consequence of the great mortality among the slaves, I was appointed clerk of the Bagnio Gallera, three clerks having died in less than one month. The duty of this station was to muster the slaves in the prison every evening; to report when any died or were taken sick; to see their black bread served out to them; and to go to the marine every morning, and on Friday to the outworks, to muster the slaves, to call their names over, and to report them when any were missing. But as several of the clerks of the sheepskins and charcoal died of the plagues, I was frequently obliged to do this duty, which kept me constantly employed, and probably was conducive to my health and may have been the means, under Divine Providence, of my being alive at the present moment.

I became secretary to the dey and regency of Algiers in March 1792. This office became vacant by the redemption of my friend Mr. D'Andreis, with whom I was acquainted in Boston. The dey remembered me and said that, as I had fulfilled the duties of the different subordinate offices of clerk of the marine, etc., I ought to be preferred to the highest post a Christian can attain. He, therefore, appointed me the same day.

Notwithstanding that the dey appointed me in consequence of my former services, he had it not in his power to exempt me from paying one thousand *sequins* to the *hasna*, or public treasury, and 383 *sequins*, the customary fee, to the officers of the government. This is paid in consequence of being entitled to redemption by any nation whatever who either concludes a peace or ransoms their citizens, even should it take place the next day after his appointment, besides other perquisites. The dey himself (strange as it may seem) loaned me five hundred *sequins*, and my generous friends, the Messrs. Skjöldebrand (the Swedish consul and brother) loaned me five hundred more, which I paid as the fee to the public treasury.

I must not forget to mention my obligations upon this occasion, but upon a former one. When I was by no means in so eligible a situation, these worthy and generous men loaned me $5,000 to purchase a prize loaded with wine, on which I made a good speculation, without any interest or reward whatever, out of pure friendship, although they knew the risk they ran; for had I died or committed any fault, real or imaginary, before they were paid, the regency would have seized all my property as their slave, and they would have lost every dollar of their money. Such unprecedented acts of generosity ought to be recorded on the tablet of our memory forever, never to be effaced. My gratitude to them is eternal and knows no bounds. The property I accumulated enabled me to purchase the vessel of which I took command when I came to Philadelphia in 1796 to bring the articles to secure the peace.

Negotiations in Barbary

ON THE 13th of August, 1795, a Spanish boat arrived from Alicante [in Spain] and brought letters from Joseph Donaldson to Messrs. Skjölde-brand and O'Brien, and from Mr. Montgomery[1] to me. In concurrence with the opinions of Messrs. Skjöldebrand and O'Brien, I waited upon the dey and informed him that an American gentleman, at Alicante, requested to be permitted to kiss His Excellency's hand on terms of peace. The dey asked if it was the ambassador he had so long expected. I answered that it was not but that he was sent by him as his precursor—that the ambassador had gone to France on public business and very proba-bly to arrange the pecuniary matters requisite to carry the treaty into effect, provided this gentleman concluded any. The dey said he did not understand the reason why so many changes and delays had been made and asked me if I would undertake the responsibility of the person who was desirous to come to Algiers, that he actually had full power to negotiate peace and the ransom of captives.

I answered my head for it: "*Effendi*,[2] that he has; otherwise, he would not ask permission to come here. But at the same time it is incumbent on me to inform Your Excellency that those powers are lim-ited to a specific sum, which he cannot surpass.

Therefore, if Your Excellency does not intend to lower your first demands—and that very considerably—you had much better not give him permission to come at all."

"Do you want a peace (*jabba*) for nothing?" asked the dey, somewhat irritated.

"No, *Effendi*," I replied, "but we want peace on the same terms that the Dutch obtained peace, which would give the president of the United States an opportunity of proving to you, Excellency, and your family, the high sense he entertains of your justice and moderation, and to compensate you for your influence with your predecessor in our favor. Although we reaped no benefit from it, we have not forgotten it."

"If you did not benefit by my good will, it was your own fault," replied the dey. "But what good did you ever do us to expect to obtain peace on the same terms as Holland, who has been supplying us with stores for a century when we were at war with Spain?"

"Permit me to ask Your Excellency what harm did we ever do you? Have you not taken thirteen sail of our vessels and 131 of our people, whom you have made slaves, and have I not been more than ten years in captivity, which I would consider as time well spent if I could be the medium of establishing peace and harmony between our nations."

"So you may," replied the dey, "but you must

pay for it," his mustachios curled indicative of a squall, as O'Brien would say.

"We wish to pay you, *Effendi*, and to make you feel how much we respect and esteem you; but not on the same scale as Spain, Portugal, and Naples, who have been at war with you since the commencement of the Hegira.[3] In our country we have no religious test, nor enmity against those of your religion. You may build mosques, hoist your flag on the tower, chant the symbol of your faith in public, without any person interrupting you. Mussulmen may enjoy places of honor or trust under the government, or even become president of the United States; and ought not these circumstances to be taken into consideration? You do not enjoy any of these privileges in any Roman Catholic country, or indeed in any other; and if you make those nations pay high for peace, it is on the principle of retaliation, because they have made you pay millions in defensive measures; but we have never been at war with you."

"Let him come," answered the dey. "I will hear what he has to say himself."

I informed the dey that my word would not be sufficient, that it would be necessary to send him a passport, under the seal of the regency, for his security.

"That is not customary," answered the dey, "and has never been granted by this regency to the ambassadors of any nation. It would look as if we were suing for peace and not them."

I informed His Excellency that it need not be made out in Turkish, that I would write one in English which would answer the same purpose, as we would keep it a profound secret from every person but those immediately concerned.

After a little more persuasion, the dey gave me permission. I wrote it in his apartment and put the seal to it, kissed the dey's hand, and retired. I then wrote a letter to Mr. Donaldson and enclosed the passport and gave them to Mr. Skjöldebrand, who chartered a Ragusan[4] brig for $400 to go to Alicante and bring Mr. Donaldson to Algiers. At two PM of the same day, I went down to the marine and put our dispatches on board, prohibited the captain from taking letters from any person, and waited until the captain of the port hauled his vessel out of the mole and made sail.

The celerity of those transactions prevented our enemies from calculating consequences or having time to oppose our measures; for in six hours after we received Donaldson's letters, the answer, with the dey's passport, were on their passage to Alicante. I was very sensible of the risk I ran in offering myself to the dey to guarantee not only his arrival but the extent of his powers. Had he refused to come to Algiers, I should not have fared well. The dey, like other chief magistrates, if the measure was attended with success, would assume the credit, but if the reverse, would throw the stigma on those who recommended or promoted it. Skjöldebrand, and everyone else, kept behind the curtain. I was the only ostensible person employed on the business, and I was entirely in the dey's power. He had often been disappointed by the United States before and his patience was almost exhausted. His ministers, disappointed of their expectations, would induce the dey to believe that he had been trifled with, and consequently insulted, and would appear ridiculous in the eyes of his people. The blame must have fallen on somebody, and who could it have fallen on but me, who was the only person exposed. It is certain that if either of the aforesaid events had taken place, I would have lost my head, or, probably, my body would have been made a luminary to light my soul in its ascent from the Jews' burial place to the mansion of bliss in Mahomet's paradise.

I had now the influence of the Spanish consul, Don Juan Garrigo, and the father administrator, who were all agents of Portugal, to combat. The British consul was an Englishman and, consequently, an enemy, but fortunately had not much energy or influence. The French consul did not openly oppose us; but the intrigues of the agents of the Chamber of Commerce of Marseilles had great weight, who were opposed to the United States obtaining peace with the Barbary States, because it would interfere with their interest in the carrying and in the grain trade. The Dutch and Swedes had lately renewed their treaties of peace and were not in much danger of any altercation taking place at present; the latter were our private friends but declined any public agency in our affairs.

Denmark and Venice, fearful of the blow falling on one of them—as it seldom happens that peace is made with one nation without the consul of another being sent away, as the prelude to war—contented themselves with raising reports prejudicial to our interests and to induce the dey to believe that the United States had neither the means nor the inclination to comply with his demands. Thus situated when Donaldson's letters arrived—which acknowledged that he had powers, although they were not defined—and knowing that a more favorable opportunity than the present would not probably occur for a number of years and believing the dey was really disposed to abandon the extravagant terms he had heretofore insisted on, I determined to run any risk to bring Mr. Donaldson to Algiers as soon as possible, and thus to prevent the agents of other nations from having time to injure our interests by intrigue, which under other circumstances would appear to have been too precipitate. The dey, in the meantime, informed me of the suggestions of our enemies, which gave me an opportunity to counteract them.

On the 20th of August, having previously obtained permission from the dey, I bespoke a neat little house in the vicinity of the Swedish consul for the reception of Mr. Donaldson on his arrival. But Peter Erick [Skjöldebrand] requested me, as a very particular favor, not to take a house so near theirs, as it would be considered as a preconcerted plan by the rest of the consuls, and that he might as well receive him in his own house, which he would be very happy to do, were it not for the jealousy of the other consuls. I therefore complied with his request, and the next day informed His Excellency that I could not procure a house for the ambassador and requested to be permitted to make use of one belonging to the regency. He said it was not customary but that he would pay the ambassador of America as much respect as possible, was it for no other reason than to pique the British, who were our inveterate enemies and on very bad terms with him. He desired me to ask the *vikilharche* of the palace for the keys of the caliph's new house, which I received and gave them to Micaiah Bacri, to have [the house] cleaned and whitewashed, and I furnished two rooms at my own expense, for which I received little thanks.

The dey, ever impatient, began to suspect that

Donaldson would not come to Algiers, which gave me an opportunity to find a door to creep out in case he did not come. When Donaldson wrote to us, he mentioned that he had intended to have sent Mr. Philip Sloan[5] with his letter but that the governor of Alicante had refused to let him embark without receiving an order from his court at Madrid. This may serve to show the interest which Spain took in the affairs of Portugal and the desire she had to frustrate our peace. Sloan had been one of the dey's attendants, was redeemed by the Dutch, and had taken letters to America and returned to Europe with Col. Humphreys.

When I informed the dey that the governor of Alicante had prevented him from coming over in the packet, and told him that Sloan had been in America and had returned with the ambassador and, consequently, had he arrived, he could have given him an account of the causes which had prevented his coming in person to Algiers, [the dey] was so exasperated that he ordered the town crier to proclaim that—except the vessels that were loading in port—no person should ship even an onion for Spain and that all intercourse should be suspended. I found it to our advantage to foment this discord and told the dey that in case our ambassador did not come, it would be in consequence of the Spaniards, informing him that the terms exacted for peace from the United States were nearly the same

The central courtyard of a large Algerian house

as those demanded from Portugal, which he had refused to lower; and that he [the ambassador], supposing His Excellency would not be more favorable to the United States, thought it would be useless for him to come at all; but that what I said was only conjecture, that he might come yet.

"Did not I tell you," said the dey, "that those that add can subtract and that let the ambassador come and we would agree? Did not I tell the agents of Portugal that I would not abate one *asper*[6] of my first demand, and are those answers the same? Can you see no difference in them?"

I said that I saw a vast difference in them.

"Then why did you not inform your ambassador of it—what do you think I said it for?"

I answered that I did not find myself responsible or justifiable in divulging anything His Excellency might say without receiving his express orders so to do.

"As a general rule you are right," answered he, "but in this case you might have deviated. But I see you have a head, and your ambassador will receive information from elsewhere, although you may not divulge my secrets. I am going to prayers," said he.

From this date to the 2nd of September, I had daily conferences with the dey, who had become impatient and doubtful whether the ambassador would come or not. I advised His Excellency to have patience, at least until the vessel returned; that common politeness would induce the ambassador to send an answer; and if he did not come, if the dey would state his ultimatum, I would take it over to Alicante myself.

"Yes, and never come back again," said the dey.

"Your Excellency has never had any reason to doubt my veracity—I would do what I promised; but my countrymen remaining behind me is a sufficient guarantee for my ransom. Besides, I could have been free long ago if I had thought proper to accept my ransom from the British." I then explained two instances to him of my refusing to be redeemed, which I could easily perceive increased his good opinion of me.

"But what terms could I state that would make the ambassador come?"

"I don't know precisely but what the United States expects a peace on the same terms as the Dutch and will make you a private present of $100,000 or $50,000 to your family, as a mark of your friendship and an acknowledgment of the favors they have or may receive from Your Excellency."

"It is a mere trifle," said the dey, and got up from his seat—not in a bad humor, as his whiskers did not curl, neither did his beard stand erect. I thought I could perceive a latent spark of satisfaction illumine his countenance.

In this train were affairs when I was relieved from great anxiety by the appearance of the Ragusan vessel we had sent for Donaldson, with an American flag at the main and a flag of truce at the fore, and her own colors flying. I immediately informed the dey that the vessel was in sight and that from the colors flying, I knew the ambassador was on board.

"I am glad of it," said he. "Bring him on shore to the house prepared for him. I am going to my country seat to see my wife."

"Her ladyship will not be forgot in the terms of peace," answered I. The dey looked over his shoulder and smiled.

The brig anchored in the bay. While going down to the marine to get a boat to bring Donaldson on shore, I was met by Capt. O'Brien and Micaiah Cohen Bacri, who wished to go on board with me. The former was stopped, as no slave except the dey's chief clerk is allowed to go out of the mole; but upon my becoming responsible for his return, he was permitted to go with me. On Thursday, the 3rd day of September, 1795, Mr. Donaldson landed and was safely deposited in the house prepared for him, at three PM.

Joseph Donaldson Jr., Esq., was a man upwards of 50 years old, of a forbidding countenance, and remarkably surly. His disposition was more soured by a fit of the gout and the roughness of the pavement; besides, the length of the walk was sufficient to have tried the patience of a man in good health, followed as we were by a crowd of people to see what sort of an animal the American ambassador was, and Donaldson had an unconquerable antipathy to be stared at. He was dressed in decent plain clothes, a cocked hat such as was worn in the Revolutionary War, much resembling those that are painted to grace the portraits of Frederick II; his right leg muffled in flannel, shod with a large velvet slipper; and his right arm leaning on a crutch to support him. The weather was very warm. The agony which Donaldson was in occasioned by the gout, and the mortification which he felt at being stared at, together with some children running across him, put him in a paroxysm of rage which he endeavored to suppress, while the perspiration ran down both sides of his face and almost blinded him. His ludicrous appearance, joined to the contortions of his countenance, and the observations of the Moors who are fond of giving nicknames to all that have any defects, excited my risible faculties so much, that it was with the greatest exertion that I confined them within the borders of common decency. The idea, at the same time striking me, that if Donaldson had a patch on his eye and O'Brien a wooden leg they would be Commodore Trunnion and Lt. Hatchway[7] personified, did not lessen the excitement.

At length we arrived at the caliph's new house—now Mr. Donaldson's new residence—and he had to climb up a long flight of marble steps of stairs to

A street scene in Algiers

his apartment. The cold of the marble increased the pain he was in, [so that] when he threw himself on a couch—his hat on one side and his crutch on the other—[he] uttered a string of ejaculations and execrations so equally mixed together that I could not discover which predominated.

"What is the matter?" said the Jew, with a look of astonishment.

"Nothing at all," said O'Brien. "The ambassador is only saying his prayers and giving God thanks for his safe arrival."

"His devotion is very fervent," replied Micaiah.

By this time, a good dinner which I had ordered from my tavern arrived, to which, with some fruits of the season and some good wine, we sat down; Mr. Donaldson appeared more reconciled to his situation and the pain of the gout was considerably abated. After dark, Peter Erick called to see him and stayed to a late hour, when our affairs were discussed from the arrival of John Lamb in 1786 to the present time. I put him in possession of my journal, containing all the negotiations that had taken place since my arrival in Algiers in 1785, and that part of my correspondence which would be useful to him.

NOTES

1. Robert Montgomery was the American consul at Alicante, Spain.

2. *Effendi*: a title of respect.

3. The Hegira was the Prophet Muhammad's flight from Mecca to Medina in 622, the beginning of the Muslim calendar.

4. Ragusa: the Italian name for Dubrovnik, Croatia. At the time, Ragusa was nominally under Venice.

5. Sloan was a mariner captured with the *Dauphin*.

6. Asper: a copper coin; the smallest unit of Ottoman currency, worth approximately one-twelfth of a cent.

7. Commodore Trunnion and Lt. Hatchway were characters in Tobias Smollett's satirical novel *The Adventures of Peregrine Pickle* (1751).

Mr. Donaldson's Audience
with the Dey

ON FRIDAY the 4th of September, being Mus-
sulmans' Sabbath, no business is done in the
palace. Nevertheless, knowing the utility of dispatch in order to prevent our enemies from having
time for intrigue, I obtained permission from the
dey to present Mr. Donaldson to him in the morning. At seven AM, he presented his credentials,
which I read and explained to the dey and observed
that all I had promised to the dey had been complied with: the ambassador had arrived and had
power to treat for peace.

"Yes," replied the dey, "but peace is not made
yet."

"That depends upon Your Excellency entirely," I
said. "If you ask more than we have to give, no
peace will be made; but if you ask within our limits,
peace may be concluded within four hours."

"It is *Jima* (Sabbath)," replied the dey. "We will
see about these affairs tomorrow." We retired after
compliments.

There were present at this audience Micaiah
Bacri, Mr. Sloan, and the Swedish consul's dragoman, who attended to get a present should peace be
concluded. Nevertheless, at nine AM, the dey sent

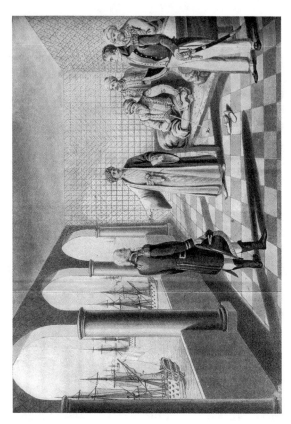

Western envoys meet with the dey of Algiers

and asked me if I was certain that the ambassador had full power to treat with him on terms of peace. I replied that I had read and explained his credentials to His Excellency, and therefore he was as well-informed on the subject as I was.

"Then take to him the terms that you made out by my orders last year, and let me know what he thinks of them."

"He will reject them, and if Your Excellency does not lower your demands to what has been paid by other small nations, he will go about his business and nothing will be done," I replied.

"I command you instantly to take those demands to your ambassador and to bring me his answer and his proposals in return, and don't say another word. I will have this business settled immediately."

When I went to kiss the dey's hand, my foot slipped on the marble pavement. "Can you not stand?" said the dey.

"Yes, but the weight of Your Excellency's proposal made me stumble." I was informed that the dey laughed heartily at this reply, and told it to his ministers after peace was concluded.

I took the dey's first proposals to Mr. Donaldson, amounting to the enormous sum of $2,247,000 and two frigates of thirty-five guns each for peace; an annuity of stores to the value of twelve thousand *sequins;* and ambassadors', consular, and biennial presents, such as are given by Sweden, Denmark, and Holland. Donaldson was in despair. He said he had done wrong to come to Algiers at all; that any offer that he could make would be an insult to the dey; and that he, therefore, would not make any.

Messrs. Skjöldebrand, O'Brien, and myself endeavored to persuade him to make some proposal to the dey, be it ever so small, and that Cathcart would take the risk upon himself to take it to the dey. I answered that as I had the dey's orders to bring him an answer, it would be better to offer him something than not to offer him anything, and advised Mr. Donaldson to read the copies of my last letters to Montgomery. After he had done so, we sat down in conclave and produced proposals number two, which offered the dey $543,000 for peace and the ransom of our captives.

I took the proposals to the dey, accompanied by Mr. Sloan, Micaiah Cohen Bacri absolutely refusing to accompany us. He said the offer was so small in proportion to the dey's demands that he would not take it to the dey for the difference; that he had not forgotten the treatment he had received when he was assisting Holland to renew her treaty; and that he was determined not to run any risk in the future. This put me in mind of the roasting the dey had promised him, and, putting on a very melancholy countenance, I requested Mr. Donaldson that in case I should be burned and he escaped a roasting, which I would endeavor to prevent as I was fond of good company, to save some of my ashes and send them to the museum at Philadelphia. But Donaldson did not like the joke and less when Peter Erick informed him that both the French and Venetian consuls had been threatened, as well as Micaiah Bacri.

I presented proposals number two to the dey and explained them to him. He first smiled with contempt and then broke out in a rage. "What do you mean by bringing such proposals to me," said the dey. "Do you want to make game of me?"

"No, these are the ambassador's proposals, not mine. His powers are limited and he can offer no more; and this offer is more than you got from the Dutch."

"You are a liar and an infidel," said this tyrant. "Your ambassador's powers are not limited; for the French consul has sent to inform me that he has carte blanche and can give what he pleases for peace."

"If Your Excellency had told the French minister that he was a liar and an ignorant fellow, he would have richly deserved it, for the president of the United States has not the power that he has informed you our ambassador has. Our divan[1] makes the appropriation for every expenditure, and the president and those employed by him cannot surpass it. Therefore, the ambassador has offered all that he is authorized to give; and if it is not accepted, he has no alternative but to wait for fresh instructions, which he will not receive in less than a year."

"*Senza feda* (without faith)," said the dey, "you have not been so long in Algiers for nothing. If you had not dictated those terms, how should that man, who only arrived in Algiers yesterday, know how to appropriate the different sums specified in his proposals?"

I replied that I was an American; that I drew pay from my country; that I was in duty bound to give our ambassador all the information which I possessed; but, at the same time, as a grateful servant to the dey, he would be pleased to observe that His Excellency and his family had been well taken care of and had been considered our principal—and, indeed, only—friends.

"Read your proposal again," said he. I complied. "$100,000 for me and $50,000 for my family; *sequins*, you mean?"

"No sir, dollars."

"Go out of my sight immediately, thou dog without a soul," said he in a passion, "and never presume to bring such trifling terms into me again under pain of my displeasure"—i.e., a bastinadoing, at least.

We retired to Mr. Donaldson's house, where we met Messrs. Skjöldebrand and O'Brien, and informed them of the result of our conference. Donaldson said the business was at an end, that he had gone as far as his instructions and would go no further.

Then said I, "Mr. Donaldson, the sooner you pack up your clothes the better. For I assure you that peace is not attainable on your terms, although it is probable it may be for forty or fifty thousand dollars more."

At two PM, the dey sent for me and scolded like a virago for having the presumption to bring such terms from Mr. Donaldson, and accused me of having coalesced with the lame ambassador to trifle with him and to insult him. I told the dey plainly that I was placed in a very disagreeable situation: that he accused me of being partial to the ambassador, and the ambassador seemed to think that I espoused his cause—the fact is, I had neither done the one or the other. I knew my country wished for peace, and I endeavored to procure it for her by all means in my power.

The dey answered by desiring me to sit down and write, when he dictated proposals number three amounting to $982,000, which was a pretty good fall from his first proposals. I took these to Mr. Donaldson, who rejected them.

He desired me to inform the dey that he would not give one dollar more for peace. I told him the consequence would be that the dey would get in a passion, and that he would be ordered out of the country, that I probably would receive a *regalo* [gift] of five or six hundred bastinadoes on the soles of the feet for the service I had rendered him. He said if he was ordered out of the country, he had no remedy but to go, and that if I received a bastinado-ing, I would have the consolation of having received it for having endeavored to promote the interest of my country.

I was piqued a good deal and, in fact, was under the necessity of taking the answer to the dey. But in order to mortify Donaldson for his ill-timed obsti-nacy, I told him that I would endeavor to reverse the tables on him; that I had property enough to pay my ransom or would be redeemed by Portugal, if I thought proper to espouse their cause; that I would place him in a position to receive the basti-nadoes which he thought so light about; and that he might console himself by knowing that it was an excellent cure for the gout.

I took Donaldson's answer to the dey. He seemed exasperated to a high degree and threatened to give me five hundred bastinadoes if I ever came to speak to him on the subject again, and desired me to embark the *tupal* (lame) ambassador on board the vessel he came in the next morning at daylight, and tell him to leave the regency without delay, as he would permit no person to remain here to trifle with him as he had done. I found that this was an improper time to remonstrate with the dey, deferred any further communication on the subject until the morning, went and gave the dey's message to Donaldson, and told him if he wished to save himself from disgrace he would attend to the dey's orders.

We then informed Mr. Donaldson that he had not placed that confidence in us which we merited, that he had never informed us of the extent of his power. Sloan said that Col. Humphreys had stated to him that if Mr. Donaldson should exceed his orders [by] fifty or sixty thousand dollars, it would be of no moment, considering the magnitude and importance of the object in view; and that therefore as citizens of the United States who had nothing in view but the interest of our country, we did not think ourselves justifiable in letting the negotiation be broken off while we had it in our power to prevent it.

He at last acknowledged that he did not imagine that the dey would have acted so precipitately; that Cathcart had so much energy or had exerted himself so much as he is now convinced he had done; that he was limited to $650,000, including all expenses; and that further he could not go. I answered that if he would leave it to me, I would guarantee the peace and ransom for fifty or sixty thousand dollars less. This was agreed to . . . and proposals number four, amounting to $585,000, were made out, signed, and sealed for me to take to the dey early in the morning, at the time Mr. Donaldson was ordered to embark. Sloan and Micaiah promised to go with me but said they would not interfere. This I consented to, for I had discovered that Mr. Donaldson seemed distrustful of my influence and I wished to have witness to my conduct.

After our mode of proceeding was adjusted, I requested Mr. Donaldson to give orders to his servants to pack up his clothes and to make a bustle, as if he was really going to embark in the morning. Mr. Skjöldebrand promised to send a message to Bashara, who acted as agent for Ragusa, to request him to give orders to the captain who brought Donaldson here to hold himself in readiness to depart at a moment's warning. I then sent for the chief of the *pisqueras* (porters) and told him the ambassador was going away in the morning, to send some of his people to carry his things on board, and then sent to the slave prison to inform our people that Mr. Donaldson would take care and forward any letters they might wish to send by him. My aim by these proceedings was that the dey might hear, by a circuitous route which would not create suspicion, that Mr. Donaldson was going to embark and to do away [with] the idea that he possessed unlimited powers or had a carte blanche, as the French consul had induced him to believe; and it had the desired effect.

Thus prepared, on Saturday, September 5th, 1795, at seven AM, I took Mr. Donaldson's proposals number four to the dey, accompanied by Mr. Sloan and Micaiah. I informed him that the American ambassador was ready to embark and would be at sea before twelve o'clock; that he had surpassed his limits in his last offer; but to avoid, as much as was in his power, the negotiations from being broken off, he had added the whole extent of his fortune to the last proposal and had sent it for the dey's consideration. I read the proposals, and he replied that the addition was trifling and said that this morning the French consul had again sent his dragoman to inform him that the ambassador had carte blanche. I desired Micaiah and Sloan to mark that assertion and informed the dey that I had refuted that falsehood already, and, I had thought, to His Excellency's satisfaction; but at present further discussion was unnecessary from the fact that our ambassador would be on board in an hour if His Excellency rejected these proposals and would be a very disagreeable proof how much His Excellency had been imposed on, and that a regular complaint would be preferred against Mr. Valliere[2] by our ambassador at the Court of France.

"I have abated two-thirds of my first demand," replied the dey, "and if he cannot comply with my last proposals, he may embark when he pleases."

I then reminded His Excellency of his promise to

let the prisoners be redeemed independent of peace, which now seemed to be unattainable. The dey affected to be in a great passion, said a great deal to little purpose, but came to no conclusions. I said that I was grieved beyond measure that our friendly offers were rejected; that we were a nation at a great distance from his, which would take a year to write to and to receive letters from; that we had never been in arms against any Mussulman nation; but that now we would be obliged to arm in our own defense and would necessarily become the enemies of those who had rejected our friendship.

At this moment, Sloan pulled me forcibly by the coat, in order to prevent me from saying any more until the dey was in a better humor. The dey observed it, when I answered, "I came here to speak truth. I have been well treated by the dey for a number of years, and no selfish consideration shall prevent me from endeavoring to prevent him being imposed on by the French consul, or any of our enemies, who under the cloak of friendship are equally his. America will never sue for peace again but will arm in her own defense; but His Excellency has promised to let the captives be redeemed, which I now implore from his clemency. We have been here more than ten years, *Effendi;* let us go, for the love of God."

I then stooped to kiss the dey's hand, which,

contrary to my expectations, he held towards me, and [he] seemed buried in thought, whether convinced that he had been imposed on by the French consul or not, I don't know. But his aspect changed and, after taking a pinch of snuff, the dey desired me to read over the proposals again to him, line by line, which I did and observed that, as he said that I dictated the appropriations to the ambassador, he would observe that His Excellency, at least, was liberally considered; that $240,000 was appropriated for the use of himself and family alone; that, in the aggregate, $585,000 was a large sum, and $279,500 more than had been paid by the Dutch; and that even on the score of precedent, the terms were advantageous to the regency.

"Yes," answered the dey, "you know how to *gabbar* (cheat, deceive, persuade); should I now reject your terms and send your ambassador away, your enemies would rejoice and you would become the laughingstock of all the consuls and Franks [foreigners] in Algiers. Go and tell your ambassador that I accept his terms, more to pique the British, who are your inveterate enemies and are on very bad terms with me, than in consideration of the sum, which I esteem no more than of pinch of snuff," at the same time blowing one away which he held in his fingers. "But recollect that the annuity in stores, presents on the arrival of an ambassador, consular and biennial presents are to be paid the same as is paid by Holland and Sweden and Denmark."

We answered that it was so understood, kissed the dey's hand, and paid him many compliments, probably with more sincerity than compliments are paid in general. And we went to give an account of the result to Mr. Donaldson, who, being informed, replied, "Aye! (with an oath) he has agreed at last, has he?" I requested him to keep up the deception until he returned from the palace, lest some of our enemies should injure us; for notwithstanding the dey's promise, peace was not perfectly established before our flag was displayed and saluted. The *pisqueras* were kept in attendance as if really he was going to embark, and at ten AM, we were ready to attend Mr. Donaldson to the palace to confirm the agreement.

NOTES

1. Divan: the governing council in Algiers. Cathcart uses the term familiar to the dey to describe the U.S. Congress.

2. Césaire-Philippe Valièrre was France's consul in Algiers.

Terms of Peace and Ransom

Bᴜᴛ Mɪᴄᴀɪᴀʜ, who remained in the palace and who had not spoken one word to the dey during the whole negotiation, now brought a note of the stores demanded by the dey for peace—the same as the Swedes had paid. This demand Skjölde-brand and all of us recommended Mr. Donaldson to reject at once, as the Swedes had not paid any cash to the treasury for peace; and, as we had promised to pay $100,000, the dey could not expect us to pay both in cash and stores. I went with Micaiah to the dey and explained this article to him, when after some altercation he agreed that the stores should be valued, which was done by the Turkish secretary, and $60,000 was deducted from the $100,000 to be paid to the treasury.

Thus, everything arranged, at eleven ᴀᴍ, Mr. Donaldson—accompanied by Sloan, Micaiah, and myself—waited on the dey, when, by Mr. Donaldson's request, I confirmed in the name of the United States all the stipulations of the terms of peace, dated September 8th, 1795, and transmitted to Col. Humphreys on the 11th of the month.

Previous to going into the palace, I had taken a silk jack [flag] that Mr. Donaldson had brought with him and put it round my waist and, after compliments, presented it to the dey, saying that as peace was established, I hoped our flag would be saluted as soon as possible. The dey said, "You seem determined that your flag should be hoisted today, or you would not have brought it into the palace; go have it hoisted as usual on such occasions. I will not disappoint you."

The dey desired me to tell Mr. Donaldson that he might take his countrymen from work at the marine, if he thought proper, but at the same time observed that he thought they had better remain, for if they were to get drunk and insult any of the Turks, he would be obliged to punish them even against his will or they might turn Moors [convert to Islam]. Donaldson answered that he did not wish to take them from the marine but that he did not care if they all turned Moors. This last paragraph I refused to translate to the dey, as I thought it very uncharitable and improper.

The dey then passed some encomiums on my conduct, said Donaldson might thank me for obtaining peace on such moderate terms, and desired him to write in my favor to our ambassador at Lisbon and our prince (president, he meant). But this being too delicate an affair for me to translate, I kissed the dey's hand and left Sloan to interpret between them.

I went down to the marine, and at meridian [noon], a large American ensign was hoisted at the main. Mr. Donaldson's silk jack in the place of the flag of truce, which was hauled down, was hoisted at the fore, and her own jack and ensign flying on board the Ragusan brig that Mr. Donaldson came over in. Then peace was proclaimed and the American flag saluted with twenty-one guns; and thus in about forty-two hours after the arrival of Mr. Donaldson, peace was established between the regency of Algiers and the United States of America—to the astonishment of every person in Algiers, friends as well as foes—by a lame old man who understood no language but his own, without funds or credit, and surrounded with enemies.

From the marine, I went to Mr. Donaldson's house, congratulated him, and dined with him (on my own dinner) and Mr. Skjöldebrand. After dinner, although the Jews of Algiers are more strict in observing the ceremonies of their religion than they are in any other country, Micaiah and David, his nephew, were busy all day preparing the peace presents and did not go to the synagogue until the evening. Such power has self-interest over an Algerine Jew that it makes him forget his God and break through all precepts, both human and divine.

In the evening, Capt. O'Brien requested me to get permission from the dey for him to be sent to Col. Humphreys with the treaty and Mr. Donaldson's dispatches. This request, I must confess, tried my fortitude as much as anything I had ever experienced, for I was tired of the humiliating situation I had been so long in and actually had intended to be the bearer of the treaty myself, if the dey would permit me. I therefore hesitated a good while before I gave any answer. Capt. O'Brien, understanding the cause of my embarrassment, interested my patriotism and pride in his favor. He said that the situation I was in gave me an opportunity of rendering very essential service to my country, especially as Mr. Donaldson was incapable to transact his own business; that by my resigning my post, some person might be appointed who would be an enemy to our interests; and, if any unfavorable event took place, that as a patriotic citizen I would incur great censure; besides, the dey had promised me to use his influence with the regency of Tunis in our favor, which probably he would not do was I to go away; that the sacrifice which was demanded of me would ever redound to my honor; and both O'Brien and Skjöldebrand declared that they would represent my conduct to Col. Humphreys and to our executive in such a manner as would not fail to receive their thanks and approbation. Therefore, considering the duty I owed my country and the friendship that had existed between O'Brien and myself during a ten-year captivity, I consented but, I must own, with reluctance.

On Sunday, September 6th, I accompanied Mr. Donaldson to the palace and delivered our peace presents to the dey. A great many of the presents were procured from the dey himself, especially the articles which were distributed to the officers of the third and fourth rank.

In the evening, I asked the dey's permission for O'Brien and pointed out to him what great utility it would be to have a person on the spot who was acquainted with the quality of the stores which were wanted in Algiers, and he gave me permission at once. But I left O'Brien in suspense for some time as a punishment for his want of confidence and duplicity. As he supposed that I wished to carry the dispatches myself, he endeavored to supplant me by the agency of the Swedes and Jews. I likewise got four passports from the dey to protect as many American vessels with our stores from capture by all the Barbary States, including Morocco, for one year.

FRIDAY, 11TH, AT 10 AM. By Capt. O'Brien's particular request, I introduced him to the dey. This is the first time he had been in the palace since the day he landed; and the first time he ever spoke to the dey, he kissed the dey's hands and feet (I did not like that humiliation). The dey said he was an old man and recommended dispatch, saying that if he died, his successor would not be so friendly to America as he had been, and maybe would undo all that he had done, if the business was not concluded—and much he cared. He wanted the fee but did not care a cent for the client. O'Brien promised, most faithfully, to use every exertion in his power to carry the treaty into effect and took his leave.

I gave Capt. O'Brien ten Spanish doubloons ($160) of my own, to pay his expenses and to purchase some decent clothing and a packet for Col. Humphreys.

Here ends the account of our negotiations with Algiers, which produced our first treaty of peace with that regency. But the stipulations of that treaty are yet to be carried into execution, which will be a work of no small difficulty.

Peace Procured

I HAVE ALREADY STATED that Mr. Donaldson arrived at Algiers on the 3rd; that I made the treaty and took it to Mr. Donaldson for his signature on the 7th; and that O'Brien sailed with it on the 11th of September, 1795. On the 13th, Mr. Donaldson retired to the Swedish consul's country seat four miles from the city, leaving us in anxious expectation for the arrival of the funds, as he had assured us that Col. Humphreys had informed him that they were ready to embark a great part of them at Lisbon.

[OCTOBER] 6TH. We received letters from Mr. Etienne Cathalan[1] informing us that the news of peace had arrived at Paris and all the ports of France. Mr. Donaldson has received information that O'Brien arrived at Malaga on the 17th [September], landed on the 19th, and set off for Lisbon on the 20th, so that twenty-five days after Donaldson's landing in Algiers, the treaty would be in Lisbon for the inspection of Col. Humphreys.

SUNDAY [NOVEMBER] 8TH. This day, procured a truce for the United States with Tunis for eight months, guaranteed by the dey of Algiers; translated it; and took the original to Mr. Donaldson, who kept his bed with the gout and colic.

[NOVEMBER] 20TH. Donaldson still confined.

The American mates and sailors laid siege to his chamber and insisted on his procuring them leave to stay in town, as they said that they had as much right to be exempt from hard labor as the masters— and I think they had full as much. Donaldson told them that he could do nothing for them at present, to go to their quarters and have patience a little longer, and they would be redeemed. They cursed him for an old hickory face,[2] etc., and hoped that he would be brought up standing before another month, and left him. I wrote to Col. Humphreys and informed him of the truce with Tunis which took place on the 8th but did not send a copy of the truce, as Mr. Donaldson had not returned the original translation.

DECEMBER. This month very little alteration took place in our affairs, except that the dey's impatience increased daily. Every time I had any business with him, he vented his spleen on me. He said that three months was time enough for money to arrive from Lisbon; that by my persuasion he had listened to the old *tupal* (lame) ambassador and was prevented from concluding an advantageous peace with Portugal; that I had deceived him; and that his people were discontented and his patience was nearly exhausted.

On the 17th, I received answers to several of the circulars which I had sent to our consuls in Europe, one from our consul at Leghorn being a prototype of the others. Mr. Donaldson was either confined by bad health to his chamber or, when well enough, was at the Swedish consul's country seat. I had not only to bear the reproaches of the dey but likewise of our own people, who accused me for not getting leave for them to remain in the city exempt from labor. This I at first could have done with ease, but now it was impossible, for the dey had frequently threatened to send the masters to hard labor if the funds did not arrive very soon; and when leave could have been procured, Mr. Donaldson discouraged it and refused to be responsible for their conduct; therefore, it would have been very improper for me to have done it.

January 1st, 1796. This eleventh year of my captivity was ushered in by a siege. Mr. Donaldson was confined with the gout when the American mates and seamen took possession of his house, said it was public property, that they had as much right to stay in it as he had, and absolutely refused to go any more to work in the marine.

I was in the dey's palace when a complaint was lodged against them, and the dey actually ordered them to be put in chains. But I interceded for them, and the dey pardoned them but declared that in future if they did not behave better, he would chain them two and two together. I went out and informed them what the dey had said; and they abused me for the part I had taken in their favor, and said it was as much my fault as it was old hickory's that they were continued at hard work at the marine.

The dey's impatience increased daily and, as he considered that I was the chief promoter of the peace with the United States, not a day passed that I was not threatened and reviled, and sometimes scandalously abused; for, as Donaldson had never been to the palace since the presents were delivered, I was regaled with the part of the abuse which would have fallen to his lot had he made his appearance. Mr. Skjöldebrand advised Mr. Donaldson to dispatch a packet to Spain, with letters to Col. Humphreys, to learn the reason why the funds had not been forwarded; but as the Spanish packet was daily expected, it was determined to wait her arrival in hopes she would bring us some good news from headquarters at Lisbon.

But on the 3rd, the dey obliged him to alter his resolution, for he sent him positive orders to freight a sandal[3] and to send her to Spain to procure information direct from the ambassador at Lisbon why the money had not been forwarded according to promise, and promised to wait until the return of the sandal. But [he] declared that if the stipulations of the treaty were not then complied with—in part, at least—and assurance given him, such as he could rely on, that no unnecessary delay would be made in forwarding the remainder, that he would turn the old *tupal* ambassador out of the country, undo everything that had been done, cut off my head for having persuaded him to make peace with the United States in preference, and then make peace with Portugal on the same terms he had made with us—or even for less—in order to have the great sea open to his cruisers, by which he would have it in his power to be amply revenged on us for our breach of faith by the capture of a number of our vessels, etc.

Mr. Donaldson, as usual when there was any difficulty, left the business to me and requested me to charter a sandal, which I did. A certificate was procured from Mr. Donaldson that she was employed as a packet by the American ambassador at Algiers, which was certified by the dey's order by all the consuls, and a bill of health for the American sandal packet the *Independent*, Philip Sloan, master. The American flag was hoisted on board, and she was ready to sail in the evening; but Mr. Donaldson's dispatches were not ready.

On the 4th, I informed the dey that the sandal only waited his permission to sail, when he dictated a letter to Col. Humphreys and, while I was writing it, abused me, old *tupal*, Col. Humphreys, and the whole American government—*Blushidente Vashintone* (President Washington) and all—as a set of imposters who had deceived his predecessor and now had deceived him, and swore by his beard that he would not be trifled with much longer. I enclosed his letter in one of my own to Col. Humphreys, and the sandal sailed at meridian manned with twelve Moors and commanded by Capt. Sloan.

JANUARY 28TH. The long-expected Spanish packet arrived from Alicante and brought letters from Col. Humphreys dated December 14th, informing us that funds could not be secured at Lisbon and that O'Brien had been sent in the brig to London to endeavor to procure them, and were informed that Sloan had arrived at Alicante on the 6th, likewise that Mr. Montgomery had gone to Lisbon on our affairs.

*   *   *

In this state were affairs on the 4th of March, 1796, when Mr. Barlow arrived on board the American brig *Sally*, Captain March, from Alicante. This was the first American vessel that had arrived since the Declaration of Independence, those that were captured excepted. The weather was very boisterous and the winds contrary, which prevented the vessel from coming into the mole and obliged her to anchor in the bay at least four miles from the city. Prior to the arrival of Mr. Barlow, the Jews had reported to the dey that he was at Marseilles and had been appointed consul for the United States at

Algiers. This report I endeavored to suppress; but the Jews insisted that it was true, for he had the consular presents with him, which he had purchased at Paris, and read to me the letters they had received from their correspondents.

The dey ordered me to go on board and bring Mr. Barlow on shore. I informed His Excellency that the weather was so bad that a boat would be in danger of being lost; that I would bring him on shore the next day, when I hoped the weather would be more moderate. Accordingly, on the 5th, I procured a large boat with eight oars from a Venetian ship that lay in the mole and brought him on shore completely drenched, as the sea ran very high in the bay. He landed in the marine and went into the city immediately to change his apparel. I introduced him to Mr. Donaldson precisely six months after the signature of our treaty with Algiers. As soon as I changed my clothes, I informed the dey, who asked why I had not informed him that I was going on board for him [and] that he might have been saluted with five guns as is the custom when any of the consuls of other nations land.

I had consulted Mr. Barlow and informed him what the Jews had reported to the dey. He requested me to inform His Excellency that he was not appointed consul yet, but that probably he might be hereafter. I therefore informed [the dey] that Mr. Barlow's commission had not arrived yet from the

United States; that when it did, I would inform him, when it would be time enough to give the consular salutes. The dey was in a very bad humor—said that he knew what to do with the Americans and ordered me out of his presence.

On the 8th, the weather had become moderate, the brig hauled into the mole, and Mr. Barlow's effects were landed. He gave me a letter from Mr. Sloan of the 1st and sent Micaiah Cohen Bacri to the dey to request an audience, which the dey absolutely refused to give him.

28TH OF MARCH. Mr. Philip Sloan arrived by land from Cherchell [in Algeria], a town forty miles to the westward of Algiers, where the sandal, in which he came from Alicante, had put in with contrary winds. Our agents requested me to accompany Mr. Sloan to the palace in order to explain to the dey the purport of Col. Humphreys' answer to his letter, of which he, Sloan, was the bearer.

The American consul at Alicante had brought a credit with him on Madrid for the necessary funds, but at present the exportation of money was so strictly prohibited in Spain that, unless the dey would write to the king of Spain to grant permission to embark it at Alicante, it would avail us naught.

At six PM, we waited on the dey, who, as soon as he saw Sloan, asked him abruptly if he had brought the money or any account of it. I told him of Col.

Humphreys' disappointment and requested him to permit me to read his letter to him and by that means introduce what is noted above. The dey got out of patience, called both Sloan and me "dogs without faith"; gave me a hearty slap on the left cheek; took Col. Humphreys' letter and threw it with all his force out of his apartment; and ordered us to quit his presence, threatening if ever we came to him again on such an errand to be the death of us both. I said, "Strike, *Effendi*, but hear. Things are not always what they appear to be." But this tyrant drew his *attagan* that was under the pillow on his seat; and we had no alternative but to make a precipitate retreat, taking the letter with us which Sloan had taken up in his flight (as the dey did not follow us out of his room), which he returned unopened to our agents—nor was it ever opened afterwards.

The dey even refused to admit Mr. Barlow to an audience for more than a month after his arrival [and] had ordered his cruisers to arm preparatory to a declaration of war against the United States. To gain time, Mr. Barlow promised the dey a present of a frigate of thirty-six guns to wait only three months longer for the funds to arrive. This time was deemed insufficient by every well-informed person, but Mr. Barlow said he "would trust to the chapter of accidents," as we could not be in a worse condition than we were then in.

On the last of April, the dey informed me that the regency had been so often trifled with by the agents of the United States that he had no confidence in their promises; that he did not believe that the United States would satisfy them; but that he would send me with a letter from himself to the president of the United States and would wait nine months for his answer, provided that I would assure him that the frigate and stores would be built in that period. I told him that the frigate could not be built in that time, but I would promise that the stores, or a great part of them, would arrive in less than nine months. He then ordered me to be ready to sail in eight days from that date, and I departed with his letter to the president of the United States, and Mr. Barlow's dispatches, on the 8th of May, 1796, having been in captivity from the 25th of July, 1785, nearly eleven years.

Never was a parting more truly affecting. It is impossible for me to describe the situation I was in at parting with Mr. Barlow and my worthy and disinterested friend Mr. Skjöldebrand; but more distressing was it to me to part with my disconsolate brother sufferers and leave them on that inhospitable shore; indeed, it was one of the most affecting scenes that can possibly be comprehended. Words are insufficient to describe my sensations in such cases. Silence describes our feeling much better than the greatest eloquence. At meridian, made sail after having endured every indignity that a fertile-brained Mahometan could invent to render the existence of a Christian captive unsupportable, and having gone through every scene of slavery from a bricklayer's laborer and carrying heavy stones from the mountains, to being the first Christian secretary to the dey and regency, during the trying period of ten years, nine months, and fourteen days, the remembrance of which makes me tremble with horror.

NOTES

1. Etienne Cathalan was a French citizen serving as U.S. consul in Marseilles.

2. Old hickory face: slang expression; hickory was a tough or rugged wood, not pretty.

3. Sandal: long, narrow, two-masted boat.

Accounting of Captures

List of the Americans captured since the king of Spain made peace with Algiers on the 30th of June, 1785, with what became of them.

SCHOONER *MARIA* OF BOSTON, CAPTURED JULY 25, 1785

Isaac Stephens, by general redemption, 1796

Alexander Forsyth, by general redemption, 1796

James Leander Cathcart, left with dispatches, May 8, 1796

Thomas Billings, alias John Gregory, redeemed, 1796

James Harnet, died in the mad house, 1793

George Smith, redeemed by friends, 1793

SHIP *DAUPHIN* OF PHILADELPHIA, CAPTURED AUGUST 2, 1785[1]

Richard O'Brien, left with dispatches, September 1795

Andrew Montgomery, in general redemption, 1796

Philip Sloan, redeemed by the Dutch, 1794

Peter Loring, died of the plague, June 27, 1794

John Hull, taken by a Neapolitan cruiser, 1796

Charles Colvil, redeemed by his friends, 1790

John Robertson, redeemed by his friends, June 12, 1791

William Patterson, redeemed by his friends, January 3, 1794

Peter Smith, died of plague, January 18, 1787

Robert McGinnis, died of plague, 1787

John Doran, died of plague, July 1, 1787

Capt. Zacheus Coffin, died of consumption, July 2, 1787

Edward O'Reilly, died of plague, May 8, 1788

William Harding, died of plague, June 6, 1788

Jacobus Tessanaer, died of plague, July 13, 1793

Of twenty-one captives taken in 1785, nine died of these two crews; twelve returned home at different times. No more Americans captured until October 1793, when the British made a truce for Portugal; thereby, the Straits of Gibraltar were left open.

Notes

1. Earlier, Cathcart gave the date of the *Dauphin*'s capture as July 30; other sources say August 1.

Book II

American Captives in Tripoli

BY
Jonathan Cowdery

A bey of Tripoli

INTRODUCTION

Dr. Jonathan Cowdery was 32 years old when he entered the navy on January 1, 1800, during the quasi-war with France. Born in 1767 in Sandisfield, Massachusetts, in the Berkshire Mountains, he was the eldest of ten children. Marrying Mary Bryant of Massachusetts in 1789, they had two children, both named for men of science: Franklin Benjamin Cowdery, born in 1790, and Isaac Newton Cowdery, two years later. It is not clear what happened to Mary; she may have died giving birth to their second child. If so, this may have prompted him to join the navy.

In any case, by 1803 Cowdery was serving as surgeon's mate, or assistant, to John Ridgely, the ship's medical officer. Ridgely stayed on in Tripoli after the other prisoners left, serving as American chargé d'affaires.

Although Cowdery contracted an eye disease in Tripoli that severely affected his sight, he remained in the navy. He served on gunboats in New York until 1807, when he was assigned to Norfolk, Virginia, where he spent the rest of his life. In 1833, he became surgeon general of the navy. Having remarried in Norfolk, Cowdery and his second wife had no additional children. His son, Franklin, became a newspaper editor in New York state. Cowdery died in 1852.

Excerpts from Cowdery's journal appeared in American newspapers while he was still captive in

Tripoli. The full journal text went through three editions between 1806 and 1810 and then fell out of print for almost two hundred years until its relatively recent republication in an anthology of captivity narratives.

It was not unusual for such accounts to appear, giving Americans firsthand knowledge of the prisoners' circumstances. While narratives from the point of view of the officers were more common than those of ordinary sailors whose captivity was much harsher, the Philadelphia *captivity was unique in leaving accounts from each: Cowdery's describing his experience as an officer and William Ray's refutation from his very different experience as a common sailor. Both are included in this volume.*

Preface

The particulars of the unfortunate capture of the *Philadelphia* frigate by the Tripolitans have already been before the public. She ran on a bank abreast of the harbor of Tripoli on the 31st of October, 1803, at eleven AM, and kept up a brisk cannonade with the gunboats of that regency until four PM, when, failing in their efforts to get her off, they surrendered to superior force. The *Philadelphia* mounted forty-four guns and had 350 men; she was afterwards got off by the Tripolitans and moored in their harbor, but was destroyed by Capt. Stephen Decatur Jr. in a schooner, with three boats, a part of our Mediterranean squadron, who boarded and burnt her upon the night of the 16th of February, 1804, four months after her capture.

On the capture of the *Philadelphia*, the Tripolitans demanded $1,690,000, for the release of our captured brethren! They, however, have been very glad to take $60,000 for their release and to enter into new bonds for future good behavior.

This much premised, we now proceed to Dr. Cowdery's journal, which he commences immediately after his capture.[1]

*   *   *

The Philadelphia on the rocks off Tripoli

AFTER THE FLAG of the *Philadelphia* was struck and the officers and crew were waiting the pleasure of their new masters, the Tripolitan chiefs collected their favorites and, with drawn sabers, fell to cutting and slashing their own men, who were stripping the Americans and plundering the ship. They cut off the hands of some, and it is believed several were killed.

After this battle amongst themselves was a little over, we were ordered in the boats to be carried on shore. One of their officers, whom I had taken by the hand and who promised me his friendship, came to me, took me by the arm, and told me I must go. I asked him to let my boy go with me, which he refused. I then took hold of my small trunk, which contained my best clothes; he gave me to understand that I could not take it but should have everything taken care of and restored to me. He took hold of my hand and hurried me over the side of the ship, while his other hand was employed in rifling my pockets, from which he took about ten dollars. I had concealed some gold in my clothes, which he did not find. I then went down into one of their boats, from whence I was to pass into the next, which was almost full of our officers and men. I made all haste to get into it, for I observed that the Turks in the boat where I then was, were stripping my messmate, Dr. Harwood,[2] and the carpenter, Mr. Godby; but I was soon stopped by three of the ruffians, who stood over me with drawn sabers and cocked pistols, and wrested my surtout [overcoat] from under my arm.

Whilst they were picking its pockets and quarreling with each other for the booty, I sprung for the next boat, which was waiting for me. In my way, I met a little fellow, who seized me and attempted to take off my coat; but I hurled him into the bottom of the boat and jumped into the one which was waiting, amongst my fellow officers, where I thought the Turks³ more civil. They then set off for the town, compelling our men to row the boat and standing with drawn sabers over our heads.

When we had got near the shore, they ordered our men to stop rowing. Two of them came to me and gave me a severe blow on the side of the head. They then searched me and took a case of surgeon's instruments from my pocket. They took my pocketbook, but finding it contained nothing but papers, they returned it. One took my silver pencil, and another, the handkerchief from my neck. They then began upon Mr. Knight, sailing master, Mr. Osborne, lieutenant of marines, and all the officers in the boat; plundered their pockets; and took the handkerchiefs from their necks.

They then landed us at the foot of the bashaw's palace, where we were received by a guard, who conducted us into the palace before the bashaw. He viewed us with the utmost satisfaction and had us conducted into an apartment, where we found the captain and several officers who [had] arrived in another boat just before us. Here was a table set in the European style. The servants appeared to be Maltese and Neapolitan slaves. Here we supped, after which it was announced that another boat had arrived with our officers and men, who were before the bashaw.

Capt. Bainbridge requested me to go and look for Dr. Harwood, whom it was feared was killed. I found him with the carpenter before the bashaw, stripped of everything but their shirts and trousers. They afterwards informed us that they were stripped in the boat where I lost my surtout; and when they got within a few rods of the shore, they were thrown into the sea and left either to drown or swim ashore.

The bashaw's servant gave them dry clothes, and we were all again conducted before the bashaw and formed into a half circle. He was seated on his little throne, which was decorated in the Turkish order, and made a handsome appearance. He is a good-looking man, aged about thirty-five. He counted us, viewed us with a smile, and appeared highly pleased with us.

We were then conducted by the minister of exterior relations and a guard to the house formerly occupied by the American consul—a very good house, with a large court, and roomy enough for our convenience. We were seated here about nine o'clock in the evening. Capt. Bainbridge got permission from the bashaw to send for the Danish consul, who paid us a visit and offered every assistance in his power. We slept upon mats and blankets spread upon the floor, which was composed of tiles.

NOVEMBER 1. This morning the Danish consul, Mr. Nissen, paid us another visit. Capt. Bainbridge engaged him to furnish us with provisions and such other necessaries as we might want. Our dwelling was furnished in a plain style, and we were supplied with fresh provisions that were tolerably good. We were allowed to go to the front door and to walk on the terrace, or top of the house, which commanded a handsome prospect of the harbor, the sea, the town, the palace, and the adjoining country. Here we could see our ship on the rocks—full of Turks and surrounded by their boats—and a constant stream of boats going to and bringing off the plunder of the ship. We could see these robbers running about town with our uniform coats and other clothing on. The minister of exterior relations promised to be friendly and collect as much of our clothing and effects as he could and return them to us.

NOVEMBER 3. The bashaw sent for the carpenter to go on board the ship. He went and found six feet of water in the hold. The carpenter's crew and fifty men were ordered and carried on board to work at night. A gale of wind and heavy sea hove the ship off the rocks, and the carpenter returned.

NOVEMBER 4. In the morning Lts. Hunt and Osborne and myself were at the Danish consul's observatory, on the top of his house, upon a plane with and adjoining ours, which together made a large and handsome walk. We were looking at the ship with Mr. Nissen's glass, when our dragoman [interpreter] came and informed us that the bashaw had ordered us not walk upon the terrace anymore. We immediately returned to our house.

NOVEMBER 5. Our new masters came and closed up the passage which led to the top of the house, and a guard was set at the front door to prevent our going into the street. The minister sent his chief secretary with a parole of honor,[4] written in French, which we all signed.

NOVEMBER 6. We found that we were not allowed to go out, notwithstanding our signing the parole of honor. The minister of exterior relations sent us word that he had got eight of our trunks, which we might have for twelve hundred dollars. We did not take them, nor thank him for his hospitality. We purchased new blankets, sent to us by the Danish consul. The English consul, Mr. M'Donald,[5] paid us a visit and offered us every assistance in his power.

NOVEMBER 8. The Jews [had] purchased some

of our clothing and offered it to us at an enormous price, but we purchased but little of it. The bashaw sent for Capt. Bainbridge and told him that John Wilson[6] had informed [him] that Capt. Bainbridge, before hauling down the colors, threw over[board] nineteen boxes of dollars and a large bag of gold. Capt. Bainbridge assured him it was false and gave his word and honor that there was no money thrown over to his knowledge, but that the money in question was left at Malta. In the evening, the bashaw, not being satisfied, sent for the captain's servant and ordered him to be flogged if he did not tell the truth concerning the money. The boy denied having any knowledge of it. After repeating the threat several times, and the boy insisting that he knew nothing about the money, he was acquitted. Wilson had turned traitor and given the enemy all the assistance in his power. He now acts as overseer over our men.

November 9. Our captain established a credit with the Danish consul, who supplied us with necessary provisions and with cloth for mattresses. A guard was posted at our door, to prevent our going into the street or purchasing any books or clothing.

November 10. Several Turks came and informed Capt. Bainbridge that the bashaw had been told that Capt. Rogers, who commanded the U.S. frigate *John Adams*, treated the Tripolitan prisoners taken last summer very bad and that they feared we should suffer for it.

We have plenty of pomegranates, dates, and oranges. The Danish consul visits us every day.

NOVEMBER 13. The minister of exterior relations sent his dragoman to Capt. Bainbridge and informed him that, if he would send an immediate order to Commodore Preble to deliver up the Tripolitan prisoners captured by Capt. Rogers last summer, amounting to about eighty in number, we might remain where we were; but if he did not comply, we should fare worse. Capt. Bainbridge replied that he could not command Commodore Preble and, therefore, could not comply with his request. At nine in the evening, a Tripolitan officer came armed with two pistols and a saber and said, "Tonight, nothing; tomorrow, the castle." We accordingly prepared for the castle.

NOVEMBER 14. Breakfasted early, to be ready for our new habitation. At nine AM, a guard came and ordered us to the castle. We formed agreeable to rank and marched to the castle. We were huddled into the most gloomy cell, among our men, where there was hardly room for us to stand. Here we spent the day without food and were scoffed at by our foes until night, when, to our happy surprise, we were conducted back to our old place of abode. The minister of exterior relations sent for

Capt. Bainbridge and affected great surprise at our going to the castle, saying that he knew nothing of the measure, which we all knew to be false. He told Capt. Bainbridge that we should remain where we were until he heard from his people, the prisoners, in the hands of the Americans.

NOVEMBER 17. Visited our sick, who were quartered in a small house without a floor, near the palace and about half a mile from our lodgings. The Danish consul supplied the sick with fresh provisions, by the request of Capt. Bainbridge.

NOVEMBER 20. The minister permitted us to purchase our clothes. We got but a few, and at a high rate. One of our men, by the name of Thomas Prince, turned Turk [converted to Islam] and was admitted into the palace.

NOVEMBER 21. After visiting our sick, I was permitted to go with our dragoman about the town to purchase medicine; we found but a few articles. A man of 116 years of age came to have me cure him of deafness.

NOVEMBER 24. The bashaw refused to furnish necessary clothing for the sick or anything for them to eat but sour, filthy bread. Capt. Bainbridge contracted with the Danish consul to supply the sick with beef and vegetables for soup every day.

NOVEMBER 27. Our men complained of their hard usage in being compelled to lie on the cold, damp ground, to eat bad bread, to work hard, and to be bastinadoed by their drivers.

November 30. One of our men in a fit of despair attempted to kill himself but was prevented by the Turks when in the act of cutting his throat. The wound did not prove mortal. I was permitted by the minister to call on the Spanish physician for medicine for Dr. Ridgely, who was then sick.

December 5. The bashaw sent for me to prescribe for himself and two officers of his bodyguard, and ordered me to get such medicine as was necessary of the minister, who had a medicine chest.

December 6. Visited the sick at the palace and found them all better. I was received and treated very politely. The minister sent for me to cure him of a blindness in the left eye. I prescribed for him with very little success.

December 7. Visited the ambassador of Constantinople, who was affected with the intermitting fever. Found my patients at the palace almost well.

December 8. Received several natural curiosities of Tripoli from Mr. Nissen.

December 9. Visited the Turkish ambassador and found him better. He asked many questions about America and treated me with coffee.

December 10. Visited the Turkish officer, where I found a captain of one of the grand seignior's[7] ships of war, who came to Tripoli to carry presents to the grand seignior. The Tripolitan captain who took the brig from *Philadelphia*, Capt. Morris, was also there. He was very inquisitive about our country and our navy.

December 12. Was called on by the general of the marine to visit his principal secretary. Before I was permitted to give any medicine, the Turks—six in number, with Hamet, our dragoman—summoned the sick man and offered a prayer to Mahomet. The sick man then told me that if I would cure him, he would be very thankful and would speak to the bashaw in our favor.

December 15. The bashaw had a schooner launched which was built by the Spanish carpenters. She was tolerably handsome and calculated to carry six guns. When she was launched, three guns were fired from the batteries, and the consuls hoisted all their colors. At sunset, a firing from the batteries announced the commencement of the Mahometan Ramadan, continuing a lunar month in which they neither eat, drink, nor smoke while the sun is above the horizon, but feast at night. In walking through the town to visit my patients, I found the mosque and principal houses illuminated and the people rejoicing. Passing the coffee house with our dragoman, Lysle, a renegade Scotsman who was now the Tripolitan admiral, called me in to drink coffee with him and was very polite.

December 16. Visited the marine secretary

and found him in a state of great debility. Could not prevail on him to take any medicine or the least kind of nourishment. He said he would rather die than offend Mahomet by breaking the Ramadan but would take whatever I should advise at night.

DECEMBER 20. The market was so poor that we could get nothing for dinner but a shoulder of poor dromedary.

JANUARY 1. Was called to visit the bashaw's child, about eleven months old. The bashaw seemed much affected on my pronouncing the child dangerous and wished me to pay every attention to it, saying that anything he could afford should be at my service.

JANUARY 2. Found the bashaw's child better, at which he [the bashaw] expressed great satisfaction and offered me a horse and a servant to go to his gardens, about two miles from town. I preferred walking and took our dragoman with me. As I passed out at the gate of the city, I saw a man's head sticking on a pole. On enquiry, I found that it was the head of one of the bedouins, who, about a year before, had killed the son-in-law of the bashaw, who commanded the army in collecting the taxes in the back part of his dominions. About a quarter of a mile from the gate, the road passed through a burying ground full of graves.

After this, I came into a well-cultivated country, which was laid out in squares from one to six or

A harem in Tripoli

eight acres, each surrounded with date trees interspersed with orange, fig, olive, lemon, and other trees. On coming to Adm. Lysle's garden, we found him there and he invited me in. It was very beautiful. He loaded us with fruits, offered me access to it whenever I chose, and said I was welcome to anything growing in it. I concluded to postpone going to the bashaw's garden until another day.

January 3. Went to the bashaw's garden, where I met the minister and the prince—the bashaw's eldest son. They politely conducted me through the garden, which was ornamented with a great variety of fruit trees loaded with fruit, particularly with oranges, lemons, and limes. John Hilliard died in the evening.

January 4. William Anderson[8] died.

January 12. The bashaw's eldest daughter was married to Selim, the bashaw's chief *casleda,* or treasurer. Wilson, who was one of our quartermasters, and lately turned traitor and Turk, received five hundred bastinadoes for quarreling with the noted Lysle.

January 14. The minister of foreign affairs, Ciddi Mahomet Docize,[9] visited our prison. The month's fasting (Ramadan) ended this day at the change of the moon. The Tripolitans fired a salute from our ship, which lay moored in the harbor within sight of our window.

January 15. The feast called *Byram*[10] commenced. Every gun in Tripoli was fired in honor of the day. Every Turk put on his best suit, and there was a general rejoicing.

JANUARY 16. Capt. Bainbridge and Lt. Porter were invited and accordingly visited the bashaw, with all the consuls.

JANUARY 17. The *Byram* ended this evening— the consuls, the ships in the harbor, and the castle displaying their colors during the three days. The rejoicing was great, but neither elegance nor taste were discoverable.

JANUARY 18. By permission visited the triumphal arch, which was built at the time the Romans conquered this country. It is dedicated to Augustus Caesar, is very large, built of fine marble, and is full of engravings and inscriptions in tolerable perfection. It stands near the marinery.

JANUARY 19. The bashaw's agent sent us a present of tea, coffee, and sugar, and a lamb, probably to induce us to buy a quantity of old clothes taken from us, for which they asked six hundred dollars.

Diet at this time: two eggs and a piece of bread, with rainwater, for breakfast and supper; poor beef or camel's flesh, bread, and sometimes boiled cabbage, with rainwater, for dinner.

FEBRUARY 3. Was conducted to the castle to visit the bashaw, whom I found after passing several sentinels, about fifty fierce, yelping dogs, and three heavy doors loaded with irons and bolts, which

The Roman arch in Tripoli

were opened for us by armed mamelukes.[11] Prescribed for the bashaw's disorder.

FEBRUARY 6. The bashaw sent for me to come to his room in the castle. He shook hands with me, received me with much politeness, and requested me to pay every attention to his family as a physician.

FEBRUARY 10. The bashaw gave the officers permission to walk out into the town and country, but not to visit the consuls nor the batteries. Our dragoman, Hamet, was ordered to walk with us and direct us where to go. We went out six at a time.

FEBRUARY 16. Prescribed for the bashaw's eldest daughter. Her husband offered me many civilities. At five PM were informed that two English merchantmen were standing in [heading] for the harbor. They proved, however, to be two vessels under the command of Capt. Decatur. About eleven at night, we were alarmed by a most hideous yelling and screaming from one end of the town to the other and a firing of cannon from the castle. On getting up and opening the window which faced the harbor, we saw the frigate *Philadelphia* in flames.

FEBRUARY 17. The Turks appeared much disheartened at the loss of their frigate. A strong guard was put at our door, and we were forbid going out. I was forbid visiting our sick. It was reported that an American schooner and three boats set fire to the ship. Two Turks escaped who told this news. They said that eight Turks had charge of the ship, and they supposed the other six were carried off by the Americans. Our dragoman informed us that we were to be removed from our present habitation into the castle.

FEBRUARY 18. A guard of about twenty Turks was at our door. I asked permission to visit our sick and was refused. A gloomy aspect continued on the faces of the inhabitants for the loss of the frigate.

FEBRUARY 19. Again asked permission to visit our sick and was refused.

FEBRUARY 20. Permitted to visit the sick. Found the town full of country militia, and our guard doubled.

FEBRUARY 21. Our prison was kept full of Turks to guard us. The bashaw, having got a little over his fright, consented to let us remain where we were.

FEBRUARY 24. We were forbid sending letters to our friends, without first showing them to the bashaw or his ministers. The last letters we received were broken open by the latter before they were delivered to us.

MARCH 1. We were conducted to the castle.

MARCH 2. Found our habitation very dark and smoky, having no light but what came through a grated skylight.

MARCH 3. Not allowed to visit the sick, and our dragoman was forbid carrying letters to us.

MARCH 4. Capt. Bainbridge received a letter

from the ministers, reprimanding him on account of three men who floated ashore a few days after the burning of the frigate. The Turks pretended that they were murdered after they were made prisoners by the Americans.

MARCH 6. In close confinement. Hamet, our dragoman, was taken from us. The bashaw suspected him of being too friendly to us.

MARCH 7. The Tripolitans got the guns from the remains of our frigate and mounted them on their batteries. In trying them, several of the gun carriages broke down, and one of the guns burst and killed one Turk and wounded four.

MARCH 14. The Turks seemed much alarmed and placed a strong guard at our door, for what reason we knew not.

MARCH 16. The bashaw sent word that I should have anything I wanted, free of expense.

MARCH 17. Ordered not to send our clothes out to wash.

MARCH 24. I was taken out of prison to visit a mameluke's wife and child. The minister of foreign affairs paid us a visit and said many clever things.

MARCH 26. A truce was held between Commodore Preble and the bashaw.

MARCH 28 TO APRIL 13. I was violently afflicted with the dysentery, during which time the bashaw expressed much anxiety and offered me every assistance.

APRIL 15. We felt the Syroc [sirocco] wind, which was very oppressive.

APRIL 24. John Morrison died, in consequence of a hurt he received a few days before while at work under the directions of his new masters. The bashaw permitted me, with two of my fellow officers, to go to his garden, conducted by a guard of two Turks armed with pistols and sabers. This precaution, they pretended, was taken to prevent the wandering Arabs and Moors from robbing us; but it was probably done to prevent our escaping to the squadron, then cruising the harbor in sight.

MAY 7. Our boys caught a large scorpion in the small yard of our prison.

MAY 11. Our squadron appeared off the town. The Turks were at their quarters. They had twelve gunboats armed, manned, moored out in the harbor.

MAY 16. Ten of our officers took a walk to the gardens under escort of a guard. They returned with a variety of flowers and ripe apricots.

MAY 20. A party of us, under escort of four Turks, walked to the desert, about four miles from our prison. We ascended a large bank of sand, where we had an extensive view of the country. The deserts have a singular and grand appearance. They extend to Mount Atlas, which we could see at the distance of two days' journey. The sand is in heaps, like snowdrifts in our country. There was not a house nor any other object to be seen, not a thing growing to interrupt the sight; but it appeared like an ocean of sand. On our return, we visited several gardens, where we got oranges, lemons, apricots, and a variety of flowers. We were treated with sap of the date tree, which tasted much like mead.

MAY 29. A party of us, under escort as before, took a walk into the desert. On our return, we dined in the bashaw's garden under the shade of orange trees. The dinner was prepared in the Turkish style, and we ate with wooden spoons—it was simple and good. We visited several gardens and were treated with as much respect as could be expected or desired from a foe who held us as prisoners of war. On returning to town we saw two of our brigs at anchor off the harbor, seeming to defy all the force of Tripoli.

JUNE 4. We are plentifully supplied with squashes and cucumbers.

JUNE 18. The bashaw's eldest wife, called the queen, was delivered of her ninth child. She was twenty-three years of age. Her first child was born when she was in her eleventh year. It was said to be common to marry at ten.

JUNE 27. Mr. Hodge, our boatswain; Mr. Douglas, the sailmaker; and Mr. Fountain, the first master's mate, were taken from the prison and set to work by order of the bashaw.

JULY 15. The bashaw, his wives, and guards removed to their country seat at his garden. The season was very warm and our confinement continued. We purchased figs, watermelons, muskmelons, and cucumbers.

JULY 18. I was called to visit the bashaw's eldest son, the bey of Tripoli (termed the Prince of Wales of Tripoli by the English consul) at his palace, about three miles from town. I found him in a lofty and airy apartment, lying on a mattress and surrounded by his attendants. I prescribed for him and was highly entertained in the Turkish style. Saw two old women, said to have been a former bashaw's wives.

JULY 19. The bey was well enough to return to Tripoli. He called at the door of our prison, which was unlocked and the bolts and bars unloosed. I was conducted to him, when he expressed great satisfaction at having recovered his health, thanked me for my attendance, and promised to alleviate our misfortunes, as far as was in his power. I was then sent back to prison. The bashaw and bey spent a day alternately in town, on account of the expected attack by the Americans.

JULY 31. I was carried with my trunk and bed to the castle, where a room was provided for me, and the bashaw informed me I must attend the Americans and his family as a physician.

AUGUST 3. The American squadron, under Commodore Preble—consisting of one frigate (the *Constitution*), two brigs, three schooners, and seven gunboats—at about two PM, commenced an attack on the batteries and gunboats of Tripoli. I stood on the top of the castle, where I had a fair view of the engagement. Three of the enemy's gunboats were captured by the Americans. Two Turks swam on shore and were carried before the bashaw, who gave them a suit of clothes and a few dollars. They said that many were killed on both sides.

AUGUST 5. The American squadron anchored off Tripoli, I was ordered to dress the wound of a mameluke, who had his hand shattered by the bursting of a blunderbuss. I amputated all his fingers but one, with a dull knife, and dressed them in a bungling manner, in hopes of losing my credit as a surgeon in this part of the country, for I expected to have my hands full of wounded Turks in consequence of the exploits of my brave countrymen.

AUGUST 9. At about twelve o'clock, the alarm gun of Tripoli was fired. The Tripolitans all took their stations and went through the Mahometan prayer, by kneeling and kissing the ground several times, with their faces towards the east, all with as much regularity as the exercise in a well-disciplined army.

Their military maneuvering was a scene of the utmost confusion. I got permission to go on the top of the castle, where I had a most extensive view of the sea and land, and saw the American squadron approaching the town. At about one o'clock the attack commenced, and the battle soon became vigorous, with a tremendous cannonading on both sides.

I now beheld the melancholy catastrophe of the explosion of one of our gunboats. I saw the mangled bodies of my countrymen precipitated into the air. For a few moments a general silence took place, when the firing recommenced with unabated vigor. I saw the shells explode and set fire to the town in many places; but the houses being principally built of stone, mud, and mortar, the fire did but little damage. The shells and shot, however, battered the town very much and almost destroyed some of the houses. The firing ceased at four PM when the ship *John Adams* joined the squadron.

The bashaw has a bombproof room in his castle, where he stayed during the action. On hearing of the explosion of our gunboat, he ventured out to take a peep, with the precaution of having a *marabewt,* or priest, to seal a small piece of paper on the top of his head, with a Turkish or Mahometan scrawl with assurances that it would entirely secure him from all danger; but he soon returned to his cell. The Turks all wear a paper of this kind, sewed up in a little velvet bag, with assurance from the *marabewt* that it would protect them in the greatest danger. The *marabewt* gets a sum of money for these blessings. If a Turk gets wounded or killed, it is supposed the blessed paper was too old or not placed in a proper manner. In the time of action, the *marabewt* gets upon some secure place and cries to Mahomet in the most dismal yells to let them conquer their enemies and beckon to the vessels to run on shore or be destroyed. Such of our crew as were able were put to work and drove about like horses or mules.

August 10. Lewis Heximer, who lately turned Turk, went by order of the bashaw and told Capt. Bainbridge the particulars of the two late actions. The bashaw informed me that the late commander of the schooner *Vixen*, Lt. Smith, was commodore of the gunboats in the late action and was killed by a musket shot through his head. Our men complained of being drove and beat about at an unmerciful rate, in consequence of which they petitioned the bashaw in the following terms:

To His Excellency, the Grand Bashaw of Tripoli:
The petition of the whole of the American prisoners most humbly showeth:

That your humble petitioners, when doing with all their power as they are commanded, are most cruelly beaten by our wardens, stoned, insulted, and spit upon by the soldiers and others; required to carry burdens impossible for us to sustain; and chased and bruised until we are, or soon shall be, unable to labor at all.

From the many acts of justice, kindness, and generosity we have experienced from Your Excellency, we cannot suppose that such conduct is authorized by your commands; or that we should be punished for what is out of our power to perform; or for the actions of others, which we have no agency in and which we cannot prevent.

Returning Your Excellency our sincere and humble thanks for your bounty and privileges heretofore shown, and relying on your goodness and protection, we therefore most humbly pray that Your Excellency would interpose your royal authority and grant us a speedy relief. And your petitioners, as in duty bound, will remain Your Excellency's most humble, faithful, and obedient servants.

On the petition being explained to the bashaw by Heximer (or Hamet Amerikan, his new name), the bashaw forbid the Turks striking the prisoners.

AUGUST 11. The bashaw sent for me, and, agreeably to his orders, I took a seat by his side. He began conversation about my country and our squadron, which was then in sight and consisted of eighteen. He said that for two dollars he could repair all the damages that the bombardment did to his town; that but one man was hurt by the shells; that what he had been offered for the American prisoners was but fifty dollars per man; that he would make them earn that sum in two months. He asked me what I thought my country would give for me. I told him I did not know. He said he would not take twenty thousand dollars for me; to which I replied that I might then expect to remain in slavery for life. He patted me on the shoulder and said I must then content myself to stay with him. I asked to go and see our men, but he refused, saying the Moors and Arabs would kill me if they could catch me.

AUGUST 12. Our squadron hoisted a flag of truce, sent in a brig and schooner, and fired a gun. The bashaw did not, and swore he would not, answer it, and said he would not treat [negotiate] with Commodore Preble. A truce, however, was afterwards held. Consul O'Brien wished to come on shore but was refused.

AUGUST 15. Another truce was held, when the bashaw demanded one million dollars for our ransom. One hundred and twenty thousand dollars were offered and refused.

AUGUST 17. The bashaw informed me that fifteen Americans were found drifted ashore at the westward of the town and that one of them was an officer with an epaulet on the right shoulder. We supposed they were men destroyed by the explosion of the gunboat at the late engagement. I asked permission to go with two or three of our men and bury them, and the bashaw told me I might go the next day.

Our squadron lay at anchor off the harbor. The inhabitants had chiefly moved out of the town, through fear of another bombardment; and the bashaw ate, drank, and slept in his bombproof room. Several tribes of the backcountry inhabitants had lately come and offered their services to the bashaw—not more than one thousand men. Many of them had muskets without locks but had a sort of match to put fire to them. They were almost naked, half-starved, and without discipline. When they are going to battle or appear before the bashaw, they run to and fro, shaking their rusty muskets over their heads, all crying *"Halaout buoy"* (I am my father's son).

Every tribe has a priest, or what they call *marabewt*, whose badge is a small green flag, which is carried in his hand or stuck up at his tent. They pretend great skill in prophecy, in which the people put the utmost faith. They prophesy success in battle and, for a small sum of money, insure anyone against wounds or death in fighting a Christian. They often go on eminences [hills] and beckon and sing to the American vessels to run on shore. They prophesied that another American vessel was to go on the rocks, and the bashaw fully believed it.

AUGUST 18. Was not permitted to bury our dead. Our squadron stood out to sea. At evening, the bashaw went to his country seat and the bey came in to keep the throne till his father's return. They never both leave the castle. When the bashaw leaves it, the gates are shut till his return, for fear of

A dancer and a piper in native costume entertaining in Tripoli

incursion upon the throne. In the evening, the moon shining very bright, the prince or bey ordered out the band of music, which was very ordinary, and made Christians, Turks, Arabs, and Guinea Negroes dance before him, according to the mode of their respective countries, at which he seemed highly diverted.

AUGUST 19. Between nine and ten o'clock in the evening, Mr. Church, a respectable English gentleman, was shot through the head in the street, on his return from visiting his neighbors.

AUGUST 24. In the morning, between two o'clock and daylight, two of our small vessels hove about thirty shells, as was supposed, for the round fort, but they all fell short of the mark. Such attempts served rather to encourage than to intimidate the Tripolitans, and the bashaw was in high spirits on the occasion.

AUGUST 26. At about four PM, the fellow who murdered Mr. Church was executed near the spot where the crime was committed. It had therefore been a custom in this country, when a person had committed murder, to fly to a tomb of a *marabewt* (or priest) where they were protected from justice, and a fee to a *marabewt* would procure them absolution. This fellow fled to a place of this kind immediately after killing Mr. Church.

The English consul, Mr. Langford, on being informed of the murder, addressed the bashaw and demanded justice. The bashaw then found out, by a boy who accompanied the murderer when he committed the crime, the particulars of the affair and immediately sent a file of men and ordered them to prevent any person carrying food or drink to the murderer. They watched him until night, when the bashaw sent his *marabewt*, who coaxed him away, brought him to the castle, and confined him in irons.

The next day, the bashaw called his divan [governing council], when it was decided that the prisoner was guilty of willful murder and ought to suffer death. It appeared, by the evidence and confession of the prisoner, that Mr. Church had lent a sum of money to a Spanish carpenter in this place; that Mr. Church had pressed him for payment; and that the carpenter's wife hired the Turk to kill Mr. Church for forty dollars. The villain took his watch from his pocket after he had shot him.

The boy who accompanied him and carried a lantern was bastinadoed with five hundred blows. The carpenter's wife was ordered to leave Tripoli.

AUGUST 27. Our squadron stood towards the harbor.

AUGUST 28. About four o'clock in the morning, I was awakened by a heavy and incessant fire of cannon and the whistling and rattling of shot all around me. On getting up, I found that our gunboats were close in and were firing upon the town and batteries. Every gun in Tripoli that could be brought to bear was returning the fire. The Tripolitan gunboats were close under the castle for protection.

The firing continued until a few minutes after sunrise, when one of the largest gunboats ventured out with an intention of boarding the nearest American boat. As soon as she got within pistol shot, the Americans discharged their piece, loaded with grape[shot], and killed four and wounded two of the enemy; they then put about and retreated. At the same time, Commodore Preble bore down and gave the batteries to the westward of the town two broadsides. The squadron then stood out and anchored off the harbor. The damage done to the town was considerable. A large vessel was sunk in the harbor and others damaged. Many men were killed and wounded.

AUGUST 29. The bashaw sent me to his palace in the country to see his eldest son, the bey, whom I bled in the foot. He requested me to spend the day and dine with him, which I did. He endeavored to have the dinner in the Christian style. It was set on a table and consisted of a large dish of boiled rice and stewed fowls, out of which we both ate—he with a wooden spoon and I with a silver one, without knife or fork. The prince's servant stood by him and pulled the fowl in small pieces with his fingers for the prince to eat. I made use of my fingers and

Tripolitan musicians

teeth to get mine in pieces. Our dessert was dates and watermelons. Our drink was *lagby*, or the juice of the date tree, which we drank out of a large gold cup. He showed me the garden and took great pains to entertain me.

AUGUST 30. A truce was held. I took a ride upon a mule about eight miles to the westward of the town, in company with my guide, Hamet; a Turkish officer; and several footmen. I there saw a boat, which drifted on shore, with a dead man and several muskets and swords in it. The man appeared to have been shot through the body with a cannon-ball, which had also pierced the bottom of the boat. The Turkish officer collected about twenty Arabs, who hauled the boat upon the beach, dragged the dead man out of it, stripped him entirely naked, and left him on the beach.

I tried in vain to hire the Arabs to bury the body; they said it was contrary to their religion to bury a Christian. I asked permission to get him buried by our countrymen, some of my fellow prisoners, but was refused. I found that our men who were destroyed by the explosion of the gunboat on the ninth lay in a state of putrefaction on the beach. They were scattered on the shore for miles and were torn in pieces by dogs. The bashaw had frequently promised me that these men would be buried but refused to let me take some of our men to go and bury them.

SEPTEMBER 2. At about four PM, our squadron commenced another attack on the town in which eight of our gunboats drove sixteen Tripolitan gunboats under the battery on the east side of the harbor, while the commodore bore down and gave the batteries at the west end of the town several broadsides. Many of his shot came into the town and castle. Two bomb ketches were employed in heaving shells into the town, which did considerable damage to several houses and entirely destroyed the house of the Spanish carpenter, the bashaw's naval contractor.

I observed the utmost confusion and random firing among the Tripolitans. It appeared they were almost out of powder. Two of their guns burst, one of which was an eighteen-pounder of the late *Philadelphia* frigate. The men, women, and children ran out of the town in the utmost terror and distraction.

SEPTEMBER 3. Had been to see the prince in the country and was returning about ten o'clock in the evening, with the bashaw and suite, when we saw a most extraordinary light or flash and heard heavy report. We all wheeled about and made for the place we had left; but the bashaw soon altered his mind and proceeded to town, while I went to the country palace and stayed all night. The explosion was a fire ship, sent into the harbor by Commodore Preble, which did but little damage.

The Turks found ten dead men near the place where the vessel blew up, on the evening of the third. The bashaw and his people had a thanksgiving to Mahomet on the occasion. Their ceremony was prayer in doleful tone and singing, accompanied with the sound of an instrument made by drawing a skin over a hoop.

SEPTEMBER 6. More men were found, three of which appeared to be officers. By permission, I took our boatswain and a gang of men and buried these bodies a little east of the wall of the town. All that I saw who appeared to have been killed by the explosion amounted to fourteen. The bashaw's son-in-law told me that six more had been found drifted on the western shore, but I could not ascertain the truth of it.

SEPTEMBER 7. John M'Donah died of a consumption, with which he had long been ill.

SEPTEMBER 9. The bashaw took me with him and his suite to his country seat, where we spent the most of the day. About five PM, we went to see the great *marabewt*, or Mahometan priest, in whom the bashaw had great faith and thought he could foretell events.

It was said by the Turks that he foretold the stranding and capture of the *Philadelphia* and that he got offended with the bashaw and caused and foretold her being burnt. But I had heard nothing of these mysteries until a little previous to this. He now said that the commodore's ship, the *Constitu-tion*, would never return to America; that she would either be blown up or run on shore; and that the bashaw would have success in his warfare with America. It appeared that this great prophet was a sojourner and that he only came to Tripoli when the bashaw was in want of a prophet.

He was encamped on the sandy desert, at a tomb of an ancient *marabewt*. The tomb had a house over it, with several rooms, and was encircled with sev-eral green trees. It was about two miles back of the gardens. We found this great *marabewt* standing on a large mat, which was spread on the sand under the shade of a large mulberry tree. About thirty of his attendants stood back of him, paraded in form of a crescent. I was ordered to pull off my hat, and all approached him from the west—the bashaw, with some of his most truly attendants, in front. When we came near to him, we all dismounted. The bashaw ran to him, kneeled before him, and kissed his hand. The mamelukes followed his exam-ple. The *marabewt* then sat down and was followed by the bashaw and his suite, forming a circle on the mat.

During this time, I stood by my mule, about five rods from the scene, with my hat in my hand. I was soon called and ordered by the bashaw to take off my shoes and feel the *marabewt*'s pulse. I left my shoes at the edge of the mat, or holy ground, and stepped on. I laid my hat on the edge of the mat in preference to laying it on the sand, but it was immediately taken off. I was then ordered to approach His Holiness and kiss his hand. I felt his pulse; but before I had time to prescribe for him, he put his hand against me and gave me to understand that I must go off the holy ground. Immediately stepped off, put on my shoes, took my hat, and went to my mule.

The bashaw called me back and asked what I would do for the *marabewt*. I recommended bleeding, but the *marabewt* shook his head and gave me to understand that he wanted nothing of the *kelp* (dog). I was then told to withdraw, which I did, and took a walk round the tomb, which I found to be very ancient. The bashaw spent about half an hour with the *marabewt*, when he kissed his hand and we all returned to the country. The bashaw apologized for the impoliteness of the *marabewt* and said that they had a foolish antipathy to all but Mahometans.

OCTOBER 22. None of our cruisers were to be seen from the top of the castle. The Tripolitan gunboats were disarmed, and the bashaw's gunners were employed in drawing the charges from the cannon on the battery. Many of the guns now stood in the sand, as they did when Commodore Preble first attacked the town. On being fired two or three times, they recoiled into the sand so deep that they could not be worked and were abandoned. The bashaw told me that if he had three frigates, he would blockade America. He said he could do it as easily as a frigate and schooner could blockade Tripoli!

OCTOBER 26. A great scarcity of grain. Our crew had no bread for three days. The bashaw gave orders to all the market people not to sell grain to anybody but his household. There was no bread to be had for money. A dispute took place between the bashaw and the renegade Lysle about the purchasing of some barley. Lysle was considerably intoxicated and insisted on his right to purchase grain in the market. The bashaw was highly affronted and flew at him with all his might, struck him, and ordered his mamelukes to disarm him and put him in prison, which they strove to obey and carried him off.

The bashaw, however, soon ordered him released and then ordered his servant, who was supposed to be the cause of the quarrel, bastinadoed with five hundred blows, which was immediately put into execution.

NOVEMBER 9. The bashaw had an epileptic fit, and his people thought he was possessed with the devil. They performed many ceremonies to cast him out, which they said succeeded. The Turks said they saw many ghosts the night before and that a *marabewt* drove the devil out of the bashaw.

DECEMBER 6. Our men suffer for the want of

provisions. The bashaw does not allow them either victuals or cash. They get but a small allowance of bread—and that on the credit of their own country. They are beat unmercifully and compelled to work hard every day.

DECEMBER 7. I was informed that, through the influence of many Turks, the bashaw had given orders to Sarcy, our master, to treat the American prisoners with the utmost cruelty in order to induce the United States the sooner to make peace. He was impatient for his money.

DECEMBER 10. Our men all agreed not to work unless they were fed, and, accordingly, when the wardens went to the prison and ordered them out, they all refused. The wardens whipped them until they were tired and then went to inform the bashaw, who immediately ordered them bread and oil, and they went to work.

DECEMBER 21. At evening, the bey, the eldest son of the bashaw, was married to his first cousin, eldest daughter of the bashaw who was driven out of Tripoli by the present bashaw. The bride was said to be very handsome and but twelve years old.

Our boatswain, carpenter, sailmaker, and first master's mate, who had the liberty of the town for a few months, were put in close confinement with our other officers, on suspicion of attempting to raise the crew to take the town.

DECEMBER 25. The bashaw's son-in-law, Selim,

who had charge of the stores, was detected in selling a quantity of cordage to a Tunisian merchant. The bashaw ordered him five hundred bastinadoes; but Selim fled to a *marabewt* for protection and escaped punishment.

JANUARY 24. Renegade Wilson, who pretended to be a great engineer, was ordered by the bashaw to fire hot shot at a mark but succeeded indifferently. The bashaw, however, was highly pleased, gave Wilson eight dollars, and promised to reward him in proportion to his exertions in his future warfare. Wilson engaged to teach the Turks how to throw bombs, hot shot, and hand grenades, and to alter and improve the fortifications, etc.

JANUARY 25. The bashaw sent me to visit the wife of Alla Mameluke. She was once a wife or concubine to the bashaw, who gave her as a wife to his favorite. She was sister to a wife of the emperor of Morocco, about eighteen, and very handsome. She was in childbed travail, attended by a number of Jewish women. She was delivered of a son, her first child, to the great joy of all the Turks in the castle, male and female. It was proclaimed by a loud yelling, with clapping of hands to and from the mouth, by the women of the castle.

JANUARY 28. The bashaw was informed by Wilson, the renegade, that our crew were all armed and about to rise upon the town. Search was made and the report found to be false. But the bashaw was much intimidated and an additional guard was placed over us.

FEBRUARY 1. George Griffiths, one of our crew, having informed the bashaw that he could build an air furnace and cast guns, shot, etc., [was] furnished with a mason and nine of our crew and set to work, with a promise he should have a hundred dollars for the first shot he should cast. After expending about five hundred dollars in the experiment, Griffiths this day attempted a blast in his furnace; but with all the wood and coal that the bashaw could furnish, he could not melt the iron, and the furnace cracked in several places. It afterwards appeared that Griffiths had no intention to cast any shot.

FEBRUARY 5. While a number of our men were at work at the north corner of the castle, a large body of the wall fell and killed Jacob Dowerdesher. The only consolation we received from the Turks was that he was *amka devic* and *sansafedah*—that is, "D——n his mother; he has got no faith," *Romo kelp*—"Christian dog."

MARCH 1. An American frigate appeared off the harbor. The Turks were all at their quarters and were manning their gunboats.

The bashaw was preparing an armament to go against some of his refractory tribes on the borders of Egypt.

MARCH 4. Hassan Bey, the bashaw's chief mameluke, was appointed to command the expedi-

Arab horsemen exercising in the Tripolitan desert

tion towards Egypt, on the borders of the dominions of Tripoli. Hassan and his officers were attended by the bashaw and several stands of colors to a *marabewt* about three miles from town, to receive absolution and assurances of victory in the intended expedition. A great part of our crew, and many Turks and Jews, were employed in packing up ammunition, etc., for the camp.

MARCH 5. Two frigates and a brig, supposed to be American, appeared off the harbor. The people of Tripoli were preparing and moving their effects into the country, expecting a siege by the Americans.

MARCH 12. Swallows appeared. Apple, peach, and plum trees were in blossom, and peas in market.

MARCH 17. Walking by the house called the American house, I perceived that it was full of Turks, and a strong guard was at the door. On inquiry, I found that they were the sons and nearest relations of the bashaw's officers, who had gone in the expedition to the frontiers. The bashaw kept these people as hostages for the fidelity of his officers, whom it appears he was afraid to trust, lest they might join in the rebellion and come against Tripoli. It was said that His Highness had received a letter stating that the Americans were making great preparations to attack Tripoli. A tent was pitched on the battery of the castle and orders given to keep watch all night, and every night afterwards. Orders were also given to make every preparation to repel the Americans.

MARCH 18. The bashaw sent his son-in-law into the country for troops to protect Tripoli.

MARCH 19. It was reported and generally believed that the Americans had been to Alexandria in Egypt, where they had got the ex-bashaw and four thousand Egyptians and carried them to Syracuse, where they were to be landed to act in concert with the Americans against Tripoli.[12] I perceived many private councils and long faces amongst the Turks.

MARCH 21. A frigate and brig appeared off the harbor. The bashaw told me he suspected Commodore Barron was dead, as he had not heard from him for a time. Not long before, he told me that he had heard of the death of his brother, the ex-bashaw (Achmed [Hamet] Qaramanli). He seemed highly pleased at such news. Several of the sons and dearest friends of his chiefs in the country were brought into the castle, as hostages for their fidelity to the present bashaw. Symptoms of dissatisfaction appeared amongst the people.

MARCH 22. Two Negroes were hung at the gate of the city for robbery.

The bashaw's son-in-law, who had been sent into the country to collect troops to protect Tripoli, returned without success. The people refused to fight for the bashaw, because he had made unusual demands for money and even had stripped their wives of their jewels. For several days, it had been reported that ten thousand troops were to muster on the beach near the town; and His Highness was to make a speech to encourage them to fight for him against the Americans and his brother. I prepared myself to see these troops, but to my disappointment not one of them appeared.

APRIL 7. One of our cruisers appeared. A large gunboat was launched, which was built by renegade West, who was one of our crew turned Turk.

APRIL 12. The bashaw received an unfavorable letter from his agent at Malta concerning the armament of the Americans. The Spanish consul presented the bashaw three hundred stands of arms and a number of pistols, and, it is said, advised him to keep up the war and force the Americans to pay his demand. It was concluded that the bashaw's women and children should stay at the castle during the summer. They said that if they must be taken, they would rather fall into the hands of the Americans than the Arabs.

APRIL 13 TO 16. The bashaw declared that if the Americans drove him to extremities, or attacked his town, he would put every American prisoner to death.

APRIL 19. The bashaw interrogated me concerning the force of my country; he asked me how many marines the United States kept in pay. My answer, for good reasons, was ten thousand!

"How many troops?" he asked.

"Eighty thousand," said I, "are in readiness to march to defend the country at any moment; and one million of militia are also ready to fight for the liberty and rights of their countrymen!"

At this, His Highness assumed a very serious look, and I returned to my room.

APRIL 27. A very oppressive Syroc wind. Several companies of Arabs had arrived within a few days: about three hundred horse and seven hundred foot.

MAY 3. The bashaw and suite went very early this morning to the great *marabewt*, of whom some particulars have been mentioned. He was to continue with the bashaw during the contention with the Americans. He now assured the bashaw that the American frigates would be destroyed and that the gunpowder of the whole squadron would be so damaged that the Americans would not be able to fire a gun. He agreed to attend the bashaw, to keep the balls and shells from hurting him. He received large sums of money from the bashaw.

MAY 14. I received a note from Capt. Bainbridge stating the inconvenience which the officers labored under by being in close confinement and by breathing unwholesome air. I spoke to the bashaw on the subject and humbly solicited that our officers might be removed to the American house. The bashaw replied that the war between him and my country at first was about money, but now it was whether he or his brother should be the bashaw; and that the Americans had bound themselves to his brother in such a manner that it was not in their power to make peace with him; but that his brother and the Americans were determined to take Tripoli and take off his head. He swore by the prophet of Mecca that if the Americans brought his brother against him, he would burn to death all the American prisoners except me—that my life should be spared, because I saved the life of his child when very sick.

He went off in a great passion and mounted his horse. His mamelukes and guard, to the number of about forty, attended him, and they took a ride to his country palace. They returned about sunset, and the minister of exterior relations and the bashaw were in private conference.

MAY 19. A spy employed by the bashaw arrived from Malta and Syracuse. He brought news that the American squadron sailed for Alexandria in Egypt about twenty days before; that it consisted of four frigates, three brigs, three schooners, twenty-four gunboats, six bomb ketches, and several transports; that they were to take on board the former, or ex-, bashaw, and to proceed along the coast of Tripoli and take the principal towns; and then to attack and take the town of Tripoli and put it in possession of the ex-bashaw. The bashaw and his people seemed much agitated at this news.

MAY 21. The bashaw with his attendants rode into the country. According to custom, he took with him on a mule two boxes, said to contain twenty thousand *sequins* (forty thousand dollars). But I did not believe they contained that sum. They were light. I had lifted them both! And they were carried to and from the mule by one slave. Another mule was loaded with the packages of the bashaw's clothing. The bashaw always went thus provided, through fear that he might be served as he served his brother, the ex-bashaw, who was denied to return to the castle when the present bashaw usurped the throne.

During the absence of the bashaw, his eldest son, the bey, had his amusement. He ordered two carpets spread on the south corner of the castle. On one of the carpets, the bey and his attendants seated themselves with a band of music, consisting of two men with tambourines and one with a sort of drum. Murat, his uncle, and myself were seated on the other carpet. Three large Negroes were brought and ordered to perform before the bey. The music then struck up and the three Negroes commenced [their] dance with many ridiculous airs, whirling round, shaking their heads, and roaring like mad bulls.

A sandstorm in the Tripolitan desert

This continued about half an hour, when they appeared to be raving mad. They ran about, as if to tear in pieces everybody they met. One of them made a leap at me but was prevented from reaching me by the bey, Murad, and another Turk, who jumped between us. Two other Turks caught hold of the Negro and held him, when I, by the advice of the bey, went to the top of the north end of the castle, where I could see the sport in safety. During the frolic, I saw those Negroes chase several Christians; and I was told that they often tear all their clothes off and hurt them much by biting, etc.

MAY 22. I was informed that, in a letter which the bashaw received the evening before, it was stated that Hassan Bey and his army were taken in Derne by the Americans and Ciddi Hamet,[13] the ex-bashaw. I was desired not to mention it, because it was a great secret; and the bashaw did not wish to let his people know it. I was also informed that the bashaw called a council of his chiefs and proposed to put all the American prisoners to death, but it was agreed to postpone this measure for that time.

MAY 23. Twenty-five of our men were sent with a cart for timber into the country. The wind from the desert was very heavy and hot. The men almost perished in the sand, which flew and drifted like a snowstorm in our country. They stopped through fatigue and asked their driver, who was a Turk, for liberty to drink at a well which was near them. The

Turk replied that they were *Romo kelps*, Christian dogs, and said they should have no water. He gave them all a severe beating with a large club, which he always carried with him to drive them with, and made them go on with the cart, which the poor fellows had to drag, loaded with timber, through the burning sand. They returned towards night almost perished.

MAY 24. At night, the bashaw dispatched a boat with powder, musket balls, and money for his troops, who were collecting to oppose the approach of his brother Hamet, the ex-bashaw. The eldest son of Hamet was confined in the castle by order of the present bashaw. The bashaw was so much agitated at the news of the approach of his brother that he this day declared that if it was in his power now to make peace and give up the American prisoners, he would gladly do it without the consideration of money. His funds were so low that his steward ran in debt for the supply of the kitchen. He gave his mamelukes, domestics, and myself but one meal per day. The rich Turks in town took turns in supplying his few troops. He heartily repented for not accepting the terms of peace last offered by our country.

MAY 26. Three frigates in sight. At about eleven AM, the smallest came near in and hoisted the banners of peace. The bashaw asked his head men of the town, who were with him in his gallery, whether it was best to hoist his white flag. All except one, the chargé d'affaires for Algiers, declared in favor of it and of making peace if possible. They expressed great contempt towards the Algerine consul for his advice and said that whoever would advise the bashaw not to hoist the white flag at such a critical moment must be his foe and not his friend.

The Algerine soon disappeared and left the castle. The Spanish consul soon after came to the castle; and the bashaw sent him in one of his handsome boats, with Shous Hammad, to the frigate. They returned at evening with the joyful news of a prospect of peace. There was a visible change, from gloominess to joy, in the countenance of all the Turks.

MAY 27. Both Turks and Christians were all anxiously looking out for the frigates. It was said that Col. Lear had promised to come on shore this morning and that the Spanish consul was preparing a dinner for the gentlemen who were expected to come with him. We were all agitated alternately by hope and despair. The terraces and every eminence in town were covered with people of all classes and ages who were looking for the wished-for peacemaker. But not a frigate nor a sail hove in sight during the day.

MAY 28. All looking out again for our squadron. A brig hove in sight in the morning, which we all at first thought was the flagship. On discovering it was a brig, a gloominess again appeared on every countenance. The Turks began to think that the frigate had gone to fetch the whole fleet, which they heard consisted of sixty sail of different sizes. They thought that the flag of truce was only a plan of the Americans to find out the force of Tripoli, etc. But at sunset, three frigates and a brig appeared, which revived our hopes. The bashaw showed the greatest anxiety for peace. He was sensible of the danger he was in from the lowness of his funds and the disaffection of his people.

MAY 29. Three frigates and a brig bore down upon the town and displayed the ensigns and signals of peace, which were immediately answered from the castle. The Spanish consul, Fafah the Jew,[14] and several Turks went on board and did not return until late at night, when it was reported that negotiations for peace were going on rapidly.

MAY 31. The Spanish consul [Don Gerardo Joseph de Souza] and Shous Hammad went on board the commodore and returned at night. The bashaw sent me to inform Capt. Bainbridge that peace was agreed on, which I did to the great joy of the officers.

JUNE 1. The truce continued. Bainbridge went on board the commodore and returned at night. Our men were still driven to hard labor, and our officers kept confined.

JUNE 2. I received a letter from Capt. Bainbridge stating that the terms of peace were agreed on and that we should soon go on board the squadron. I immediately read this letter to our crew, who were so overjoyed that many of them shed tears. They were still drove to hard work and many of them flogged.

JUNE 3. The articles of peace were signed and salutes fired from the frigates and batteries.

JUNE 6. I bid the bashaw a final adieu, at which he seemed much affected.

NOTES

1. It is not known who wrote this introduction.

2. Nicolas Harwood was a surgeon's mate on the *Philadelphia.*

3. Westerners often characterized all Muslims as "Turks"; in the case of North Africa, most of the soldiers and officials would have originally been Turkish, rather than Arab or Berber.

4. Prisoners of war signed a parole of honor, agreeing to abide by certain rules in exchange for not being incarcerated.

5. Cowdery means Bryan McDonough, the British consul at Tripoli.

6. John Wilson, the German-born quartermaster on the *Philadelphia,* converted to Islam.

7. The grand seignior, or grand vizier, was the Ottoman sultan's prime minister. The Ottoman Empire was a Turkish sultanate founded in the thirteenth century by Osman I and ruled by his descendants until its dissolution after World War I.

8. William Anderson: the captain's clerk on the *Philadelphia.*

9. Cowdery means Muhammad D'Ghies.

10. The three-day festival of *qurbana bairami,* in Turkish, follows the month-long fast of Ramadan and commemorates Abraham's sacrifice of his eldest son—Ishmael in the Muslim tradition; Isaac in Judeo-Christian tradition.

11. The mamelukes were usually Caucasians enslaved by the Ottomans to serve as soldiers throughout the empire.

12. In this and the following paragraphs, Cowdery is misinformed. These are references to the Eaton expedition.

13. Achmed Sidi was the deposed pasha who marched on Derne with William Eaton.

14. Leon Farfara, a Jewish banker.

BOOK III

Horrors of Slavery; or
the American Tars in Tripoli

BY
William Ray

A cologee, or guard, *of Tripoli*

INTRODUCTION

*William Ray, born in Litchfield, Connecticut, in
1771, aspired to be a man of letters. But men of letters
have to earn a living, so at age twenty-two he entered
business, quickly ran into debt, and set out for Pennsylvania hoping for better opportunities.*

*On the way, Ray grew ill and expended all his cash
paying for room and board. He reached Philadelphia
"without a shilling—without any friend or acquaintance—unable to labour, and too proud to become a
mendicant," as he noted in* Horrors of Slavery. *From
the banks of the Delaware River, he spied the flag flying from the* Philadelphia, *and on June 13, 1803, he
was "pressed into the maritime service of the United
States." He said he was pressed, or forced, because he
was "compelled by an irresistible, horrific band of
complicated wants, commanded by imperious necessity, more formidable, and as rapacious as a British
press gang." Two weeks later, on July 5, the* Philadelphia *went to sea. Within four months, Ray would be a
prisoner of war, captured when the* Philadelphia *ran
aground in Tripoli.*

*Ray had high hopes for his voyage; other writers
have found their muse at sea. Though quickly disillu-
sioned about life aboard ship—the physical conditions
were appalling and the officers brutal—intellectually,
Ray thrived. He wrote poetry about the ship, the crew,*

and his new hero, Capt. William Bainbridge. If the Philadelphia *met a hostile ship, "the Moor, Tripolitan, or Algerine," Ray predicted that, like "stern Ulysses, as Achilles bold, or warlike Hector in the days of old, the martial look of Bainbridge shall inspire the dauntless ardour of heroic fire."*

Ray was off the mark. Though Bainbridge did have a martial look, it was more often directed against his own sailors than the enemy. Bainbridge had a reputation as a cruel captain, and his officers and midshipmen emulated his example. When Ray published his book of poetry in 1821, he acknowledged how wrong he had been about Bainbridge.

In captivity, Ray continued to write. His poems "Elegy on the Death of Hilliard" and "The American Captive in Tripoli" appeared in the Portfolio of Philadelphia and in the New York newspapers, even while he remained in Tripoli.

But Ray's more important writings were on behalf of the crew. In August 1804, the sailors wrote to Bainbridge asking to have their wages increased and rations improved. He replied that he had nothing more to give them, though Commodore Preble had sent him small amounts to cover the needs of all the crew and officers.

Two days later the crew sent another letter, in William Ray's handwriting, suggesting that Bainbridge appoint men to supervise the sailors' messes, ensuring that rations were equitably distributed. Bainbridge told the crew to appoint their own mess *captains and also pledged to get more bread, meat, and vegetables for the men. The crew thanked Bainbridge for his intercession, and though they did not receive more provisions, their wages "were more punctually paid."*

After peace was secured, most of the American prisoners in Tripoli were evacuated aboard the President, *but Ray was assigned to the* Essex. *When he asked to be transferred, he was told the* Essex *would sail for home in about six weeks. In fact, it extended its cruise. But Ray obtained a good position as captain's clerk and found the duty easy and the living of the best kind. The ship visited Tunis, Algiers, Tangier, Malaga, Cadiz, and Gibraltar before finally arriving in Washington, D.C., in August 1806.*

Ray spent the rest of his life in upstate New York, finding more success writing than in various business ventures. He published Horrors of Slavery *in 1808; served as editor of the* Reveille, *a newspaper in Elizabethtown, between 1812 and 1816; and published* Poems *in 1821 and a novel,* Sophia. *Ray served in the War of 1812 with the Plattsburgh militia. He married, had one child, and died in 1827.*

Horrors of Slavery *has become the primary source for the condition of the captive sailors in Tripoli. Ray's perspective was much different from Cowdery's. He accused Cowdery of ignoring the ordinary sailors while he treated the pasha's family, played chess with the crown prince, and strolled in the pasha's gardens.*

When Ray published a collection of his poetry, he prefaced the elegy on Hilliard with Cowdery's cold comment, "John Hilliard died in the evening," noting that Cowdery had spent that January day at the pasha's country estate and bluntly charging the doctor with negligence.

Ray wrote to his former commander in January 1807, hoping that Bainbridge would subscribe in advance to Horrors of Slavery *and perhaps use his influence to help sell copies. Unfortunately for both men, Bainbridge was at sea when Ray wrote to him. Ray took Bainbridge's silence to mean refusal to subscribe to his work, and so the portrait of Bainbridge in the book is not flattering: the captain is seen as indifferent to the plight of the crew and insensitive to their suffering.*

Bainbridge was infuriated by Horrors of Slavery. *He wrote to the secretary of the navy blasting Ray as "an ungrateful wretch who has no character to lose." Despite Bainbridge's denunciation,* Horrors of Slavery *had three editions between 1808 and 1811.*

Exercising Ship

IT WAS ABOUT the 26th of August, if I mistake not, when we arrived in Gibraltar. We lay here a few days when the frigate *New York,* Commodore Morris; the *Constitution,* Capt. Preble; and the *John Adams,* Capt. Campbell, arrived from the Mediterranean. The brig *Vixen,* Lt. Smith, also arrived from Baltimore.

Information was received that a vessel with Barbary colors was cruising off the Rock, and we went in pursuit of her. It was in the afternoon when we came in sight of her. She bore away, and we gave chase. Our ship was under English colors.[1] We fired a number of guns before she would come to. About sunset we came within hailing, and our captain ordered one of our seamen, who could speak Spanish and the lingua franca [common language], to speak her. When he accordingly did and asked where she was from, they answered, "Morocco."

"Where are you bound?"

"Morocco."

"What news?"

"The emperor of Morocco has given us orders to capture all American vessels."

"Have you taken any?"

"Yes, we have captured a brig."

"Where is she?"

"Ahead."

"Are any of her men on board?"

"Yes, the captain and four men."

You may judge something of their consternation and confusion when we let fall our English ensign, hoisted the American, and order them to strike. They instantly doused their colors and humbly deprecated [prayed against] our vengeance.

Being ordered, they sent their boat on board of us, with their officers and captain of the American brig. Mr. Cox, our first lieutenant—with several midshipmen; about forty sailors; and a sergeant, corporal, and eight marines—was sent on board to take command of the prize. The prisoners were disarmed and put under hatches, with sentinels over them.

The ship carried twenty-two six-pounders and about one hundred men. Their guns were badly mounted, the ship filthy, and the men meager, grisly, and shabby. They had onions of the mildest flavor and largest size I ever beheld; I believe they were nearly six inches in diameter. Their sea-bread was from barley-meal, baked in large loaves, cut into slices, and dried in an oven like what we called rusk.[2] Their beef or mutton was boiled; cut into small pieces; mingled with flour, fat, and oil; and packed into kegs. Rice, oil, olives, and dried fish composed the remainder of their esculent [edible] stores.

Our frigate, now in company with the prize, steered for the brig and came in sight of her the following day in the afternoon. She led us a chase and was very unwilling to come to; but when we came within hail, the affrighted master of her cried out, "Morocco! Morocco!" and struck his colors.

It was pleasing to witness the ecstasies of our countrymen on being thus unexpectedly and happily rescued from the power of their fierce predaceous [predatory] captors. They had been stripped of their clothing, robbed of their chests and cash, plundered of everything valuable in their cargo, and confined below in irons.

We took the brig in tow, the prize in company, and sailed for the Rock. Knowing themselves to be pirates and conscious of their crimes, the Moorish captives manifested great concern for their lives by frequently putting their fingers across their throats and asking us, by interpreters, if we did not think they would all lose their heads.

At the Rock of Gibraltar, the prisoners were all sent on board of the *Philadelphia*. Lt. Cox remained on board the Moorish ship as prize-master. The prisoners were kept on board of the frigate for a considerable time and then sent to their own ship again. While they were with us, they were treated as prisoners of war—not insulted or abused, not put in irons, and had as much provisions allowed them as they could devour. Notwithstanding they were

Mahometans and, by their religion, interdicted [prohibited from] the drinking of spirituous liquors and the eating of pork, many of them would indulge in excess the former and swallow with voracity the latter, in preference to any other meat.

To supply the place of Mr. Cox as first lieutenant of the *Philadelphia,* Mr. Porter came on board, and Mr. Renshaw[3] to fill the vacancy of Mr. M'Conough, who remained with Mr. Cox. James Ingerson, David Shays, Nathaniel Brooks, and Charles Rylander, having been shipwrecked on the coast of Portugal, were sent by an American consul, in a Portuguese ship, to the American consul at Gibraltar. They were Americans from Boston; had suffered much; and earnestly solicited him to provide them a passage to America, which he promised and which was no more than his official duty to fulfill.

But the perfidious misanthrope, instead of sending them on board of some of our shipping then lying in harbor and bound to America, sent them to our frigate, then bound up the Mediterranean on a two-years' cruise. The treacherous consul told them that the ship to which he would send them was bound to America, and they were unsuspicious of any device until they were safely on board of us and informed to the contrary by our crew. Was this any better than impressing? The consul's name is Gavino, and his conduct ought to be execrated by every American seaman. Him these four unfortunates may thank for their chains in Tripoli.

They applied to Capt. Bainbridge, informed him of the consul's finesse, and sued for permission to leave the ship and seek one bound to their native shores. But he told them that, as they had been sent by order of the American consul, he could not possibly discharge them, encouraged them with the hope of our not being long out, and endeavored to persuade them to enter on the ship's books. But they were chagrined and contumacious [disobedient], and positively refused either to enter or do duty.

Some time in October we sailed for Malta, in company with the *Vixen,* and arrived there towards the latter part of the same month. Here we landed several boxes of dollars, which we took in at Gibraltar . . . . We now sailed for Tripoli and, for what reason I know not, parted with the brig.

On the 31st day of October, early on Monday morning, a sail was discovered on our larboard[4] bow, and orders were immediately issued to give her chase. She made towards the shores of Tripoli, and we soon distinguished that she carried Barbary colors. The white walls of our destined residence in captivity soon hove in sight. Every sail was set and every exertion made to overhaul the ship and cut her off from the town. The wind was not very favorable to our purpose, and we had frequently to wear ship.⁵ A constant fire was kept up from our ship, but to no effect.

We were now within about three miles of the town, and Capt. Bainbridge not being acquainted with the harbor, having no pilot nor any correct chart, trusted implicitly to the directions of Lt. Porter, who had been here several times and who professed himself well-acquainted with the situation of the harbor. We, however, went so close in that the captain began to be fearful of venturing any farther and was heard, by a number of our men, to express to Lt. Porter the danger he apprehended in pursuing any farther in that direction, and advising him to put about ship. Lt. Porter answered that there was no danger yet and that he would give them a few shots more. A moment or two afterwards, just as we were preparing to come about, she struck upon the shoals and remained fast!

The impudent pirate now, for the first time, hove to and returned fire. Lt. Porter looked much like the paper on which I am now blackening his name. Dismay was conspicuous in every countenance. The sails were put aback, anchors cast ahead, and other means exerted to throw her off, but without effect. Three gunboats were immediately under way from the wharves; and one of them, coming within reach, began to spit her fiery vengeance.

I could not but notice the striking alteration in

the tone of our officers. Burling was taken from our bastille [prison], the coal-hold. It was no time now to act the haughty tyrant, no time to punish men for snoring, no time to tell men they had no right to think; but every man could now snooze and cogitate as much as he pleased. It was not "go you dam'd rascal"—but "come, my good fellow, my brave lads."

The forecastle guns were run abaft on the quarterdeck, the guns on the main deck hauled aft, but to no effect. The gunboats kept throwing their balls; but they all went too high, none of them touched our hull, and but very few went through the rigging. It was thought if our guns were thrown overboard, it might cause her to swing clear. It was accordingly done, excepting those on the quarterdeck and in the cabin; but no hopes were visible. Her foremast was cut away—all would not do—she seemed immovable. Her stern was partly demolished, to make way for our guns to bear upon the enemy better, but our shot had little or no effect.

Mr. Hodge, the boatswain, suggested the experiment of casting a stern anchor, but this attempt was rejected by the officers, and he afterwards persisted in his opinion that if this method had been adopted, she might have been thrown off with facility. Now was the juncture at which we required the aid of the brig we had left.

It was a little past twelve o'clock when we struck

the shoals; and we continued firing at the boats and using every means in our power to get the ship afloat and annoy the enemy, when, about four o'clock, the Eagle of America fell a prey to the vultures of Barbary—the flag was struck!

Many of our seamen were much surprised at seeing the colors down before we had received any injury from the fire of our enemy and begged of the captain and officers to raise it again, preferring even death to slavery. The man who was at the ensign halyards positively refused to obey the captain's orders when he was ordered to lower the flag. He was threatened to be run through, and a midshipman seized the halyards and executed the command, amidst the general murmuring of the crew.

There was only one gunboat that could bear upon us, although there were two more lying to leeward, between us and the shore, afraid to come nigher. It is true there were two or three more making ready and getting under way, but it was afterwards thought they would not have attempted to board us for that night; and by the next morning she was afloat!

In fact, the Turks were so pusillanimous that after our colors were struck, they dared not, for they did not attempt to come any nearer, until we sent a boat and persuaded them that it was no farce, no illusion, assuring them that our frigate had in reality struck to one gunboat, and entreated them to come and take possession of their lawful booty!

While the boat was gone, the clothes, chests, and provision barrels were brought on the gundeck, and every man was allowed free access. The ship was scuttled, and water let into the magazine; the cabin furniture destroyed; battle-axes, pikes, cutlasses, pistols, muskets, and all implements of war thrown overboard. All hands were then called to muster on the quarterdeck. Capt. Bainbridge read a clause in the articles of war, stating that our wages would continue while we were prisoners of war; encouraged us to hope for ransom by our country; and advised us to behave with circumspection and propriety among our barbarous captors.

To witness the odd appearance of our provident tars at this solemn hour would have excited risibility in the muscles of an expiring saint. Some of them with three or four pair of trousers, and as many shirts on, with handkerchiefs stuffed with handkerchiefs round their necks, and their bosoms crammed with clothes and provisions, bore the resemblance of Blunt, in puppet show, or Falstaff, in comedy.

NOTES

1. Using false colors to confuse the enemy was a common practice.
2. Rusk: a hard, crisp bread.

3. James Renshaw, later commodore, was the victor of Lake Champlain during the War of 1812.

4. Larboard: left side of the ship. After the introduction of steam engines made ships noisier, *larboard* was changed to *port* to avoid confusion with *starboard.*

5. To wear ship is to bring the ship about with the wind astern, unlike tacking in which the ship turns into the wind.

Remarks on Dr. Cowdery's Journal

I SHALL NOW take some notice of extracts from Doctor Cowdery's journal, as published in the *Balance* of Hudson and republished in the *Albany Register*. As far as he adheres to strict veracity I shall coincide with his observations, but when he deviates from correctness, or exaggerates on facts, take the liberty of differing with the learned doctor's diary.

He says, *After the signal of the* Philadelphia *was struck and the officers and crew were waiting the pleasure of their new masters, the Tripolitan chiefs collected their favorites and, with drawn sabers, fell to cutting and slashing their own men, who were stripping the Americans and plundering the ship. They cut off the hands of some, and it is believed several were killed.*

It is true there was a sort of mutiny and clashing of arms amongst them; but for my part I never saw any hands amputated, nor do I believe there were any lives lost. For myself and a hundred others were in the ship much longer than the doctor, and none of us ever saw or heard of this carnage amongst ourselves.

After they had borrowed about ten dollars of the doctor and wrested his surtout [overcoat] from under his arm, he says, *Whilst they were picking its pockets and quarreling with each other for the booty, I sprung for the next boat, which was waiting for me. In my way, I met a little fellow who seized me and attempted to get off my coat; but I hurled him into the bottom of the boat . . .*

This was certainly the most heroic action that has ever been read of any of the *Philadelphia's* officers. Surrounded by those horrific brigands, with *drawn sabers and cocked pistols,* for a man, at such a critical and fearful crisis, to have the courage to collar an enemy, on his own ground, must be considered as a specimen of heroism not very common to be found among empirics¹ of our navy. And when the doctor mentions hurling the *little fellow,* the reader, not acquainted with the person of the said doctor, would really suppose him to be a mammoth of a man—quite the reverse.

He further says, *They then began upon Mr. Knight, sailing master, Mr. Osborne, lieutenant of marines, and all the officers in the boat; plundered their pockets; and took their handkerchiefs from their necks.*

They then landed us at the foot of the bashaw's palace, where we were received by a guard, who conducted us into the palace before the bashaw. He viewed us with the utmost satisfaction and had us conducted into an apartment, where we found the captain and several officers, who [had] arrived in another boat just before us. Here was a table set in the Euro-

pean style. The servants appeared to be Maltese and Neapolitan slaves. Here we supped, after which it was announced that another boat had arrived with our officers and men, who were before the bashaw.

Capt. Bainbridge requested me to go and look for Dr. Harwood, whom it was feared was killed. I found him with the carpenter before the bashaw, stripped of everything but their shirts and trousers. They afterwards informed us that they were stripped in the boat when I lost my surtout; and when they got within a few rods of the shore, they were thrown into the sea and left either to drown or swim ashore.

The bashaw's servant gave them dry clothes, and we were all again conducted before the bashaw and formed into a half circle. He was seated on his little throne, which was decorated in the Turkish order, and made a handsome appearance. He is a good-looking man, aged about thirty-five. He counted us, viewed us with a smile, and appeared highly pleased with us.

We were then conducted by the minister of exterior relations and a guard to the house formerly occupied by the American consul—a very good house, with a large court, and roomy enough for our convenience. We were seated here about nine o'clock in the evening. Capt. Bainbridge got permission from the bashaw to send for the Danish consul, who paid us a visit and offered every assistance in his power. We slept upon mats and blankets spread upon the floor, which was composed of tiles.

Although the doctor here makes no discrimination between men and officers, it must not be understood that he includes the former when he says *we*, excepting servants—no, no, it was only the officers who were treated to a supper, lodged in this comfortable mansion, and had mats to sleep on. You will, therefore, please to remember that when the doctor says *we*, it is the very same as if he had said *we officers only*; for he does not think proper to descend to the task of relating how the crew were provided for, or whether they were but half alive or all dead.

I must therefore inform the interested and humane reader that, as soon as we were huddled into the boats, all, or the most of us, were stripped of all our clothing excepting a shirt, trousers, and hat. Some, however, who were in the first boat, under the eye of our officers, fared a little better and kept the most of their clothes.

When we came near the shore, we were all precipitated into the foaming waves, for the wind blew very fresh, and left to the free exercise of our talents at swimming or wading ashore. At the beach stood a row of armed men on each side of us, who passed us along to the castle gate. It opened, and we ascended a winding, narrow, dismal passage, which led into a paved avenue, lined with terrific janissaries,[2] armed with glittering sabers, muskets, pistols, and tomahawks. Several of them spit on us as we passed.

We were hurried forward through various turnings and flights of stairs until we found ourselves in the dreadful presence of his exalted majesty, the puissant [powerful] bashaw of Tripoli. His throne, on which he was seated, was raised about four feet from the surface, inlaid with mosaic, covered with a cushion of the richest velvet, fringed with cloth of gold, bespangled with brilliants. The floor of the hall was of variegated marble, spread with carpets of the most beautiful kind. The walls were of porcelain, fantastically enameled, but too finical [ornate] to be called elegant.

The bashaw made a very splendid and tawdry appearance. His vesture was a long robe of cerulean silk, embroidered with gold and glittering tinsel. His broad belt was ornamented with diamonds and held two gold-mounted pistols and a saber with a golden hilt, chain, and scabbard. On his head he wore a large white turban, decorated with ribbons. His dark beard swept his breast. He is about five feet ten inches in height, rather corpulent, and of a manly, majestic deportment. When he had satiated his pride and curiosity by gazing on us with complacent triumph, we were ordered to follow a guard.

They conducted us into a dreary, filthy apartment of the castle, where there was scarcely room for us to turn round. Here we remained an hour or two dripping and shivering with the chills of the damp cells and the vapors of the night. The Neapolitan slaves were busily employed in bringing us dry clothing to exchange for our wet. We rejoiced to see men who wore the habiliments of Christians and sincerely thanked them for their apparent kindness. We thought them disinterested, generous, and hospitable, for we expected to receive our clothes again when dry; but the insidious scoundrels never afterwards would make us any restoration. The clothes which we gave them were new, and those which they brought us in exchange were old and ragged.

We were then taken to a piazza, nearly in front of the bashaw's audience hall, where we lodged for the night. It was floored with tiles and arched above, but open on one side to the chilling blasts of intemperate night; and, as many of us had wet clothes on and nothing to cover us with—add to this the gloomy prospects before us and the painful apprehensions of chains, stripes, and dungeons—and you may well suppose we had not a very refreshing night's repose.

In the morning, about eight o'clock, an old sorceress came to see us. She had the complexion of a squaw, bent with age, ugly by nature, and rendered frightful by art. She looked round upon us and raised a shrill cry of *bu-bu-bu-bu,* struck her staff three times upon the pavement, and then went through and examined us. There was a black man amongst us, and him she selected and placed aside from the rest. We supposed she had chosen him for herself, but he remained in the castle as one of the cooks for the mamelukes.

This frightful hag is held—by the bashaw and all the Tripolitans—in the highest veneration, not only as an enchantress, but as a prophetess also. It is said by them that she predicted the capture of the *Philadelphia* and believed by them that the ship struck the shoals in consequence of her incantations.

The potent bashaw presently made his appearance, and we were ordered to rise and pull off our hats. He walked past us, into his balcony, and we were permitted to ramble for a while, through the various divisions of this chaotic pile. Some of our men had saved a little cash from the ruffian hands of our hostile pillagers, but there was nothing eatable to be purchased in the castle. We had eaten nothing for twenty-six hours and began to feel our appetite. The Neapolitans, by paying a certain share of the profits, were permitted to retail *aqua-deut*,[3] a spirituous liquor distilled from the fruit of the date tree and similar to our whiskey. This they kept to sell in their cells in the castle, around the doors of which our shivering men thronged; and such as had money shared it with such as had not. But these villainous, mercenary knaves, taking advantage of our ignorance in the price of the liquor and of the money which they gave us in change, allowed no more than about one-fourth of the real value of a dollar.

We were now collected together again in front of a large window, which looked into a back yard. The bashaw; his son; the renegade Scotsman, "Commodore" Lysle; and several of the bashaw's officers appeared at the window. And the commodore began to interrogate us respecting our captain, etc. He asked us whether we thought our captain a coward or a traitor. We answered, "Neither."

He replied, "Who, with a frigate of forty-four guns and three hundred men, would strike his colors to one solitary gunboat must surely be one or the other."

We told him that our ship being fast on the shoals, we had no chance to defend ourselves, having thrown our guns overboard; and that, although we were in no immediate danger except from one gunboat, we judged, and feared, that as soon as night favored their designs, they would surround and cut us to pieces, giving no quarter.

He said there was no necessity for throwing our guns overboard; that we might have known she would be got off as soon as the wind shifted; and assured us she was already afloat—that if we had not struck our flag, they would not have ventured to board us, and highly ridiculed our captain's cowardice, if, in fact, it was owing to want of courage. He persisted in the idea that the ship was given up by design, for, he said, the captain not bringing a pilot with him and leaving the brig, when he acknowledged himself unacquainted with the harbor, and then running so nigh in so precipitately were circumstances weighty enough to overbalance all doubts of his treachery, or, at least, indubitable evidences of his want of judgment and proofs of his pusillanimity.

The bashaw was very inquisitive to know the number of shipping and strength of America. We gave him surprising accounts of both. The commodore asked us if there were any mechanics amongst us and said that such as were willing to work at their trades should be paid for their labor; if not, they would be compelled to do other work. He was informed there were ship carpenters and blacksmiths amongst us. They were selected from the rest, counted, and then mingled with us again.

We were then collected in a body and marched through dark and winding alleys to the principal gate of the castle, different from the one at which we entered. Passing out of this, we were conducted to an old magazine, as they called it, filled with sacks of grain, meal, lumber, and useless combustibles, which we were ordered to remove to another old building, not far distant. This was the first of our labor. Our drivers began to display their

ferocity by beating several of our men who were
rather dilatory in obeying their new boatswains.

When we had finished removing the rubbish, we
were given to understand that this was to be the
place of our confinement. It had once been occupied as a prison by the Swedish captains who had
shared a fate similar to ours. The prison was about
fifty feet in length, twenty in breadth, and twenty-
five in height, with a skylight and two front, grated
windows. It had a most dreary appearance, was dark
and fuliginous [sooty]. Not a morsel of food had
we yet tasted, and hunger, like the vulture of
Prometheus, began to corrode our vitals.

Towards evening, some coarse white bread was
brought, and we were all ordered out of the prison;
and as we were counted in again, each one received
a small white loaf of about twelve ounces. This was
all we had for the day. About sunset our keepers
came and ordered us all out, to be counted in. We
were under the disagreeable apprehensions of being
separated and sold into distant parts of the country,
and at every call of all hands, painful sensations
would disturb our breasts. We were counted in, one
by one, and as we passed the grim jailer were under
the humiliating injunction of pulling off our hats.
Those who refused this devoir [duty] were sure of a
severe bastinadoing. We had nothing to keep us
from the cold, damp earth but a thin, tattered sailcloth. The floor of the prison was very uneven,

planted with hard pebbles, and as we had nothing but a shirt to soften our beds and nothing but the ground for a pillow, and very much crowded in the bargain, the clouds of night shed no salutary repose.

Let us now return to our officers. Doctor C. says, *This morning* [November 1] *the Danish consul, Mr. Nissen, paid us another visit. Capt. Bainbridge engaged him to furnish us with provisions and such other necessaries as we might want. Our dwelling was furnished in a plain style, and we were supplied with fresh provisions that were tolerably good. We were allowed to go to the front door and walk on the terrace, or top of the house, which commanded a handsome prospect of the harbor, the sea, the town, the palace, and the adjoining country. Here we could see our ship on the rocks—full of Turks and surrounded by their boats—and a constant stream of boats going to and bringing off the plunder of the ship. We could see these robbers running about town with our uniform coats and other clothing on. The minister of exterior relations promised to be friendly and collect as much of our clothing and effects as he could and return them to us.*

The doctor does not think it worth mentioning that almost the whole crew were suffering intolerably, by hunger and nakedness; and it is very evident that he thought more of uniform coats than of his naked countrymen, who had no coats to put on. He says, also, that the ship was lying on the rocks, which was positive mendacity, for she floated clear early that very morning! And I have observed, in all the public letters, that this circumstance has been carefully concealed.

This day, Capt. Bainbridge wrote a letter to the secretary of the navy with the lamentable tale of our misfortunes, containing a brief statement of the circumstances of our capture; requesting that arrangements might be made to meet the exigencies of himself, the other officers, and officers' servants; and adding, "that the remainder of the crew would be provided for by the regency."

How did he know this? What assurance had he from the bashaw that he would provide for us, any more than for himself and his favorites? It is true, he might suppose that the bashaw would put us to labor if we were not provided for by our government, and that, for his own benefit, he would allow us sufficient food to sustain existence; but, was this any reason that no further notice should be taken of us, that government should make no appropriations for the mitigation of our sufferings? How did he know but that benevolent characters in America might institute charitable contributions for the palliation of our miseries? How did he ever know but that Congress might interpose for our relief? Or, how did he know but that the department of the navy might see fit to allow us some part of our rations or wages?

But his declaration that we would be provided for by the regency precluded, at once, the necessity of any executive, legislative, public, or private aid whatsoever. No doubt, had Capt. Bainbridge made a just statement of our situation to the Department of the Navy, representing that we were wholly dependent on the clemency of a faithless fratricide for the support of life, and soliciting, in our behalf, as well as for his train of servants, that some provision might be made for us, a liberal and patriotic spirit would have granted us laudable and adequate alleviation until a ransom or enfranchisement could be effected. For certainly those who were compelled to labor were under greater necessity for temporary aid and governmental munificence than those who were cloistered in idleness.

At numerous times, when we were on the very brink of starvation and petitioned Capt. Bainbridge for some part of our pay or rations, he invariably gave us to understand that it was entirely out of his power to do anything for us. No wonder, when he had impressed not only the government but all the people of the United States with the belief that we stood in no need of assistance. The fact is an obvious one: he had committed a most flagrant blunder and, to parry off the shafts of obloquy, would hold up the idea of moderation in his demands and frugality in his expenditures of the public money.

Or, if not, his conduct evinces a total disregard

and dereliction of his crew. How could an officer feast and fatten on the public benefaction and, at the same time, be unmindful of his men, who had an equal claim on the government for similar favors? How could he be the means of debarring that claim by asserting that we would be provided for without it? Had not the captain as much reason to expect that the bashaw would make provision for him and his officers, and his officers' servants, as for us? Or were the men whom he had brought into this distress, by his blunders, totally unworthy of his regard?

We were completely ignorant of this duplicity until we returned to America, and verily thought that Capt. Bainbridge had done everything in his power to ameliorate our condition. What must we then think of a commander who would give up his men to the enemy contrary to their wishes, and then abandon them to starve or rely on the mercy of sanguinary barbarians?

November 2. Before sunrise, the horrid clanking of huge bolts announced the early vigilance of our keepers, who ordered us all out. They told the carpenters to stand by themselves, the blacksmiths by themselves also, the coopers the same; and each company were appointed to their several employments, under the direction and command of Turkish masters; but they did not effect much, for a considerable time. The remainder of our men were distributed into different gangs, as we called them—some to the castle, to carry stone, dirt, lime, and mortar, where they were making repairs. Some were sent as cooks in the castle, and ten men were taken from amongst us to be denominated cooks. Their employment was to bring water from a well, about a quarter of a mile distant, for the whole of us to drink; to bring and serve out the bread and oil to us; and sometimes to boil what the Turks call *couscous*, which is barley ground very coarse and neither sifted nor bolted [sieved], with which they occasionally fed us. Some were sent on board the frigate and remained all night. About twelve or one o'clock, the cooks were called to go for bread and presently returned with a quantity of black barley loaves, coarse and full of straws and chaff, weighing about twelve ounces each. Of these, they gave us two apiece, and, bad as they were, our men seized them with avidity. This was our allowance for twenty-four hours.

NOVEMBER 3. *The bashaw sent for the carpenter to go on board the ship. He went and found six feet of water in the hold. The carpenter's crew and fifty men were ordered and carried on board to work. A gale of wind and a heavy sea hove the ship off the rocks, and the carpenter returned.*

No doubt, as the doctor says, there was six feet [of] water in the hold; but he ought to have mentioned that the ship was scuttled by us. Otherwise,

The manner of bastinadoing

it conveys the idea that the ship filled in consequence of the shock at first, or injury on the shoals.

If our men, and all the Turks, have not uttered willful falsehoods or been very egregiously mistaken, the ship was hove off the rocks the very next morning after she was captured. This morning, after a large company was sent to the ship and the most of our crew disposed of in different avocations and at various employments, a considerable number of us were told, after having been counted, to return into the prison and be ready at a moment's warning for any emergency. Some of them, however, strayed away, went into the town, and returned intoxicated. Our keepers perceived it and proceeded to exhibit exemplary punishment and sate, at once, their thirst of revenge.

The instrument with which they prepare a man for torture is called a baston. It is generally about four or five feet long and as thick in the middle as a man's leg, tapering to the ends. At equal distances from the center it is perforated in two places, and a rope incurvated, the ends passed through the holes and knotted. This forms a loop. The person is then thrown on his back, his feet put through the loop, and a man at each end of the stick—both at once—twist it round, screw his feet and ankles tight together, and raise the soles of his feet nearly horizontal.

A Turk sits on his back, and two men, with each

a bamboo or branch of the date tree—as large as a walking staff and about three feet in length, hard and very heavy—strip or roll up their sleeves and, with all their strength and fury, apply the bruising cudgel to the bottoms of the feet. In this manner they punished several of our men, writhing with extreme anguish and cursing their tormentors. They were then hampered with a heavy chain at each foot, but the next day they were taken off.

Our men began to complain much of hunger, having for this day but the two loaves of filthy, black, and sour bread. Some of them, however, who had the good fortune to save a little money, were permitted to go to the market to purchase vegetables. Their market makes a wretched appearance. On each side of the main street in the town, commencing at the principal gate, a long string of low mud-wall huts on each side [of] the way is all the market they have, at the doors of which, seated cross-legged on the ground and a blanket wrapped round them, the Turks retail pumpkins, carrots, turnips, scallions, oranges, lemons, limes, figs, etc., etc., with a thousand trinkets and haberdashers' wares.

At night, most of our men returned from the frigate and brought with them beef, pork, and bread, which was generously shared with those who had none and, though raw, devoured with voracity. The floor of our prison was not large enough to contain or admit us all, stretched at full length, and many of us were obliged to sit or stand all night. This occasioned a strife or crowding at the prison door to be the first, or at least not the last, counted in; for the first were considered as being lawfully entitled to the spot of ground for the night, and no one attempted to eject or oust them. It was surprising to witness the invincible spirit of our tars, and a person would be at a loss whether to ascribe it to a philosophic fortitude or natural apathy. In the most desponding aspect of times, they would caper, sing, jest, and look as cheerful—many of them—as if they had been at a feast or wedding.

November 4. A large number of our men were again sent and employed in bringing ashore the product of the frigate. The officers were prohibited walking on the terrace of their prison. Some of us were every day reserved for sudden avocations, to go and carry burdens in different parts of the town, and for any other enterprise. At every emergency or call for men, a wardman or keeper would enter the prison, take such as fancy or accident pointed out, and, if there was the least hesitation in obeying his commands, a severe beating was the result of such contumacy.

Four of us were chosen to be the packhorses of some unknown expedition. We were led by a grisly emissary of the bashaw through many crooked and dirty alleys, until we came to a house at which he

A woman of Tripoli

ordered us to halt. He went in, but soon returned and gave us signals to follow him. He led us through a gloomy passage to a large courtyard. Our breasts palpitated on the way, but our fears were dissipated when we found ourselves surrounded by a dozen beautiful females, who came from the piazzas above.

As the women in the streets are constantly wrapped and muffled up in blankets which conceal their shapes and faces, except one eye, this to us was a novel sight: for the ladies were exposed to view as much as the half-naked belles of our own towns. They were fantastically wrapped in loose robes of striped silk; their arms, necks, and bosoms bare; their eyelids stained round the edges with black; their hair braided, turned up, and fastened with a broad tinsel fillet. They had three or four rings in each ear as large in circumference as a dollar. Several of them were very delicate and handsome. They brought us dates, olives, oranges, and milk. They expressed or manifested great surprise at our appearance, and, like other ladies, were full of giggling and loquacity.

Our driver then bade us follow him again into another yard, where he showed us a large copper kettle and ordered us to take it up and follow his footsteps. We carried it about half a mile to another house, where there was a number of women, one of which would have killed us if she had not been prevented by our master. He made us understand that her malignity arose from her husband having been killed by the Americans, in the boat at which we fired when we were on the shoals. Here we left the kettle and returned to the prison. The streets are not paved, never swept, and are full of sharp pebbles; and, having no shoes, I suffered intolerably both by the cold and in carrying burdens, until [my feet] became indurated by use.

NOVEMBER 5. *Our new masters came and closed up the passage which led to the top of the house, and a guard was set at the front door to prevent our going into the street. The minister sent his chief secretary with a parole of honor, written in French, which we all signed.*

The Turks informed us that the reason of their closing up the passage was a suspicion that we men were concerting with the officers some plan of escape, and that the suspicion was raised from a report of this kind fabricated by the infamous Wilson, in hopes to ingratiate himself with the bashaw. Our prison door was more effectually secured at the same time.

This day, several of our seamen who were born under British colors flattered themselves with the fallacious hope of obtaining emancipation by throwing themselves under the protection of the British government and claiming from the English consul the privileges or exemptions of British subjects. For this purpose they went to him; and he registered a number of their names, promised to write to his government, and, if possible, effectuate their release. They returned highly elated with the prospect of freedom. But a large majority of our patriotic tars, who had adopted America as their country, laughed at their credulity and hissed at their project, positively declaring that they would not be released by a government which they detested, on account of its tolerating the impressment of seamen, and swearing that they would sooner remain under the bashaw than George the Third.

NOVEMBER 6. Our treatment and provisions much the same.

As I was walking the streets, on a return from carrying a bundle of faggots into the town, I met with a Mahometan who spoke English tolerably fluent. He informed me that he had been in America in the time of our revolution, a servant to General Fayette [LaFayette]. When his master returned to France, he continued in America for two years, then went to his native country and was a soldier in the French Revolution, went with Bonaparte's army to Egypt, and, when the French evacuated that country, his life was despaired of.

He was left in a wretched hospital and would have perished had it not been for the fraternal kindness of a benevolent Mussulman who took him to his house and treated him with the affectionate attention of the nearest consanguinity and who was the means of saving his life. While in a debilitated state both of body and mind, he was persuaded by his benefactor, whose importunities it seemed ungrateful to resist, to embrace the religion of Mahomet.

He was now on his way to Tunis with a traveling company, appeared to be well-respected by his comrades, was decently dressed, and seemed to have plenty of money; but he asked me a thousand questions concerning America—and seriously regretted his ever having left it, and of his transmutation of religion; but he still had hopes of making his escape. He gave me a Spanish dollar, which he insisted on my accepting, shook hands, and bade me adieu.

November 7. Several of our men were much indisposed, from sleeping on the damp ground and being almost destitute of clothes. A small apartment or cell adjoining our prison was appropriated for the use and retirement of the sick, and Dorman, who was loblolly boy[4] on board of the frigate, was appointed to attend them. Another room, contiguous to that, was the receptacle of our provisions, and the men who were called cooks were permitted to sleep in it by themselves. Another cell, at a different part of the prison yard, was set apart for the carpenters, coopers, and blacksmiths to sleep in, so that our prison was not quite so crowded as at first.

NOVEMBER 8. *The bashaw sent for Capt. Bainbridge and told him that John Wilson had informed [him] that Capt. Bainbridge, before hauling down the colors, threw over[board] nineteen boxes of dollars and a large bag of gold. Capt. Bainbridge assured him it was false and gave his word and honor that there was no money thrown over to his knowledge, but that the money in question was left at Malta. In the evening, the bashaw, not being satisfied, sent for the captain's servant and ordered him to be flogged if he did not tell the truth concerning the money. The boy denied having any knowledge of it. After repeating the threat several times, and the boy insisting that he knew nothing about the money, he was acquitted. Wilson had turned traitor and given the enemy all the assistance in his power. He now acts as overseer of our men.*

This perfidious wretch was a quartermaster on board the frigate. He was born in Germany and spoke the lingua franca very fluently. He as yet mingled amongst us and acted as a spy, carrying to the bashaw every frivolous and a thousand false tales. He had not as yet assumed the habiliments of the Turks, so that he was the more dangerous.

The bashaw rode out this day and, as he returned, was to pass with his retinue through our prison yard, which is approximate to the castle.

Wilson came and told us that it was the bashaw's orders that we should parade in single file in front of our prison, with our hats off, and when he should make his appearance, we must give him three cheers. He presently made his entrance into the yard, and being marshaled according to orders, some of our silly asses swung their hats and brayed like the animal they personated. But the most of us refused, with a laudable spirit of indignation, this mean and sycophantic testimonial of a tyrant's applause.

His return from his cavalcade was announced by the firing of cannon from the castle and crackling of muskets on the beach. He was preceded by a foot-guard at some distance. Next to the foot-guard was the high constable of the town police, mounted on an elegant Arabian gray; in his hand, he held perpendicularly before him a three-pronged scepter, richly ornamented. His majesty was mounted on a milk-white mare, sumptuously caparisoned and glittering with golden trappings. He was dressed much the same as when we first saw him, excepting a white robe which had a head like a hood and on the top a large tassel.

At his right hand rode a huge Negro, who was made one of the bashaw's principal officers and admitted to this distinguished honor for having assassinated the bashaw's brother, who was a powerful and dangerous rival. Three or four of his younger children went before him, seated on mules, with Neapolitan slaves running by their sides, holding with one hand the bridle of the mule and with the other an umbrella over the head of the child. At his left hand rode his vizier, or prime minister, his chief officers of state, and was followed and attended by his mamelukes, or lifeguards, without order or arrangement, courting his approbation by numerous feats of equestrian agility. Two large boxes slung across a mule, led by a trusty Neapolitan slave, contained his principal treasures.

NOVEMBER 10. The Turks appeared very savage and spit at us and on us, as we passed the streets. The keepers or drivers beat us without any pretext and acted more like infernal than human beings. We did not then know the cause of this alteration for the worse, but perhaps the following will account for it.

Several Turks came and informed Capt. Bainbridge that the bashaw had been told that Capt. Rogers, who commanded the U.S. frigate John Adams, *treated the Tripolitan prisoners taken last summer very bad, and that they feared we should suffer for it.*

Several of our men were sent for and interrogated very closely concerning the money Wilson had reported was thrown into the sea. But they all unanimously corroborated the assertions of Capt. Bainbridge that there was no money sunk.

NOVEMBER 11. As I was coming in at the principal gate of the town, having been out on the sands for water, I saw a hand and foot hanging at the outside of the gate fresh bleeding; and observing a cluster of people not far distant, I stepped to see the cause of their being collected. The object of their curiosity was a wretch with his left hand and right foot recently amputated, faint and almost expiring. The stumps had been dipped in boiling pitch. This is their mode of punishment for capital offenses. The miserable object is dragged out of town and left to breathe his last in the most exquisite agonies, unless some friend sees fit to compassionate [take pity on] his sufferings, and then he sometimes recovers; for you will see a great number of men in Tripoli hobbling about the streets thus mutilated.

NOVEMBER 13. This day we were employed in bringing pig iron and shot from the boats at the wharf to the magazine in the navy yard. I was very sick and complained to the principal keeper that I was unable to work; but the only consolation I received was that of being called a *kelp* (dog) and told to do as I was ordered. At night our men returned from the frigate with some more beef and pork, to which, eaten raw, hunger gave a delicious flavor.

NOVEMBER 14. *Breakfasted early, to be ready for our new habitation. At nine AM, a guard came and ordered us to the castle. We formed agreeable to rank and marched to the castle. We were huddled into the most gloomy cell, among our men, where there was hardly room for us to stand. Here we spent the day without food and were scoffed at by our foes until night, when, to our happy surprise, we were conducted back to our old place of abode.*

Poor Doctor! In this whining tale there are several misrepresentations. That the officers were in the prison, amongst us contaminating fellows, is true. But the doctor and his fellow officers—though nobody doubts their feeling very big—must be gigantic monsters indeed, if they had hardly room enough to stand in a cell at least twenty-five feet high and which contained, every night, nearly three hundred men who were chiefly absent the whole day. Neither was our prison in the castle, as he intimates. And if he remained all day without food after having eaten a hearty breakfast, it was owing to his own fastidiousness; for our men boiled some meat which was brought from the frigate and invited all the officers to partake of it, and several of them made a hearty repast. If this famous son of Aesculapius[5] had been three days at a time without food, as we often were, perhaps he might have had an appetite for black bread and salt beef.

While Capt. Bainbridge was amongst us, Wilson came with orders to get men for some kind of drudgery, when the captain accused him of informing the bashaw of our sinking the box of money; he prevaricated and attempted to extenuate, though he could not pointedly deny, the crime. The captain told him that he would have him hanged for a traitor if ever he returned to America, and in a violent passion threw his chain at him. A few days afterwards, Wilson, probably fearing the reality of his threats, put on the turban and confirmed his apostasy.

NOVEMBER 17. The Danish consul sent some fresh provisions for our sick, by the request of Capt. Bainbridge. Our bread was very coarse and musty. This day I saw one of the Mahometan saints or anchorites, who are held in the highest veneration by the Tripolitans. He was seated on a tomb within a small, smoky cell, where he kept a lamp incessantly burning, which he said was the spirit of the dead. He offered me a piece of bread in the name of the prophet, pitied my situation, and really appeared to possess philanthropy.

NOVEMBER 18. A number of us were sent to carry powder from the quay to the castle, which is about three-quarters of a mile. The powder was taken from the frigate and was still wet. I was compelled to carry a cask of it, which was very heavy; and my feet, being tender, gave me insufferable pain. What would the querimoneous [querulous] Doctor think, if he had been doomed to such hardships?

NOVEMBER 20. Thomas Prince was metamorphosed from a Christian to a Turk. He was a lad of about seventeen years of age and had a mother, as he informed us, living in some part of Rhode Island.

Our men now began to construct what they termed cots. They were formed by fastening four pieces of timber at the corners, in the shape of a bedstead, and then weaving a net of ropes like a bedcord. These were suspended from spikes driven in the wall and composed a lodging much more comfortable and healthful than the moist earth; but materials for these cots being very scarce, but few of us could be provided with a luxury so rare and inestimable.

NOVEMBER 21. Doctor Cowdery informs us that a man 116 years of age came to him to be cured of deafness. We do not know which to doubt most—the doctor's credulity or the Turk's veracity.

NOVEMBER 22. We wrote a petition to the bashaw in behalf of the sick, praying for some kind of blankets or clothing to keep them from the earth, appealing both to his humanity and his interest.

NOVEMBER 25. Sixteen of us were put to boring cannon. The labor was intense; and having neither bread nor anything else to eat until four o'clock in the afternoon, hunger and weariness were almost insupportable. Some of our men, by some clandestine means, were found intoxicated, for which they were inhumanly beaten and confined in shackles. Whenever instances of this kind occurred, *all* were sure to suffer for the misconduct of a *few*.

NOVEMBER 26. To the disgrace of human nature, be it said that although we all had an equal share of bread allowed us, some had the meanness, the selfishness, the brutality to steal from their companions in misery the only ligament of soul and body. We frequently divided our pittance and kept one loaf overnight to eat in the morning; and often when morning came, we found ourselves pillaged of our stores and nothing to silence the importunate calls of hunger. About twelve o'clock I received a small white loaf from the allowance of our officers, and never in my life did I taste a more luscious dainty.

NOTES

1. Empirics: in this context, quack doctors.
2. Janissaries: mercenary soldiers of the Ottoman Empire.
3. *Aqua-deut:* probably aquadent, a powerful brandy.
4. Loblolly boy: attendant to the ship's doctor.
5. Aesculapius: Greco-Roman god of medicine.

A Petition

NOVEMBER 27. We presented a petition to the bashaw in the following language:

To His Excellency the Grand Bashaw of Tripoli
The petition of the American prisoners most humbly
showeth—

That when your petitioners were captured in the
United States frigate Philadelphia, *they were plun-*
dered of all their clothing, and are daily sickening
and suffering most intolerably by the inclemency of
the season, and by not having anything to sleep on to
keep them from the cold, damp ground but a thin
and tattered sailcloth; and also, that your petitioners,
not receiving sufficient food and nourishment to
enable them to endure the hardships and perform the
hard tasks assigned them, are frequently most inhu-
manly bastinadoed for the lack of that strength which
adequate nutriment would restore and supply.

Your petitioners therefore pray that His Excellency,
consulting his interest as well as his honor, by con-
tributing to our relief, would graciously be pleased to
grant us more comfortable clothing and more nutri-
tious food; and your petitioners, while they continue
your prisoners, will remain your most faithful, indus-
trious, obedient, and humble servants.

NOVEMBER 28. In consequence of the foregoing petition, the bashaw ordered us two barrels of

Christian slaves at labor in Barbary captivity

pork from the frigate. It was really laughable to see with what ridiculous pride and pomposity our chief keeper performed the functions of a purser's steward, but it was not laughable to see with what greediness our half-starved crew seized and consumed their crude dividend of the meat.

NOVEMBER 29. I was sent to work in the castle carrying dirt, stones, mortar, lime, and sand for repairing the walls. A little past twelve o'clock, our overseer beckoned to me to follow him. I obeyed; and he took me to the cookhouse and ordered me to take a dish of *couscous* and follow him again. He led me through several gloomy, subterraneous cells—dimly lighted, smoked black by torches, where were large iron staples and chains, once the lot of some ill-fated object of a tyrant's wrath—until we came to a dungeon strongly bolted. My grim conductor loosened the door, and a wretch appeared, ghastly and loaded with chains. The dish was handed in without saying a word, and we returned to our labor. I durst not express the curiosity I felt to know what was his accusation. His head was afterwards struck off and carried on a pole through the streets of the city.

NOVEMBER 30. *One of our men . . . attempted to kill himself but was prevented by the Turks when in the act of cutting his throat. The wound did not prove mortal.*

This was C.R.,[1] one of the four persons previously mentioned who were taken in at Gibraltar and were so unlawfully detained. The wound however was a mere scratch, and the lycanthropy [insanity], which was the cause of it, was occasioned by taking a little too much aqua vita [liquor].

Nothing of very great importance for a considerable term of time. West, one of our carpenter's crew, had turned Turk and had a number of men employed in building gunboats, repairing gun carriages, and works of circumvallation.[2] Some of our men were assisting to repair fortifications in mason work—some sent into the country every day to cut timber for ship and boat building; some boring guns; some coining *buckamseens*[3] in the mint in the bashaw's castle, twenty-five of which are equal to a Spanish dollar; some carrying mortar from cisterns in different parts of the town.

Our rations continued the same: two black barley loaves and about three-fourths of a gill of oil per day—more or less, bastinadoing continually, and once a fortnight we received a little beef and pork.

DECEMBER 15. A number of Spanish carpenters were employed in building boats and other vessels for the regency; and on the fifteenth of December, they had a schooner ready for launching. In the afternoon, the consuls all hoisted their colors, three guns were fired from the battery, and the schooner was precipitated into the waves amidst the acclamations of a shabby multitude of idle spectators.

DECEMBER 17. As I was returning with a crock of water from the sands, not far from the large eastern gate, I saw a man walking towards me leading a child by the hand. Another Turk was just before me leading a large fiery courser, wild and prancing, by his side and, as they met the harmless child passing very near to the horse's heels, struck [the horse] with a switch. The haughty, majestic animal, as if conscious of the indignity, let fly his hoofs and dashed [the child] into eternity in the twinkling of an eye. The father of the child, as I supposed it to be, looked at him for a moment, raised him up, and, perceiving he was past all remedy, laid his right hand on his breast, lifted his left, raised his eyes to heaven, made a short ejaculation, seeming to say, "It is done—and I acquiesce in thy righteous dispensations, O omnipotent God!" He seemed perfectly composed, took the corpse in his arms, and walked pensively towards the country. The surrounding spectators beheld this pathetic scene of paternal affliction, this sudden stroke of death, with brutal indifference.

DECEMBER 20. *The market was so poor that we could get nothing for dinner but a shoulder of poor dromedary.*

What the doctor here complains of, in such dolorous language, would have been a feast and produced strains of joy with us. Had he been compelled to labor as many of us, quite as good by nature as himself, and been stinted to two small loaves of coarse, musty bread, the shoulder of a dromedary would have been a most delicious repast to the querulous gentleman and his dainty companions.

DECEMBER 22. One hundred fifty of us were sent to raise an old wreck deeply buried in the sand, near the beach, eastward from the town. It was now the coldest season of the year; we were almost naked and were driven into the water up to our armpits. We had to shovel the sand from the bottom of the water and carry it in baskets to the banks. The chilling waves almost congealed our blood, to flow no more. The Turks seemed more than ordinarily cruel, exulting in our sufferings. We were kept in the water from sunrise until about two o'clock before we had a mouthful to eat or were permitted to sun ourselves. Then brought us some bread and a jug of *aqua-deut.*

When we had snatched a short repast, we were driven again into the water and kept there until sunset. Having no clothes to change, we were obliged to sleep on the ground in our wet ones, which gave many of us severe colds and caused one man to lose the use of his limbs for upwards of a year afterwards. With such usage, life became insupportable; and every night when I laid my head on the earth to sleep, I most sincerely prayed that I might never experience the horrors of another morning.

DECEMBER 25. The different consuls' colors [flags] were all hoisted, and the Neapolitan slaves permitted to attend Mass; for there are no less than three Roman Catholic priests in this place. No relaxation was allowed us.

DECEMBER 26. Mr. Godby, late carpenter of the *Philadelphia*, had been taken out from among the officers to work in the bashaw's navy yard. He returned every night to his usual lodgings with the officers. His being employed in giving strength and furtherance to our enemy raised suspicious umbrage in the breasts of many of our officers, because they said he was not constrained to do it. Some of his messmates were Mr. Erving, sergeant of marines; Mr. Morris, purser's steward; and Mr. Leith, ship's cook. Mr. Godby returning home at night a little fuddled [drunk], began to vaunt of his liberty and the privileges he enjoyed superior to his messmates. They also had been "kissing Black Betty"[4] and no doubt gave him some pungent retort. Blows ensued, and the carpenter found his timbers too weak and something shattered by the attack.

The next morning Godby went to the bashaw and entered a complaint against the three persons above-mentioned. Wilson, the renegade, was now highly in favor with the bashaw; and the sergeant, while they were on board the ship, had given Wilson a severe drubbing for interfering with the duty of a sentinel, and this was a fine opportunity to feed revenge. Wilson acted as interpreter for Godby, and no doubt exaggerated all he said.

About ten o'clock, the three men were brought to the castle, before the bashaw. Judgment was already passed against them, and the bashaw ordered them bastinadoed. Wilson stood by and dictated the punishment, telling them, when they came to Erving, not to spare his flesh. They were all most unmercifully beaten on the soles of their feet and on their posteriors, then hampered with a huge chain at each leg and sent to the prison with us, where they remained for one night, and the next day were sent to their wonted residence. Godby was as cruel to our men who were under his command as any of their other drivers, and we all supposed he would now turn Turk.

Doctor Cowdery does not mention this in his journal, or, at least, it has not been published. What is the reason? Why, the reason is as plain and prominent as the action was dastardly and flagitious [villainous]. Godby was a warranted officer, and officers must not expose each other's secret villainies. What was the reason he was not reported to the commodore after his liberation and dealt with according to his demerit? Why, for the very reason abovementioned. Would you believe that, instead of a halter [noose], he received his full pay and rations for volunteering his services in the bashaw's employ—building gunboats, and instructing the enemy in the arts of defense and means of repelling our friends and their foes? Yes, I have never heard that he was ever even reprimanded for his conduct.

The case with us was quite different. We were compelled to work or perish in tortures. He was under no compulsion but solicited the undertaking and executed his business so effectually that he received from the bashaw one hundred dollars at a time for his services.

JANUARY 2. *As I passed out at the gate of the city, I saw a man's head sticking on a pole. On enquiry, I found that it was the head of one of the bedouins, who, about a year before, had killed the son-in-law of the bashaw, who commanded the army in collecting the taxes in the back part of his dominions. About a quarter of a mile from the gate, the road passed through a burying ground full of graves.*

The head, which the doctor here speaks of, belonged to the person whom I saw confined in the castle. That the doctor should have seen a *burying ground full of graves* is very astonishing, indeed! It is as wonderful as if he had seen a town full of houses.

JANUARY 3. *Went to the bashaw's garden, where I met the minister and the prince—the bashaw's eldest son. They politely conducted me through the garden,*

which was ornamented with a great variety of fruit
trees loaded with fruit, particularly with oranges,
lemons, and limes. *John Hilliard died in the evening.*

The doctor is as laconic in mentioning the death
of our seamen as he was remiss in attending to
them. The company of a prince in a flower garden
was much more pleasing to the doctor than the
company of a languishing sailor in a dreary cell. The
gratification of his vanity was obviously anterior to
the offices of humanity. He frequently informs us of
his prescriptions for the bashaw and his family but
seldom mentions the sickness or sufferings of his
own countrymen. Hilliard died of a flux, which
might have been greatly mitigated, if not cured, had
he received proper medical attention.

ELEGY

On the death of JOHN HILLIARD,
who died Jan. 3d, 1804, in the prison of Tripoli
[Published in the *Port Folio*]

Hilliard, of painful life bereft,
Is now a slave no more;
But here no relative has left,
His exit to deplore!

No parent, no fond brother, stands
Around his clay-cold bed;
No wife with tender, trembling hands,
Supports his dying head.

No sister follows or attends
His melancholy bier;
Nor from a lover's eye descends
The soft distilling tear;

But foes, and of a barb'rous kind,
Surround him as he dies;
A horror to his fainting mind,
And to his closing eyes.

What though no monumental stone
Bespeaks a guilty name,
By splendid trophies basely won,
Damn'd to eternal fame;

If but an honest heart he wore,
If virtue's paths he trod,
He was, so poets sung of yore,
The noblest work of God.

His fellow-pris'ners strove to cheer
His sad departing soul,
And bade the sympathetic tear
In free profusion roll.

Mourn not—'twas Heav'n's allwise behest
And merciful decree,
That gave his wearying sorrows rest,
And set the captive free.

JANUARY 4. *William Anderson died.*

He had been sick ever since we fell into the hands of the Turks. Both he and Hilliard were placed in cots, carried by four of our men, and interred with as much decency as possible on the beach, at the western part of the town, without the gates and near the wall.

JANUARY 12. The new moon appeared and the Ramadan ended. The Turks were all looking at the moon and muttering some kind of prayer or thanks. Several of the castle guns and a salute from the frigate, which now lay moored in the harbor, was fired at sunset. Joy seemed to brighten the gloomy visages of all the Tripolitans.

JANUARY 15. *The feast called* Byram *commenced.* Every gun in Tripoli proclaimed the day. The Turks all appeared arrayed in new suits of their best attire. The markets teemed with the richest productions I had ever seen them; but this, to us, was only a tantalizing prospect. Their bakers were too much engrossed with the pleasures of the feast to attend to their business, and we had nothing but the camelion's rations⁵ for this day.

JANUARY 16. When hope is nearly expiring under the torturing hand of despair, what a small anodyne will revive her. Capt. Bainbridge, in company with all the consuls, visited the bashaw, and this we considered as a presage of pacification.

JANUARY 17. The feast ended this evening. The consuls' flags, which had been flying for three days, were struck, and the people resumed their usual vocations. We were now supplied every Sunday with fresh provisions and vegetables, for soups.

JANUARY 20. Happening in at a Greek's shop, he showed me a sacred relic of the Holy Cross, which he had purchased at and brought from Jerusalem. It was about four inches long, of no intrinsic value, and yet this superstitious fanatic said he would not give it for all the wealth of the bashaw. I reached my hand to take it, but he said I must not touch it unless I had recently partaken of the Eucharist. I told him I would not give him a *buckamseen* for it. He said I was a great infidel then and asked me if all the Americans were so impious, kissed the toy with holy rapture, and put it in his bosom.

JANUARY 25. I saw a man at the castle gate undergo the shocking operation of having his left hand and right foot amputated. It was performed with an axe in the shape of a half moon, and the executioner was one of our keepers. The wretched victim never uttered a word, nor even a groan. The stumps were dipped in boiling pitch, and he was dragged to the gate and thrown on the mercy of mankind.

FEBRUARY 3. *Was conducted to the castle to visit the bashaw, whom I found after passing several sentinels, about fifty fierce, yelping dogs, and three heavy doors loaded with irons and bolts, which were opened for us by armed mamelukes.*

Decatur Boarding the Tripolitan Gunboat, *oil painting by Dennis Malone Carter*

Our men were frequently called before the bashaw, both by night and by day, and it is very strange that none of them ever saw anything of these yelping dogs. We must, therefore, suppose that the doctor in this particular is very much mistaken.

FEBRUARY 16. Towards evening two vessels were seen standing in [heading] for the harbor. Our men were much rejoiced at the sight, for they were confident they were Americans; and, as the season of the year was not favorable for an attack, they flattered themselves that very probably they had come with proposals of amicable accommodation. The bashaw had ordered us a barrel of pork and another of beef, and all of our men appeared more than ordinarily cheerful.

About eleven o'clock at night we were alarmed by the screeches of women, the clattering of footsteps through the prison yard, and harsh, loud voices of men, mingled with a thundering of cannon from the castle, which made our prison tremble to its base. Tumult, consternation, confusion, and dismay reigned in every section of the town and castle, and it was verily believed that, if we had been at liberty and armed, we might with ease have taken the castle and every fort in the town; for the most of the people in the town supposed we had already risen and taken the castle and were afraid to come nigh it. In the confusion of voices we could often hear the word *American*, and therefore hoped that some of our countrymen were landing to liberate us; but the true cause of so much clamor we did not learn until morning.

FEBRUARY 17. Early in the morning, and much earlier than usual, our prison doors were unbolted. The keepers, like so many fiends from the infernal regions, rushed in amongst us and began to beat everyone they could see, spitting in our faces and hissing like the serpents of hell. Word was soon brought that the wreck of the frigate *Philadelphia* lay on the rocks near the round fort, almost consumed by fire. We could not suppress our emotions, nor disguise our joy at the intelligence, which exasperated them more and more, so that everybody we met in the streets would spit on us and pelt us with stones. Our tasks were doubled, our bread withheld, and every driver exercised cruelties tenfold more rigid and intolerable than before.

Eight Turks had charge of the ship; two of them escaped and made the report that an American schooner and three boats set fire to the ship and carried the other six Turks away. By what we could learn, Capt. Decatur, who was commander in this heroic action, had taken some Maltese with him in the boat; and when they were hailed as they approached the frigate, they answered that they were Maltese, had been in a gale, and were in want of water. They were permitted to enter the ship, when they instantly secured the hands—all but two—and set fire to her.

FEBRUARY 18. All hands were sent to get the remains of the frigate from the rocks, under the control of Mr. Godby, who, to court favor from the Turks, struck several of our men and behaved more like one of the bashaw's myrmidons [loyal followers] than like an American fellow prisoner. They did not succeed in clearing the wreck but brought off copper, bolts, spikes, etc.

FEBRUARY 19. A tent was pitched in front of our prison and a strong guard kept over us at night, and we received no more beef or pork from the bashaw's stores. The militia began to collect from the country; they were repairing their ramparts and making every preparation to repel the expected invasion.

MARCH 1. Our officers, with a strong guard, passed through our prison yard for the castle. We were not permitted to exchange words. Capt. Bainbridge, however, bid us be of good heart, although he looked very much dejected himself. They were confined in a prison very dreary, with a grated skylight.

MARCH 4. *Capt. Bainbridge received a letter from the ministers, reprimanding him on account of three men who floated ashore a few days after the burning of the frigate. The Turks pretended that they were murdered after they were made prisoners by the Americans.*

The burning of the Philadelphia, *acquatint engraving by F. Kearney*

That mean, detestable spirit of revenge, which seeks retaliation on the innocent connections or affinity of those who have injured us, blackens and disfigures one of the most conspicuous features in the portrait of a Tripolitan. Every time there was any attack upon the place or even an American vessel in sight, we were sure to suffer for it.

MARCH 7. The Turks got the guns from the wreck of the frigate. They mounted them on their batteries, and, in proving them, several burst—killed one Turk and wounded four.

MARCH 26. Early in the morning, some of our men returned from the beach and, with joy sparkling in their countenances, informed us that a frigate with American colors was standing in for the harbor. About eight o'clock, our joy was increased by observing the flag which she carried to be a white one. The bashaw soon responded to the signal by hoisting a white ensign on the castle. What a contemptible opinion of the Tripolitans' character must we form: yesterday they would stone us and spit in our faces for the burning of the frigate, which we had no hand in destroying; and today they would flatter and caress us because there appeared a pacific signal, which we had no more agency in raising than in burning the ship. As we walked the streets, the Turks would pat us on the shoulder and say, "American *bono*" (good).

About nine o'clock, Consul O'Brien landed on

the beach and went up into the castle. In about half an hour, he returned and went on board the frigate. We could not learn the business or result of this short interview. Various were the reports and our conjectures. Some said that peace was concluded on and that the commodore had gone to Malta for the money to ransom us; but when the white flag dropped, with the most of us, our spirits flagged; and the frigate departing bore away the anchor of hope which she had brought us.

Our allowance continued the same; our men, many of them, began to be as naked as the natives of Pellew.[6] A few shirts and trousers had been alternately issued amongst us, but not sufficient for all. We made a most pitiable appearance. Many of the men had to drag a heavy wagon five or six miles over the sand, into the country and back again every day before they had anything to eat, except sometimes a few raw carrots which they plundered on the way. We were turned out every morning regularly before sunrise, and locked in at sunset. We were much afflicted with vermin; and, not having any clothes to change, the only way we had to keep ourselves from becoming insufferably filthy was to go on the beach and strip off our shirts, going naked until we washed and dried them, and then our trousers in the like manner.

APRIL 15. We felt the Syroc [sirocco] winds; they are very sultry and suffocating. The Turks do not walk the streets during the prevalence of these morbid gales.

We now began to grow economical. We found that we could sell our bread, in market, for four *paras* a loaf. Three hundred of these *paras* make a dollar; and with the avails of one loaf, we could purchase as many vegetables as three men would eat at a meal, made into a soup, with bread and oil. We put ourselves into messes, as we chose, some of three or four men each. Thus, by sparing two loaves out of our day's rations, we could purchase carrots and scallions enough to make a handsome little pot of soup, for these vegetables were very cheap.

We also contributed our mites[7] and purchased an earthen vessel, large enough to cook for four men, for about two *buckamseens*, twenty-five *paras*. We then boiled the vegetables, threw in some bread to thicken the soup, and added oil and salt. We were allowed to get some chips from the navy-yard to cook it with; and when prepared, we ate it, sitting on the ground, with wooden spoons. By this management we began to live rather more comfortably.

There are also little shops in the market in which they keep *tirsha* for sale, which is made of either carrots or turnips, cut into small pieces and boiled; then mashed with a ladle and beat with salt and water until it becomes pulpous; to which are added red pepper, pulverized, and mixed with water and a measure of oil; a lemon is squeezed into it; and over the top are strewed fennel seed. It is of the consistence of applesauce and so strong of pepper that it is quite disagreeable at first, but by frequent use, it soon becomes palatable. This is a cheap and salubrious dish, of which the poorer sort of people eat much. You will see those little hovels of shops almost constantly crowded with Turks, sitting on a ground floor, and with their fingers loading their greedy mouths.

The bashaw, to excite them to industry, occasionally called the carpenters, the masons, the coopers, and the blacksmiths into the castle and distributed amongst them a few *buckamseens*. Those who dragged at the cart were sometimes encouraged with the like gratuity.

APRIL 24. Departed this life, John Morrison, in the twenty-seventh year of his age. He was an able and skillful mariner, captain of the foretop on board the frigate, and supported the character of a true and brave American tar. His death was occasioned by a hurt which he received in assisting to load a large piece of timber on the wagon, about two miles from the town. He was brought in on a litter, by four men, and lay three days in the most excruciating pain.

The night previous to his death, Doctor Ridgely was permitted to visit him, in company with Lewis Heximer, who was one of our crew, transformed into a Turk, and now acted as interpreter to our officers. An old Algerine, who was one of our drivers, came in to see him while he was dying and insisted that nothing ailed him but that he was shamming sickness to avoid labor. He went to the dying man, told him to rise, called him an infidel and a dog, and struck him several times with his cane. How our men burned to immolate the ferocious villain! He [Morrison] was interred the following day, by the side of his late shipmates.

Part of the American fleet was now in sight, and, as has been observed, the unreasonable Turks always made this a pretext for doubling their severity. Our spirits, however, were cheered at the sight, and hope again returned to cheer our desponding bosoms till, on the twenty-sixth, the squadron disappeared. We now began to abandon all hopes of release by negotiations of peace and only expected, from the force of arms, carnage and emancipation.

MAY 11. The squadron again appeared. The Turks were in great trepidation and expected an attack. They sent us to carry powder and balls from the castle to their forts and beat us without mercy. I was now taken sick with a bilious complaint.

MAY 16. Ten of our officers were permitted to walk into the country. They passed several of our men, at a cart, and scattered them some *buckamseens*.

MAY 20. The sap of the date tree, which they call *lagby*, now began to be plenty in the market and elsewhere. It is of a whitish color, like whey, and, as it comes from the tree, has the spirit of wine. It tastes something like mead and can be bought for about three cents a quart.

MAY 27. Doctor Ridgely paid a visit to our sick and informed me that Capt. Bainbridge had exerted his influence with the prime minister and had procured me an exemption from labor. He called the keepers and told them that it was the bashaw's orders not to send me to work any more while I was a prisoner. As I never had been much accustomed to, nor was I remarkably fond of, labor, especially among the Turks, these were glad tidings of great joy.

MAY 28. A number of our men were employed in cleaning and fitting up a prison for us in a different part of the town.

MAY 29. Two of our brigs were lying off the harbor, and in consequence, as usual, we had severe treatment.

JUNE 10. We were ordered to remove to our newly prepared prison, which was adjoining the wall at the eastern part of the town. We found it much more strong, spacious, and cleanly than the other, but the yard was much smaller. About one hundred of the Neapolitan slaves were confined with us, making upwards of 350 of us in one apartment.

Our sick were kept in a separate cell, at one end of the yard, the wall of which was very high, and at the entrance was a gate of enormous weight and strength. Within the gate was a guardhouse, where a dozen armed Turks kept sentry every night, and the keepers, or drivers, in the daytime. There was a guard also on the top of the prison. This day our weekly rations from the captain were discontinued.

JUNE 18. *The bashaw's eldest wife, called the queen, was delivered of her ninth child. She was twenty-three years of age . . . . It was said to be common to marry at ten.*

This may be true, but it looks a little like mendacity.

JUNE 27. Mr. Hodge, our boatswain; Mr. Fountain, our first master's mate; and Mr. Douglas, sailmaker, were taken from their prison, in the castle, to oversee our men in their several departments. An upper story of a building, occupied by our sick in the prison yard, was fitted for, and received, them and Mr. Godby.

JULY 4. A few of us got permission to go out on the sands to purchase and drink *lagby*. The benevolent Danish consul had made me a small present to enable me to celebrate the day. We retired to a stone platform, the ruins of an ancient reservoir, under the cooling shade of a luxuriant orange tree, open to the refreshing breezes of the sea. Here we sat and regaled ourselves with this delicious beverage until we almost forgot that we, who were offering a libation to the birthday of liberty, were ourselves but wretched slaves. Towards sunset three or four of our squadron appeared in sight, and we returned to our gloomy prison with several jugs of this wholesome and cheering liquor.

JULY 15. The most of our men were employed in carrying furniture and baggage from the castle to the bashaw's seat in the country, about two miles distant. At night the bashaw and his family left the castle and went thither.

JULY 25. The *Constitution*, Commodore Preble, appeared again off the harbor. Every preparation of defense was now making by the Turks with the utmost dispatch. The American squadron now consisted of the frigate *Constitution*; brigs *Syren*, *Argus*, and *Vixen*; schooners *Nautilus, Enterprise,* and *Scourge*; two bombs;[8] and six gunboats. The whole number of men: 1,060. The bomb vessels were about thirty tons and carried a thirteen-inch brass sea-mortar and fifty men. The gunboats, twenty-five tons, carried a large iron twenty-four-pounder in the bow, with a complement of twenty-five men. They were officered and manned from the squadron, excepting twelve Neapolitan bombardiers, gunners, and sailors attached to each boat, who were shipped by permission of their government. The bomb vessels and gunboats were loaned us by his Sicilian majesty, nearly 150 of whose men were slaves in Tripoli. The commodore now proceeded to make the necessary arrangements for an attack on Tripoli as soon as the weather would permit.

Tripoli was impregnably walled, protected by batteries judiciously constructed, mounting 115 pieces of heavy cannon, and defended by more than twenty-five thousand Arabs and Turks. The harbor was protected by nineteen gunboats, two galleys, two schooners of eight guns each, and a brig mounting ten guns, all ranged in order of battle, forming a strong line of defense, at secured moorings inside a long range of rocks and shoals extending more than two miles to the eastward of the town, which forms the harbor; protects them from the northern gales; and renders it impossible for a vessel of the *Constitution*'s draft to approach near enough to destroy them, as they are sheltered by the rocks and can retire under that shelter to the shore unless they choose to expose themselves in the different channels and openings of the reefs for the purpose of annoying their enemies.

Each of these gunboats mounts a heavy eighteen- or twenty-six-pounder in the bow and two brass howitzers on her quarters, and carries from thirty-six to fifty men. The galleys have each one hundred men; schooners and brigs about the same number. For several days the weather was very boisterous, and the gunboats were in great danger of being lost.

AUGUST 1. The gale subsided, and the squadron

stood towards the coast. Every preparation was made for an attack on the town and forts.

NOTES

1. Charles Rylander was one of the men consul John Gavino sent aboard the *Philadelphia* at Gibraltar. Bainbridge had entered only one onto the ship's roster before its surrender, so he was not sure if these individuals should be counted as part of the crew and, thus, under his protection.

2. Circumvallation: building of ramparts and trenches.

3. *Buckamseen*: Tripolitan currency, roughly equivalent to four cents in 1804.

4. Kissing Black Betty: drinking liquor directly from a dark bottle.

5. Ray, referencing a fable claiming that the chameleon lived on air, is facetiously reporting there was no food that day.

6. Pellew: Palau, a group of islands in the Pacific.

7. Mite: tiny, seemingly insignificant coins, from the Biblical parable of the widow's mite.

8. Bomb: bomb ketch, mortar-carrying vessel.

Commodore Preble's Engagement with the Tripolitans

A UGUST 3. The wind east, pleasant weather, and the squadron stood in towards Tripoli. About twelve o'clock, the squadron was within two or three miles of the batteries. Some of our men who had been at work on the fortifications came running in and informed us that the whole coast was lined with our shipping. The whole town was in an uproar, every Turk had his musket and other weapons, and wild disorder rang through every arch. We were all locked into the prison and a formidable guard set over us. Their batteries were all manned, and several of their gunboats and galleys had advanced in two divisions without the rocks.

The commodore, observing this, was resolved to take advantage of their temerity. At half past twelve o'clock, the commodore bore off and made a signal to come within hail, when he communicated to each of the commanders his intention of attacking the enemy's shipping and batteries. The gun- and mortar boats were immediately manned and prepared to cast off, the gunboats in two divisions of three each. The first division was commanded by Capt. Somers, in No. 1; Lt. Decatur,[1] in No. 2; and Lt. Blake, in No. 3. The second division, by Capt.

Decatur, in No. 4; Lt. Bainbridge,[2] in No. 5; and Lt. Trippe, in No. 6. The two bombards were commanded by Lieutenant-commandant Dent, and Mr. Robinson, first lieutenant of the *Constitution*.

At half past one o'clock, having made the necessary arrangements for the attack, the commodore wore ship and stood towards the batteries. At two, signals were made to cast off the boats; at a quarter past two, signal for the bombs and gunboats to advance and attack the enemy; at half past two, general signal for battle; at three-quarters past two, the boats commenced the action by throwing shells into the town. In an instant the enemy's shipping and batteries opened a tremendous fire, which was promptly returned by the whole squadron within grapeshot distance. At the same time, the second division of gunboats, led by the gallant Capt. Decatur, was advancing with sails and oars to board the eastern division of the enemy, consisting of nine boats.

Our boats gave the enemy showers of grape and musket balls as they advanced; they, however, soon closed, when the pistol, saber, pike, and tomahawk were made good use of by our brave tars. Capt. Somers, being in a dull sailer, made the best use of his sweeps but was not able to fetch far enough to the windward to engage the same division of the enemy's boats which Capt. Decatur fell in with. He, however, gallantly bore down with his single boat on five of the enemy's western division and engaged within pistol shot, defeated, and drove them within the rocks in a shattered condition and with the loss of a great number of men.

Lt. Decatur, in No. 2, was closely engaged with one of the enemy's largest boats, which struck to him, having lost a large proportion of men, and, at the instant that brave officer was boarding her to take possession, he was treacherously shot through the head by the captain of the boat that had surrendered, which base conduct enabled the poltroon to escape.

Capt. Decatur, after having with distinguished bravery boarded and carried one of the enemy of superior force, took his prize in tow and gallantly bore down to engage a second, which, after a severe and bloody conflict, he also took possession of. These two prizes had thirty-three officers and men killed, and twenty-seven made prisoners, nineteen of whom were badly wounded. Lt. Trippe, of the *Vixen*, in No. 6, ran alongside one of the enemy's large boats, which he boarded with only midshipman John Hinly and nine men, his boat falling off before any more could get on board; thus was he left to conquer or perish with the odds of thirty-six to eleven.

The Turks could not withstand the ardor of this brave officer and his assistants; in a few moments the decks were cleared and her colors hauled down.

U.S. naval fleet, led by the frigate Constitution

foreground), bombards Tripoli

On board of this boat fourteen of the enemy were killed and twenty-two made prisoners, several of whom were badly wounded; the rest of their boats retreated within the rocks. Lt. Trippe received eleven saber wounds, several of which were very severe.

During the action, our men were taken out of the prison several times to carry powder and shot from the magazine in the castle to the forts, and were almost beaten to death—stoned and cudgeled by every Turk in the streets.

At half past four, the wind inclining to the northward, the commodore made a signal for the bombs and gunboats to retire from action and, immediately after, to tow off the gunboats and prizes, which was handsomely executed by the brigs, schooners, and boats of the squadron—covered by a heavy fire from the *Constitution*, which was two hours under the fire of the enemy's batteries. The only damage which she received was a twenty-four-pound shot nearly through the center of her main-mast, thirty feet from the deck; main-royal yard and sail shot away; one of her quarterdeck guns damaged by a thirty-two-pound shot, which at the same time shattered a marine's arm; sails and rigging considerably cut. The commodore imputed his getting off thus well to his keeping so near that the batteries overshot him and to the annoyance our grapeshot gave the enemy. They are, however, wretched gunners.

Lt. Decatur was the only officer killed, but in him the service has lost a brave and valuable officer. He was a young man who gave strong promises of being an ornament to his profession. His conduct in the action was highly honorable, and he died in a noble cause. The enemy suffered very much in killed and wounded among their shipping; but as few of the shells burst on shore, not so great execution was done as might be expected or as has been reported. This was undoubtedly owing to unskillful bombardiers. The officers, seamen, and marines of the squadron behaved in the most gallant manner. The Neapolitans, in emulating the conduct of our seamen, answered the commodore's highest expectations.

All the officers and ship's company of the *Constitution* gave full satisfaction. The commodore was much gratified by the conduct of Capt. Hall and Lt. Greenleaf, and of the marines belonging to his company, in the management of six long twenty-six-pounders on the spare deck. Capt. Decatur spoke in the highest terms of the conduct of Lt. Thorn. The boat which was first boarded by Capt. Decatur was obstinately defended and was not surrendered until seven-eighths of her crew were killed or wounded. Having manned his prize and being left with only nine Americans besides himself, he determined to board another boat. Being only ten Americans to twenty-four Turks, a scene of combat ensued of the most daring effort on the one part and determined resistance on the other. The Turks made a powerful defense and were not subdued until twenty-one of them had fallen.

Capt. Decatur was, at different times, most critically circumstanced. At one time, while engaged with the Tripolitan captain in front, a Turk in his rear aimed a blow with a saber, which one of the seamen most nobly interposed to defend and which split his skull. In a subsequent encounter, he was engaged by a Turk with a pike, which he endeavored to cut off with his sword, when the blade broke and left the hilt in his hand, and he then received a thrust in his arm. Not having time to draw a pistol until the thrust would be repeated, he closed with his antagonist, who, being the strongest man, threw him; but his activity placed him above his adversary, who drew his dagger, as Capt. Decatur did his pistol, which prevailed.

The list of killed and wounded is as follows.

Killed	Gunboat No. 2, Lt. James Decatur.
Wounded	*Constitution*, one marine.
Do. [ditto]	Gunboat No. 4, Capt. Decatur, slightly; one sergeant of marines; and two seamen.

Boatswain's mate Reuben James saves the life of Stephen Decatur Jr. as he struggles with his brother's killer, engraving after a painting by Alonzo Chappell

Do.	Gunboat No. 6, Lt. Trippe, severely; one boatswain's mate; and two marines.
Do.	Gunboat No. 1, two seamen.
Do.	Gunboat No. 2, two seamen.
Total	One killed and thirteen wounded.

The number of killed and wounded among the Turks cannot be ascertained; it is thought, however, to be very considerable. Three of their gunboats were sunk in the harbor and three captured. Two Turks swam ashore and came to the bashaw, who gave them a few dollars and a suit of clothes.

AUGUST 4. All our men were employed in repairing damages done to the forts and in carrying powder and shot to replenish them. The infuriate [furious] Turks, wherever we met them, would strike, spit upon, and stone us. From the circumstance of our giving up the *Philadelphia* to one gunboat, without bloodshed, they had until now entertained an opinion that the Americans were all cowards; but they now were impressed with a full conviction of the skill and bravery of our tars. The Turks told us that the Americans were all drunk, or they would not have ventured as they did and fought so furiously.

AUGUST 5. The squadron was at anchor about two leagues north from the town. A French privateer of four guns, which put into Tripoli a few days since for water, left it this morning and was chased by the *Argus*, which soon came up with her. The commodore prevailed on the captain of her, for a consideration, to return to Tripoli for the purpose of leaving fourteen very badly wounded Tripolitans, who were put on board his vessel with a letter to the prime minister, leaving it to the option of the bashaw to reciprocate this generous mode of carrying on the war. This act of humanity had but little effect on the minds of these barbarians, for they did not abate their cruelties to us in consequence of it.

AUGUST 7. The French privateer went out and carried a letter from the French consul to the commodore, stating that his attack of the third had disposed the bashaw to accept of reasonable terms and advising him to send a boat to the rocks with a flag of truce, which was declined, as the flag was not hoisted on the bashaw's castle.

At nine o'clock, the light vessels, the gun, and bomb boats were ordered by signal to cast off and stand in towards the western batteries, and the whole advanced with sails and oars. A light breeze from the eastward, and a strong current, obliged the *Constitution* to remain at anchor. The orders were for the bombs to take a positioning a small bay to the westward of the city, where but a few of the enemy's guns could be brought to bear upon them, but from whence they could annoy the town with shells.

At half past two PM, the bomb and gunboats having reached their station, the signal was made for them to attack the town and batteries. After the alarm gun of Tripoli was fired, the Turks all took their stations and performed the Mahometan ceremony of prayer, by kneeling and putting their foreheads to the ground, with their faces towards the east, with as much regularity as a well-disciplined military company grounding their arms. The moment the signal was made by the commodore, the bombs commenced throwing shells into the town and the gunboats opened a sharp and well-directed fire on the town and batteries within point-blank shot, which was warmly returned by the enemy. The seven-gun battery, in less than two hours, was silenced except one gun. The walls of the other forts were considerably injured.

At a quarter past three PM, a ship hove in sight to the northward, standing towards the town. The commodore made the *Argus* a signal to chase her. She proved to be the United States frigate *John Adams*, Capt. Chauncey.

At half past three, one of our gunboats was blown up by a hot shot from the enemy, which passed through her magazine. She had on board twenty-eight officers, seamen, and marines, ten of whom were killed and six wounded. Among the killed was John S. Dorsey, midshipman, and James R. Caldwell, first lieutenant of the *Syren*, both excellent officers. Midshipman Spence and eleven men were taken up unhurt. Capt. Decatur, whose division this boat belonged to and who was near her at the time she blew up, informed the commodore that Mr. Spence was superintending the loading of the gun at that moment and, notwithstanding the boat was sinking, he and the brave men surviving finished charging, gave three cheers as the boat went from under them, and swam to the nearest boats, where they assisted during the remainder of the action.

The father of Mr. Spence was purser of the *Philadelphia* and one of the American prisoners in Tripoli. All the officers and men behaved with the utmost intrepidity. Forty-eight shells and above five hundred twenty-four-pound shot were thrown into the town and batteries.

In this action twelve men were killed and six wounded, two mortally.

August 9. The commodore went on board the *Argus* in order to reconnoiter the harbor of Tripoli; he stood in towards the town and was very near being sunk by the enemy's fire. One of their heaviest shot, which struck about three feet short of her water line, raked the copper off her bottom under water and cut the plank half through. This day a number of our men fainted and dropped beneath the weight they were compelled to sustain, and they were brought half dead to the prison.

AUGUST 10. In the evening, we petitioned the bashaw.[3]

On the petition being explained to the bashaw by Heximer (or Hamet Amerikan, his new name), the bashaw forbid the Turks striking the prisoners.

But his orders were insincere and illusive, for the very next day he stood by and saw several of us severely beaten innocently, without the least apparent dissatisfaction.

AUGUST 12. At ten o'clock in the forenoon, the French consul hoisted a white flag at his flagstaff, under the national colors, which was a signal that the bashaw was ready to treat [negotiate]. The commodore sent a boat into the harbor and took this opportunity to forward to Capt. Bainbridge letters from three friends. The boat was not allowed to land, but returned in the afternoon and brought the commodore a letter from the French consul, advising that the bashaw was ready to receive five hundred dollars for the ransom of each of the prisoners and terminate the war without any consideration for peace or tribute.

This was $350,000 less than was demanded previous to the action of the third. These terms the commodore did not hesitate to reject, as he was informed by Capt. Chauncey that it was the expectation of our government, on the arrival of four frigates, to obtain the release of the officers and crew of the *Philadelphia* without ransom, and dictate the terms of peace. This is the commodore's statement respecting the truce, which no doubt is a correct one; and if it is, what a monstrous blunder has the doctor again committed.

He [Cowdery] says at this same time, *Our squadron hoisted a flag of truce, sent in a brig and schooner, and fired a gun. The bashaw did not, and swore he would not, answer it, and said he would not treat with Commodore Preble. A truce, however, was afterwards held. Consul O'Brien wished to come on shore but was refused.*

August 15. And again he says, *Another truce was held, when the bashaw demanded one million dollars for our ransom. One hundred and twenty thousand dollars were offered and refused.*

Here is a wide difference between the commodore's and the doctor's statements. The doctor has only given his patient, the public, too large a dose of exaggeration, which has proved the fatal bane of unbelief.

August 17. Fifteen dead Americans were found drifted ashore on the beach, westward of the town. By an epaulette on his shoulder, one of them was known to be a lieutenant. Doctor Cowdery asked permission of the bashaw to go with some of our men and bury them. He promised they should be buried the next day.

The beach was covered with a despicable multitude of horse and foot soldiers, with rusty muskets without locks and fired with a match. They were half-naked, meager, and totally undisciplined.

August 18. We were not permitted to bury our dead, according to the bashaw's promise. At night our squadron stood to sea.

August 19. Mr. Church, whom we called the English merchant, was shot through the head in the streets as he was returning at night to his lodgings.

August 20. The ketch *Intrepid* arrived from Syracuse with fresh provisions and vegetables for our squadron. Capt. Chauncey had brought word to the commodore that Commodore Barron was to sail for the Mediterranean four days after his departure; and, in consequence of this information, Commodore Preble expected him every moment and was waiting for his arrival to make another attack, which he believed would be final and effectual. He had dispatched the *Enterprise* to Malta with orders to our agent there to hire transports to bring our squadron fresh provisions, water, and other stores. On the twenty-second she returned, but brought no intelligence of the long-expected frigates. A ship arrived from Malta, the same day, with livestock and water for the squadron.

August 26. At three PM, the commodore weighed anchor and stood in for Tripoli. He was employed until eight PM, in making arrangements for attacking the town; all the boats in the squadron were officered and manned and attached to the gunboats. The two bomb vessels could not be brought into action, as one was leaky and the mortar-bed of the other had given way. The *John Adams, Scourge,* transports, and bombs were anchored seven miles to the northward of the town. Capt. Chauncey, with several of his officers and about seventy seamen and marines, had volunteered their services on board the *Constitution.*

At one AM, the gunboats, in two divisions, led by Capts. Decatur and Somers, were ordered to advance and take their stations close to the rocks at the entrance of the harbor, within grapeshot distance of the bashaw's castle. The *Syren, Argus, Vixen, Nautilus, Enterprise,* and boats of the squadron accompanied them.

At three AM, the boats anchored with springs [ropes] on, within pistol-shot of the rocks, and commenced a brisk firing on the shipping, town, batteries, and bashaw's castle, which was warmly returned but not as well-directed. At daylight, perceiving that the gunboats had nearly expended their ammunition, the commodore weighed with the *Constitution* and stood in for the harbor; Fort English, the bashaw's castle, [and] crown and mole batteries kept up a constant fire as he advanced.

At half past five, the commodore made a signal for the gunboats to retire from action and for the brigs and schooners to take them in tow. The *Constitution* was then within two cables' length of the rocks and commenced a heavy fire of round and grape on thirteen of the enemy's gunboats and galleys, which were in pretty close action with our boats. They sank one of the enemy's boats, and at the same time, two more, disabled, ran in on shore to avoid sinking. The remainder immediately retreated.

The commodore continued running in until he was within musket shot of the crown and mole batteries, when he brought to and fired upwards of three hundred round shot, besides grape and canister, into the town, bashaw's castle, and batteries. He silenced the castle and two of the batteries for some time. At a quarter past six, the gunboats being all out of shot and in tow, the commodore hauled off, after having been three-quarters of an hour in close action.

The gunboats fired upwards of four hundred round shot, besides grape and canister. A large Tunisian galliot was sunk in the mole; a Spanish ship had entered with an ambassador from the grand seignior and received considerable damage. The Tripolitan galleys and gunboats lost many men and were much cut.

Capts. Decatur and Somers conducted their divisions with their usual firmness and address, and were well-supported by the officers and men attached to them. The brigs and schooners suffered considerably in their sails and rigging.

The damage which the *Constitution* received was principally above the hull: three lower shrouds, two spring stays, two topmast backstays, trusses, chains, and lifts of the main yard shot away. Her sails had several cannon shot through them, and besides were considerably cut by grape; much of her running rigging cut to pieces; one of her anchor stocks and larboard cable shot away; and a number of grape shots were sticking in different parts of her hull, but not a man hurt!

The hero's life a miracle shall save,
For partial fortune will protect the brave
Through many dangers; but, when e'er they fall,
'Tis heaven in mercy that directs the ball.

A boat belonging to the *John Adams*, with a master's mate (Mr. Creighton) and eight seamen, was sunk by a double-headed shot from the batteries, while in tow of the *Nautilus*, which killed three men and badly wounded one, who, with Mr. C. and the other four, was picked up by one of our boats. The only damage our gunboats sustained was in their rigging and sails, which were considerably cut by the enemy's round and grape shot.

AUGUST 31. A vessel arrived from Malta with provisions and stores for our squadron, but brought no news of Commodore Barron or his frigates.

SEPTEMBER 2. The bomb vessels having been repaired and ready for service, Lts. Dent and

Robinson resumed the command of them. Lt. Morris of the *Argus* took command of No. 3, and Lt. Trippe, having nearly recovered of his wounds, resumed the command of No. 6, which he so gallantly conducted on the third. Capt. Chauncey, with several young gentlemen, and sixty men from the *John Adams*, volunteered on board the *Constitution*. At four PM, the commodore made signal to weigh, kept under sail all night.

At eleven PM, general signal to prepare for battle. A Spanish polacre,[4] in ballast, went out of the harbor to the commodore, with an ambassador from the grand seignior on board, who had been sent from Constantinople to Tripoli to confirm the bashaw in his title. This ceremony takes place in the Barbary regencies every five years. The captain of the vessel informed the commodore that the shot and shells made great havoc and destruction in the city and that a vast number of the people had been killed; but his accounts were much exaggerated, for very few of the shells burst, and consequently did no great injury.

The weekly allowance of meat and vegetables, which we received from the Danish consul by order of Capt. Bainbridge, had been discontinued ever since the tenth of June, as has been noticed. And in consequence of several petitions made to Capt. Bainbridge, stating that it was almost impossible for the men to exist under the severity of treatment and increased labor to which we were doomed since the invasions of Commodore Preble, we received from the Danish consul, by order of Capt. Bainbridge, one pound of beef per man, with vegetables for soups, and one loaf of wheat bread, in addition to the bashaw's allowance. The meat and vegetables we were to receive only twice a week; the bread, every day.

As I was exempt from labor, the task of superintending the drawing and dividing of the provisions was enjoined on me. There had been much dissatisfaction and murmuring among the men respecting the division of their late rations; and as every ounce of meat, to men half-starving, was considered of the greatest value and importance, to prevent any just complaints, by giving everyone his exact dividend, I classed the men into messes of eight and made them choose their messmates; then numbered the messes as on board the ship. The meat was then cut up by two of the petty officers and divided into as many heaps as there were messes; and particular care was taken that each heap should be alike in quality. Each lot was then exactly weighed and made equivalent. Our vegetables were pumpkins, turnips, and scallions, which were as exactly divided as the meat and in the same manner.

As many numbers as there were messes were then made of paper and stuck on the meat and in like manner to the vegetables. Another set of numbers was made, put into a hat, and shook together. The number of messes being called, one by one, whatever ticket each one drew entitled him to a corresponding number of meat and vegetables. This was a lottery without any blanks, and a method that prevented any more complaints. The bread was easily divided. This was a great alleviation to our hunger-pained breasts.

SEPTEMBER 3. At half past two PM, the signals were made for the gunboats to cast off, advance, and attack the enemy's gunboats and galleys, which were all under way in the eastern part of the harbor, whither they had been for some time working up against the wind. This was certainly a judicious movement of theirs, as it precluded the possibility of our boats going down to attack the town without having the enemy's flotilla in the rear and directly to windward. The commodore accordingly ordered the bomb vessels to run down within proper distance of the town and bombard it, while our gunboats were to engage the enemy's galleys and boats to windward.

At half past three PM, our boats having gained their stations to which they were directed, commenced throwing shells into the city. At the same time, our gunboats opened a brisk fire on the galleys and within point-blank shot, which was warmly returned by them and Fort English, and by a new battery, a little westward; but as soon as our boats arrived within good musket-shot of their galleys and boats, they gave way and retired to the shore, within the rocks and under cover of musketry from Fort English. They were followed by our boats and by the *Syren, Argus, Vixen, Nautilus,* and *Enterprise,* as far as the reef would permit them to go with prudence.

The action was then divided: one division of our boats, with the brigs and schooners, attacked Fort English, whilst the other was engaged with the enemy's galleys and boats. The bashaw's castle, the mole, crown, and several other batteries kept up a constant fire on our bomb vessels, which were well-conducted and threw shells briskly into the town; but, from their situation, they were very much exposed and in great danger of being sunk. To prevent which, the commodore ran within them with the *Constitution,* to draw off the enemy's attention and amuse them whilst the bombardment was kept up. The commodore brought to within reach of grape and fired eleven broadsides into the bashaw's castle, town, and batteries, in a situation where more than seventy guns could bear upon him. One of the batteries was silenced; the town, castle, and other batteries, considerably damaged.

By this time it was half past four o'clock. The wind was increasing and inclining rapidly to the northward; the commodore made a signal for the boats to retire from action and for the brigs and

Explosion of the ketch Intrepid

schooners to take them in tow, and soon after hauled off, with the *Constitution*, to repair damages.

Our gunboats were an hour and fifteen minutes in action. They disabled several of the enemies' galleys and boats, and considerably damaged Fort English. Most of our boats received damage in their rigging and sails. About fifty shells were thrown into the town, and our boats fired four hundred round shot besides grape and canister. They were led into action by Capts. Decatur and Somers, with their usual gallantry.

It is very unaccountable that among so many shells as were thrown into the town, so few of them burst. It must have been owing to want of skill and not treachery in the bombardiers. The bashaw gave a bounty for every shell that his people brought to him, and they were found in plenty. A large number went directly over our prison, and fell innoxious [harmlessly] in the sand. Three or four shots struck our prison but did no damage of consequence.

It must be remembered that most of the foregoing account of Commodore Preble's operations is taken from his letter to the secretary of the navy, and nearly in his own words. The commodore further says,

Desirous of annoying the enemy by all the means in my power, I directed to be put in execution a long-contemplated plan of sending a fireship, or infernal, into the harbor of Tripoli in the night, for the purpose of endeavoring to destroy the enemy's shipping and shatter the bashaw's castle and town. Capt. Somers of the *Nautilus,* having volunteered his service, had, for several days before this period, been directing the preparation of the ketch *Intrepid,* assisted by Lts. Wadsworth and Israel. About 100 barrels of powder and 150 fixed shells were apparently judiciously disposed of on board her. The fuses leading to the magazine were calculated to burn a quarter of an hour.

September 4. The *Intrepid* being prepared for the intended service, Capt. Somers and Lt. Wadsworth made choice of two of the fastest rowing boats in the squadron for bringing them out after reaching their destination and firing the combustible materials which were to communicate with the fuzes. Capt. Somers' boat was manned with four seamen from the *Nautilus,* and Lt. Wadsworth's with six from the *Constitution.* Lt. Israel accompanied them. At eight in the evening, the *Intrepid* was under sail and standing for the port, with a leading breeze from the eastward. The *Argus, Vixen,* and *Nautilus* convoyed her as far as the rocks.

On entering the harbor, several shots were fired at her from the batteries. In a few minutes after, when she had apparently nearly gained her intended place of destination, she suddenly exploded, without their having previously fired a room filled with splinters and other combustibles, which were intended to create a blaze in order to deter the enemy from boarding whilst the fire was communicating to the fuzes, which led to the magazine.

The effect of the explosion awed the batteries into profound silence, with astonishment. Not a gun was afterwards fired for the night. The shrieks of the inhabitants informed us that the town was thrown into the greatest terror and consternation by the explosion of the magazine, and the bursting and falling of shells in all directions.

The whole squadron waited with the utmost anxiety to learn the fate of the adventurers, from a signal previously agreed-upon in case of success, but waited in vain; no signs of their safety were to be observed. The *Argus, Vixen,* and *Nautilus* hovered round the port till sunrise, when they had a fair view of the harbor. Not a vestige of the ketch or the boats were to be seen. One of the enemy's largest boats was missing, and three others were seen, very much shattered and damaged, which the enemy were hauling on shore.

From these circumstances I am led to believe that those boats were detached from the enemy's flotilla to intercept the ketch; and without supposing her to be a fireship, the missing boat had suddenly boarded her, when the gallant Somers and heroes of his party, observing the other three boats surrounding them and no prospect of escape, determined at once to prefer death and the destruction of the enemy to captivity and torturing slavery, put a match to the train leading directly to the magazine, which at once blew the whole into the air and terminated their existence.

My conjectures respecting this affair are founded on a resolution which Capt. Somers [and] Lts. Wadsworth and Israel had formed, neither to be taken by the enemy, nor suffer him to get possession of the powder on board the *Intrepid*. They expected to enter the harbor without discovery but had declared, if they should be disappointed and the enemy should board them before they reached the point of destination, in such force as to leave no hopes of a safe retreat, they would put a match to the magazine and blow themselves and their enemies up together, determined, as there was no exchange of prisoners, that their country should never pay ransom for them nor the enemy receive a supply of powder through their means.

The disappearance of one of the enemy's boats and the shattered condition of three others confirm me in my opinion that they were an advanced guard, detached from the main body of the enemy's flotilla, [and] on discovering the approach of the *Intrepid*, that they attempted to board her before she had reached her point of destination; otherwise, the whole of the shipping must have suffered and perhaps would have been totally destroyed.

That she was blown up before she had reached her station is certain; by which the service has lost three very gallant officers. Capt. Somers and Lts. Wadsworth and Israel were officers of conspicuous bravery, talents, and merit. They had uniformly distinguished themselves in the several actions—were beloved and lamented by the whole squadron.

Far from wishing or endeavoring to detract from the merits of those immortal heroes who lost their lives in attempting to effectuate our emancipation, a strict regard to correct information, as far as it can be traced, induces me to make the following enquiries and remarks:

I would ask any reasonable person, is it probable that Capt. Somers [and] Lts. Wadworth and Israel would have voluntarily sacrificed their lives by a premature act? Or, in other words, would they have fired the train had they not been boarded by the enemy or surrounded in such a manner as to banish all hopes of escape? And if the enemy had boarded them, would they not have shared promiscuous destruction, as had been reported from conjecture? And if the enemy did suffer, or were thus destroyed, should not we have been informed of it through some of the means following?

The Neapolitans—who were servants to most of the chief men in Tripoli; who were slaves and anticipated freedom from our squadron's success; who brought us with avidity every intelligence of our enemy's loss or defeat; who perfectly understood the language of the Tripolitans—never gave us any information and, of course, never heard that any of the Turks were destroyed by the explosion of the infernal. There were many Jews and disaffected Turks, Greeks, and Maltese who were ready to communicate to us every unfavorable circumstance of the enemy, and we never heard from them that any of the Turks perished in the explosion. The Christian consuls—and especially the Danish one, who was our particular friend—never informed us that any of the Turks were killed by the explosion of the fireship.

Lewis Heximer, who had turned Turk but seriously repented of it, and who was promised and expected to be given up to us on our liberation by covertly befriending us while in full confidence of the bashaw and all the Turks, never gave us information of the kind and, of course, never heard such a report amongst the Turks. Doctor Cowdery, who lodged in the same room with Heximer, does not mention it in his journal.

Is it not therefore more than probable that, through all these channels of communication, if a circumstance so extraordinary as the destruction of one or two hundred Turks, some information of the event would have reached us? It is therefore very evident that no Turks were destroyed; and if none were destroyed, is it not full as evident that the train communicated to the magazine sooner than was expected and that the explosion happened before our men could possibly avoid a catastrophe so much to be lamented?

Doctor Cowdery says *the explosion was a fire ship, sent into the harbor by Commodore Preble, which did but little damage,* and *the bashaw and his people had a thanksgiving to Mahomet on the occasion,* which would not have been had he lost a boat and two hundred men by it. But from whatever circumstance or accident they lost their lives, it is certain that they died meritoriously; and, while valor, patriotism, and heroic actions meet with admiration, gratitude, and applause, the names of Somers, Wadsworth, Israel, and their brave companions in death will live and shine on in the annals of fame and be registered in the catalog of American martyrs in the cause of liberty.

The weather continuing to wear a threatening aspect until the seventh of September, and the ammunition being reduced to a quantity not more than sufficient for three vessels to keep up the blockade, no intelligence of the expected reinforcement, and the season so far advanced as to render it imprudent to hazard the gunboats any longer on the station, the commodore gave orders for the *John Adams, Syren, Nautilus, Enterprise,* and *Scourge* to take the bombs and gunboats in tow and proceed to Syracuse with them; the *Argus* and *Vixen* to remain with the *Constitution,* to keep up the blockade.

This day, fourteen bodies of Americans, supposed to be destroyed by the explosion of the fire ship, were interred by permission of the bashaw. John M'Donald, who had long been in a decline, departed this, he hoped, for a better life.

SEPTEMBER 10. The United States ship *Presi-*

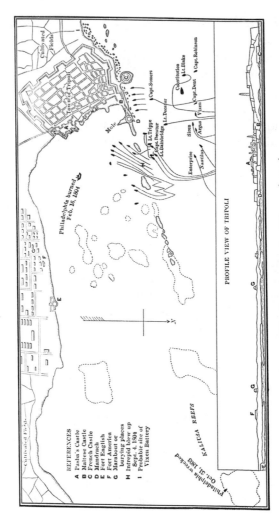

REFERENCES

A Pasha's Castle
B Maltese Castle
C French Castle
D Mandrach
E Fort English
F Fort America
G Marabout or
   burying places
H Intrepid blew up
   Sept. 4, 1804
1 Probable site of
   Vixen Battery

KALICSA REEFS

Philadelphia wrecked
Oct. 31, 1803

Philadelphia burned
Feb. 16, 1804

Cultivated Fields.

Town of Tripoli

Mole

Capt. Somers
Lt. Trippe
Capt. Decatur
Lt. Dainbridge
Lt. Decatur
Constitution
Lt. Blake
Capt. Robinson
Siren
Argus
Vixen
Capt. Dent
Enterprise
Nautilus

PROFILE VIEW OF TRIPOLI

A map of Tripoli's harbor showing U.S. naval attacks

dent, Commodore Barron, and *Constellation,* Capt. Campbell, hove in sight and soon joined company, when the command of the squadron was surrendered to Commodore Barron with the usual ceremony. Commodore Preble continued in company with the squadron until the twelfth, when three strange ships hove in sight, standing directly for Tripoli. Chase was given and two of them boarded and taken possession of by the *Constitution*—the *President* in company— about four leagues from Tripoli, but not more than four miles from land, while the *Constellation* and *Argus* were in chase of the third.

The two boarded by the *Constitution* were loaded with about sixteen thousand bushels of wheat. Tripoli was in a state of starvation, and there can be no doubt but those cargoes were meant as a supply and relief to our enemies. No further operations were carried on against Tripoli for this season.

Commodore Preble left the station and returned to America by the first convenient opportunity, where he met with that warm, generous, and honorable reception which our countrymen are ever ready to evince towards those who have distinguished themselves by valor, patriotism, and magnanimity. He left a lasting impression on the mind of the bashaw, and all the barbarians of Tripoli, of American bravery. Such unparalleled heroism appalled their savage bosoms and struck them with the profoundest astonishment. That a single frigate

Stephen Decatur Jr. in hand-to-hand combat with Tripolitans

should dare venture under the batteries in the manner that Preble did they imputed to madness, and that she ever lived to return was ascribed by them to some superior agency's invisible protection. He was considered as a prodigy of valor and dreaded as the minister of destruction. He was not an idle, *barron* commodore.⁵ His labors produced effect—he won laurels and bore them.

Respecting the damage done to the town of Tripoli, various reports have made erroneous statements. There was but little damage done to the town, for it is wholly built of incombustible materials; and they who have reported that the town was set on fire by the shells might as well have informed us that a conflagration of the Mediterranean was effected with a taper. In every attack upon the place, we were taken out in intervals, to carry powder to the different forts, and treated worse than can be represented by words. They would place a barrel of powder on a man's back and make him run every step, without resting, from the castle to the batteries—three-quarters of a mile—with a driver behind him dealing blows at every breath, amidst the pelting of stones from the soldiery and every insult and indignity that could be offered or endured.

A great number of shells and balls went over and fell near our prison, but none of them did any material damage. One ball went through our cookhouse, adjoining one end of our prison; one struck the front obliquely and spent its fury without harm; and several more glanced over the corners and terrace of it. A ball went through the Danish consul's observatory the moment he had left it, in the exact direction where he stood. It is a great pity the commodore had not found more skillful bombardiers; for, though they could not fire the houses, had they all burst, great damage as well as great consternation must have been the result. Two of the guns burst, in the last action, and killed two Turks in the castle.

Before our squadron had left the coast, and previous to the last engagement, I received a line from one of our officers mentioning that Lt. James Decatur was killed on the third of August.

Notes

1. Lt. James Decatur: the younger brother of Stephen Decatur.

2. Lt. Joseph Bainbridge: Capt. William Bainbridge's younger brother.

3. For full text of the petition, see page 146.

4. Polacre: a three-masted merchant ship.

5. Ray is playing on the name Barron, meaning "barren," as Samuel Barron was incapacitated by illness, and his brother James took over the squadron, but neither used it against Tripoli. When Ray published this book in 1808, Americans would have known James Barron as the commodore forced to surrender the *Chesapeake* to the British ship *Leopard* in June 1807, precipitating the embargo of 1808. Suspended from the navy for five years, James Barron spent the War of 1812 in Denmark, then returned to the United States after the war.

Blockade

OUR MEN were employed in repairing the damages done in the several attacks upon the forts and batteries—laying new platforms, building new gun-carriages, hauling timber and stone to build boats and erect fortifications; and nothing worthy of remark transshaped our fortune for a considerable time.

OCTOBER 21. The last day we saw any of our shipping. The Tripolitans took their arms and ammunition from their gunboats and extracted the charges from the cannon on the forts and batteries. It seems the bashaw, as yet, had but very inadequate conceptions of the force of his foe, for he this day told Doctor Cowdery (so he informs us) that if he had three frigates he would blockade America. He fancied he could do it as easily as one frigate and a schooner could blockade Tripoli.

OCTOBER 23. No bread to be had. The Turks told us that, in consequence of the blockade which our shipping had maintained, we now had to suffer, and advised us to petition to our commodore in Syracuse to make peace and take us away. The bashaw issued an edict prohibiting the inhabitants from purchasing and the venders of grain from selling to any but the castellany [castle warden].

Money would not command bread, and starvation was whetting her teeth to devour us.

Commodore Lysle, disregarding the bashaw's proclamation, purchased some barley. An altercation ensued between them. Lysle insisted on his right to purchase grain in the public marts. The bashaw was outraged, flew at him, struck him, and commanded his guard to disarm and confine him— which was done for a few hours, when the bashaw ordered him released and gave the person who had fomented the fracas five hundred bastinadoes.

For three days we never tasted bread, and for eleven days more we had but a very little, subsisting on dates pressed into a cake, and vegetables, with oil.

NOVEMBER 9. The meat and vegetables, which we had drawn by order of Capt. Bainbridge, were discontinued. Philosophers may prate what they will of the feasibility of our enjoying happiness under all circumstances and in all conditions. Let one of those sticklers for contentment be placed in our situation with an empty stomach, a heavy burden on his back, and a fell fiend at his heels, dealing flagellation at every step; and I am pretty well convinced that he would feel disposed to relinquish his tenets.

NOVEMBER 20. A great scarcity of bread still prevailed, and our men were obliged to sell the clothes which they had lately drawn, and for which they were suffering, to procure something to sustain life. The cravings of hunger predominated over the calls of external wants, and our clothes were sacrificed for a mere trifle; but trifles are of magnitude when they preserve life.

During the extremity of famine, one of our men, impelled by imperious hunger, taking advantage of the Jews' Sabbath, who had the charge of the distillery, clambered over a wall twenty feet high; broke or unlocked three doors; and got into the still-house, where a little shop was kept for retailing *aqua-deut*; and brought off a pitcher full of *buck-amseens*, which he distributed amongst his companions so profusely that he was suspected, and subsequently convicted of, the robbery. But he greased the fists of his keepers, who, for a share, put him in irons and gave him a slight punishment.

Some of our tars had the ingenuity to counterfeit the bashaw's coin. When a specimen of the fraud was shown to the bashaw, he laughed heartily and said that the Americans were all wizards and devils, and protested that if the person was detected, he could not punish, but reward, his invention.

DECEMBER 7. It was said that the bashaw, impatient for the money which he forestalled as the price of our ransom, gave orders to our wardens to treat us with the utmost severity, in order to extort from us supplications to our country for a speedy peace. For several days we had been without bread or money, for the bashaw sometimes ordered us cash when bread was not plenty; and the men were unanimously determined not to labor any more unless one or the other was allowed us.

DECEMBER 10. Our keepers, or drivers, as usual, unlocked the prison doors early in the morning and ordered us *tota fora* (all out). Not one of us moved. The most of us had now provided ourselves with cots, as before described, which were ranged one above another to the top of the prison, making it difficult for the drivers to come at us. A few, however, slept on the ground; and to those the furious elves had free access and began to beat them.

We then all spoke and told them that we were resolved, if death should be the consequence, not to turn out another day without food. They threatened to call the soldiers and fire in upon us; and when they found they could not move us by threats nor blows, they left us and informed the bashaw of our refractory conduct. They soon returned and assured us that if we would peaceably and tacitly obey their orders, we should have bread at twelve o'clock. This was agreed to, and the stipulation was fulfilled.

DECEMBER 21. *Our boatswain, carpenter, sailmaker, and first master's mate, who had the liberty of the town for a few months, were put in close confinement with our other officers, on a suspicion of attempting to raise the crew to take the town.*

It is true such a plot was in cogitation, but it was

a very preposterous one. It was meditated for us to rush into the castle when the gates were first opened in the morning, to seize on the armory and magazine, liberate our officers, secure the guard and the mamelukes, and make a prisoner of the bashaw and his family—at the same time, to plant a twenty-six-pounder, loaded with grape, at each gate and point the guns of the castle into the town.

This doubtless might have been effected with but little loss; but the question is, how long could we have maintained our ground? The Turks might have brought their cannon from the different forts to bear upon and batter the castle to prostrate ruins. Could such a plot have been carried into operation when our squadron was cruising off the harbor, it might have been terminated with success; but under the then-existing circumstances, before relief could have reached us, destruction must have swallowed us up.

DECEMBER 25. In compliance with a petition which we preferred to Capt. Bainbridge, he sent orders to the Danish consul to have us supplied with a collation [light meal] of fresh beef and vegetables, with an additional allowance of one loaf of bread per man; the whole to be washed down with a cask of wine, yielding a dividend of one quart to each individual. We also petitioned the bashaw for a respite from labor for the day, and he was graciously pleased to vouchsafe our request.

In the morning, at the usual time of unlocking our prison, the wardens came and informed us that some cordage and other articles were missing out of the bashaw's naval magazine (as they called it) and that some of the Americans were suspected of the robbery; and unless we would give information of the perpetrator, no holiday should be allowed us, but that we should spend the day in close confinement and without food. They kept us in until about ten o'clock, when—it being discovered that Selim, the bashaw's son-in-law, who carried the keys of the stores, had committed the crime by selling the cordage clandestinely to a Tunisian merchant—we were allowed to come out and bring our provisions and wine to the prison. The bashaw ordered his son-in-law five hundred bastinadoes; but he fled to a *marabewt* and escaped punition. The remainder of the day was spent, if not with the greatest festivity, with decent propriety and was ended in perfect unanimity.

We sent our thanks to Capt. Bainbridge for his compliance with our request, and on the first of January, he ordered us the same quantity of provisions and wine as before. I was told to take eight men, go to the Danish consul's, and get the wine. Our men were the tapsters [bartenders], and the consul requested me to keep an account of the measure. The good-natured, benevolent man told us all to drink as much as we wanted while it was drawing and came, several times, urging us to drink. The tapsters accepted of his liberal invitation with such unreserved cordiality that, by the time they had finished drawing, they were not able to carry the cask to the prison.

Another set of bearers was collected, and the consul made them drink until they were nearly as much intoxicated as the first; and when we were departing, he distributed a handful of money amongst the whole. Our tars pronounced him the best fellow they had ever met with and swore he must have been a sailor or he would not be so generous with his cash and his grog.

JANUARY 28. A strong guard was placed in our prison yard, and we were forbid to go out. The infamous Wilson had informed the bashaw that we were all armed and prepared to rise and take the town. They searched our prison and found the report false.

FEBRUARY 1. George Griffiths, gunner's mate of the late *Philadelphia,* having inveigled the bashaw with the project that he could construct an air furnace to cast guns, shot, and shells in, was provided with masons and nine of our crew, and set to the work. He received a doubloon on commencing and was promised one hundred dollars for the first specimen of his skill. After lavishing more than five hundred dollars in making the experiment, it this day proved abortive, by premeditated design.

A group of Tripolitan officers of the guard

FEBRUARY 13. As a number of our men were at work under a corner of the castle wall, a part of it fell and crushed out the entrails of Jacob Dowerdesher, who died instantly.

Another tar has weather'd storms and strife,
And burst the bonds of slav'ry and of life.

FEBRUARY 20. Our bread, which we drew from or by order of the captain, growing light, we petitioned him to let us receive a *buckamseen* apiece each day in the place of it, to which he complied and which we received daily until the termination of our captivity. The sum amounted to ten dollars and three quarters, which I received every morning from the Danish consul and divided amongst the men. Such as labored at the cart, and a large number who were employed in building up a corner of the castle, received a *buckamseen* a day from the bashaw; and my task was to muster them at evening and mark the number of days each one had labored, and receive and pay them the money. The men were often defrauded by the embezzling of the keepers.

MARCH 1. *An American frigate appeared off the harbor. The Turks were all at their quarters and were manning their gunboats.*

They began to resume their wonted cruelties on such occasions.

MARCH 16. The mansion lately occupied by

our officers appeared to be full of people, and a guard on the terrace and at the door. They were the nearest relatives of those officers who had gone on the expedition, and held as pledges of their loyalty, fearing they might attach themselves to his brother, the ex-bashaw.

MARCH 30. Selim, who had been sent into the country to collect or enlist troops, returned with but a handful of men. The people had been oppressed by his exorbitant demands for money, and their women had been stripped of their rings, bracelets, and jewels, and they refused to fight for the bashaw.

APRIL 27. *A very oppressive Syroc wind.*

Two of our men who were sent into the country with a cart—dragging it, loaded, over the burning sands—fainted and were brought in almost lifeless. The remainder were nearly exhausted by heat and fatigue. Several companies of Arabs passed through the town and paraded under the bashaw's balcony, in the navy yard. There were about three hundred horse and seven hundred foot, and both made but a despicable appearance.

MAY 19. Antonio, a Neapolitan slave who had recently paid his own ransom, returned from Malta and Syracuse, whither he had been sent by the bashaw as a spy.

The residue of Doctor Cowdery's journal approaches very near the truth.

MAY 23. *Twenty-five of our men were sent with a cart for timber into the country. The wind from the desert was very heavy and hot. The men almost perished in the sand, which flew and drifted like a snowstorm in our country. They stopped through fatigue and asked their driver, who was a Turk, for liberty to drink at a well which was near them. The Turk replied that they were* Romo kelps, *Christian dogs, and said they should have no water. He gave them all a severe beating with a large club, which he always carried with him to drive them with, and made them go on with the cart, which the poor fellows had to drag, loaded with timber, through the burning sand. They returned towards night almost perished.*

This is true, but no more than what occurred almost every day.

MAY 24. *The bashaw was so much agitated at the news of the approach of his brother that he this day declared that if it was in his power to make peace and give up the American prisoners, he would gladly do it without the consideration of money.*

If this be true, what must we think of Col. Lear's treaty? What must we think of sixty thousand [dollars] lavished [expended] to no purpose?

His funds were so low that his steward ran in debt for the supply of the kitchen. He gave his mamelukes, domestics, and myself but one meal per day. The rich Turks in town took turns in supplying his few troops.

He heartily repented for not accepting the terms of peace last offered by our country.

MAY 26. *Three frigates in sight. At about eleven* AM, *the smallest came near in and hoisted the banners of peace. The bashaw asked his head men of the town, who were with him in his gallery, whether it was best to hoist his white flag. All except one, the chargé d'affaires for Algiers, declared in favor of it and of making peace if possible. They expressed great contempt towards the Algerine consul for his advice and said that whoever would advise the bashaw not to hoist the white flag at such a critical moment must be his foe and not his friend.*

The Algerine soon disappeared and left the castle. The Spanish consul soon after came to the castle; and the bashaw sent him in one of his handsome boats, with Shous Hammad, to the frigate. They returned at evening with the joyful news of a prospect of peace. There was a visible change, from gloominess to joy, in the countenance of all the Turks.

And if it had this effect on the Turks, what must it have produced in the feelings of Americans in slavery? Our men were in paroxysms of joy, notwithstanding the issue was yet precarious.

MAY 27. *Both Turks and Christians were all anxiously looking out for the frigates . . . . But not a frigate nor a sail hove in sight during the day.*

MAY 28. *All looking out again for our squadron.*

. . . at sunset, three frigates and a brig appeared, which revived our hopes. The bashaw showed the greatest anxiety for peace. He was sensible of the danger he was in from the lowness of his funds and the disaffection of his people.

MAY 29. *Three frigates and a brig bore down upon the town and displayed the ensigns and signals of peace . . . The Spanish consul, Fafah the Jew, and several Turks went on board and did not return until late at night, when it was reported that negotiations for peace were going on rapidly.*

MAY 31. *The Spanish consul and Shous Hammad went on board the commodore and returned at night. The bashaw sent me to inform Capt. Bainbridge that peace was agreed on, which I did to the great joy of the officers.*

JUNE 2. *I received a letter from Capt. Bainbridge stating that the terms of peace were agreed on.*

Capt. Bainbridge came himself to our prison; called us together and communicated the intelligence of a treaty being agreed on, but not yet signed; and cautioned us not to let the prospect of liberty transport us beyond the bounds of discretion, lest the preliminaries might yet be annulled. He delivered me a letter from a friend of mine in the United States, the only one I received while in Tripoli.

JUNE 3. *The articles of peace were signed and salutes fired from the frigates and batteries.*

I shall not pretend to describe in adequate terms our various emotions for a number of days previous to this confirmation of our hopes. Sometimes our spirits were soaring—buoyant on the wings of sanguine expectation; at other times, diving into the very gulf of despair.

> *But O! what joy when the saluting sound*
> *Was heard to thunder through the arches round!*
> *Enraptur'd lays the choral hundreds sung,*
> *And that drear mansion once with gladness*
>   *rung.*

The bashaw this morning called the American renegades Wilson; West; Smith, who had a wife and four children in Boston; Heximer; and Prince, and told them that peace was now concluded, the Americans were about to leave Tripoli, and if they, or either of them, chose to go, it was left at their option. Unaware of the artifice, all except Wilson expressed their wish and anxiety to relinquish the turban and accompany us to America.

Wilson, jealous [suspicious] of the bashaw's sincerity and perhaps afraid of the threatened halter, thanked his majesty for this generous offer but told him that he preferred Tripoli to America, and Mahometanism to Christianity, and that he chose to remain and would ever continue firmly attached to his service. Wilson was honored and caressed by

the bashaw and his divan for his singular fidelity—
while the other four were sent into the country with
a formidable guard.

We had a glance at them as they passed our
prison and could see horror and despair depicted in
their countenances. A number of our men went to
the American house and remained all night with
our officers, but the greater part were locked in the
prison as usual. Our drivers were missing and a new
guard over us.

JUNE 4. Lest our men might wreak vengeance
on some of the Turks, and especially the keepers, for
past cruelties, which would have inevitably involved
us in difficulties and dangers, our men were kept
locked in the prison until the arrangements were
made to receive them all at the rendezvous, which
was not until about ten AM. Here we all received
new clothes and were sent on board of different vessels in the afternoon, where some met with the
warm reception of a good flogging before the next
morning.

The fall preceding, we had drawn a subscription
for the purpose of purchasing the ransom of a
friendly Neapolitan. We obtained considerable
encouragement at that time, but our own emancipation appearing so dubious, this humane project
for that time was procrastinated. As soon therefore
as our liberty was ascertained, we resumed the subject and obtained upwards of three hundred dollars;

wrote to Capt. Bainbridge and had the money advanced and deducted out of our wages; and enjoyed the supreme satisfaction of giving liberty to one of our fellow creatures. He was servant to our chief warden—and not a taskmaster nor a driver over us as has been reported—in which capacity he had frequent opportunities of befriending us and had rendered several of us very essential services. I have been informed, however, that when he found what severity was practiced in our service, he seriously repented of his leaving Tripoli!

We were upwards of nineteen months in imprisonment, and only six died out of more than three hundred men; and considering the hardships we endured, we had but little sickness—a sufficient proof that the climate is remarkably healthy. It was thought that the oil we mixed with all our food contributed greatly to the preservation of our health.

Index

INDEX

Index

List of The Lakeside Classics

The Lakeside Classics

The Lakeside Classics

The Lakeside Classics

The Lakeside Classics

The Lakeside Classics

IMAGE CREDITS
AND ACKNOWLEDGMENTS

The GeoNova Group: *xxvi–xxvii*

Johns Hopkins University, The Sheridan Libraries Special Collections: from *Algérie Historique, Pittoresque et Monumentale,* Adrien Berbrugger (Paris: Chez. J. Delahaye, 1843): *35, 59, 75, 80*

Library of Congress: from *A Narrative of the Expedition to Algiers in the Year 1816, Under the Command of the Right Hon. Admiral Lord Viscount Exmouth,* Abraham V. Salamé (London: J. Murray, 1819): *84;* from *Narrative of a Ten Years' Residence at Tripoli in Africa,* Miss Tully (London: H. Colburn, 1817): *118, 154, 298*

Maine Historical Society Collections: *258–259*

The Mariners' Museum, Newport News, Va.: *122*

Naval Historical Foundation: *ii, xxii, lxviii, 1, 240, 244, 263, 278, 288*

The Newberry Library: from *A Narrative of Travels in Northern Africa, in the Years 1818, 19, and 20,* G. F. Lyon (London: John Murray, 1821): *150, 164, 171, 214;* from *An Historical and Geographical Account of Algiers,* James Wilson Stevens (Philadelphia: Hogan & M'Elroy, 1797): *210*

Northwestern University Library, Melville J. Herskovits Library of African Studies: from *A Compleat History of the Piratical*

States of Barbary, Laugier de Tassy (London: R. Griffiths, 1750): *53*; from *Letters Written During a Ten Years' Residence at the Court of Tripoli,* Miss Tully (London: H. Colburn, 1819): *134, 138, 180*

USS Constitution Museum: from *White Slavery in the Barbary States,* Charles Sumner (Boston: J. P. Jewett and Co.; Cleveland, Ohio: Jewett, Proctor, and Worthington, 1853): *liv*

University of Chicago Library: from *Algeria: The Topography and History, Political, Social and Natural, of French Africa,* John Reynell Morell (London: Nathaniel Cooke, 1854): *25;* from *The Captives,* James Leander Cathcart, compiled by J. B. Newkirk (La Porte, Indiana, 1899): *4;* from *Histoire de L'Algérie Francaise,* Leynadier et Clausel (Paris: Chez. H. Morel, 1846): *22;* from *Naval Documents Related to the United States Wars with the Barbary Powers, Volume V* (Washington: United States Government Printing Office, 1944): *lxv;* from *Our Navy and the Barbary Corsairs,* Gardner W. Allen (Boston: Houghton, Mifflin and Company, 1905): *286;* from *White Gold,* Giles Milton (London: Hodder & Stoughton, 2004): *43*

University of Minnesota, James Ford Bell Library: from *Barbarian Cruelty,* Thomas Troughton (London: R. Walter, 1751): *228*; from *Historie van Barbaryen, en des zelfs zee-roovers,* Pierre Dan (Amsterdam: Jan ten Hoorn, 1684): *17, 46*

Special thanks to Harrie Slootbeek, curatorial assistant, The USS Constitution Museum, for his valuable assistance in identifying images for this volume.

DESIGNED, TYPESET, PRINTED, BOUND, AND DISTRIBUTED BY
R.R. DONNELLEY & SONS COMPANY

COMPOSITION:
ALLENTOWN, PENNSYLVANIA

SCANNING AND IMAGE PROOFING:
RR DONNELLEY
PREMEDIA TECHNOLOGIES,
ELGIN, ILLINOIS

COMPUTER TO PLATES, PRINTING, AND BINDING:
CRAWFORDSVILLE, INDIANA

ADDRESSING AND MAILING:
RR DONNELLEY
RESPONSE MARKETING SERVICES

WORLDWIDE DISTRIBUTION:
RR DONNELLEY LOGISTICS

BODY TYPEFACE:
11/12.85 POINT GARAMOND

PAPER STOCK:
50-POUND WHITE LAKESIDE CLASSICS,
BY GLATFELTER

CLOTH:
ARRESTOX VELLUM, LAKESIDE GREEN,
BY HOLLISTON MILLS, INC.